READING-TO-WRITE

SOCIAL AND COGNITIVE STUDIES IN WRITING AND LITERACY

Oxford University Press and
The Center for the Study of Writing at Berkeley and Carnegie Mellon

A series devoted to books that bridge research, theory, and practice, exploring social and cognitive processes in writing and expanding our knowledge of literacy as an active constructive process—as students move from high school to college and the community.

The Center for the Study of Writing (CSW), with the support of the Office of Educational Research and Improvement, conducts research on the development of writers and on writing and literacy as these are taught and learned in the home, in elementary and secondary school, in college, in the workplace, and in the community. In conjunction with schools and teachers, CSW develops projects that link writing research to classroom practice. A list of publications is available from CSW at the University of California, Berkeley, 5513 Tolman Hall, Berkeley, CA 94720.

READING-TO-WRITE

Exploring a Cognitive and Social Process

LINDA FLOWER   *Carnegie Mellon University*

VICTORIA STEIN   *University of Arizona*

JOHN ACKERMAN   *University of Utah*

MARGARET J. KANTZ   *Central Missouri State University*

KATHLEEN McCORMICK   *Carnegie Mellon University*

WAYNE C. PECK   *Allegheny Presbyterian Center*

New York   Oxford
OXFORD UNIVERSITY PRESS
1990

Oxford University Press

Oxford   New York   Toronto
Delhi   Bombay   Calcutta   Madras   Karachi
Petaling Jaya   Singapore   Hong Kong   Tokyo
Nairobi   Dar es Salaam   Cape Town
Melbourne   Auckland

and associated companies in
Berlin   Ibadan

Published by Oxford University Press, Inc.,
200 Madison Avenue, New York, New York 10016

Oxford is a registered trademark of Oxford University Press

Library of Congress Cataloging-in-Publication Data
Reading-to-write : exploring a cognitive and social process /
Linda Flower . . . [et al.].
p.   cm.   Includes index.
ISBN 0-19-506190-X
1. English language—Rhetoric—Study and teaching (Higher)
2. Reading (Higher education)   3. Cognition—Social aspects.   I. Flower, Linda.
PE1404.R375   1990   808'.0427'0711—dc20   89-8845

The project presented, or reported herein, was performed pursuant to a
grant from the Office of Educational Research and Improvement/Department of
Education (OERI/ED) for the Center for the Study of Writing. However,
the opinions expressed herein do not necessarily reflect the position or
policy of the OERI/ED and no official endorsement by the OERI/ED
should be inferred.

9 8 7 6 5 4 3 2 1

Printed in the United States of America
on acid-free paper

Preface

So I'm just gonna—I don't care, I'm just going to interpret them the only way I can interpret them. . . . Let's just put what the authors agreed on. *Authors agree*—We'll just—If at least two of them concur, we'll say they agree. *Authors in general agree that* . . . But then they don't agree—There's nothing you can say about this. . . .

Can I leave it at that. . . . Oh give me a break, I don't know what I'm doing. I'm only a freshman. I have no idea what to do.

—Darlene, a first-semester freshman

Darlene's college assignment asked for synthesis and interpretation. The paper she turned in—a short, simplistic review of material from her sources—failed to meet her own expectations and her readers'. And yet, a chance to look at the process behind this unsophisticated product revealed serious thinking, a complicated, if confused, decision process, and a trail of unused abilities and discarded ideas—an active encounter with academic discourse that her teacher would never see.

The study presented here takes an unusually comprehensive look at one critical point of entry into academic performance. It shows a group of freshmen in the transition into the academic discourse of college, looking at the ways in which they interpret and negotiate an assignment that calls for reading-to-write. On such tasks, students are reading to create a *text* of their own, trying to integrate information from sources with *ideas* of their own, and attempting to do so under the guidance of a *purpose* they must themselves create. Because these reading-to-write tasks ask students to integrate reading, writing, and rhetorical purpose, they open a door to critical literacy. Yet this same interaction often makes reading-to-write a difficult process for students to learn and to manage.

To provide a rounded picture of cognition in this academic context, the study examines these students' thinking processes from a number of perspectives, drawing on their think-aloud protocols of writing and revising, on interviews with and self-analyses by the students, and on comparisons of teachers' and students' perceptions of texts the students wrote. It attempts to place these observations within a broader contextual analysis of the situation as students saw it and the social and cultural assumptions about schooling they brought with them.

What this study reveals are some radical differences in how individual students represent an academic writing task to themselves—differences teachers might interpret simply as an indication of a student's ability rather than his or her interpretation of the task. Students were often unaware that such alternative representations existed or that they might hold such significance. Some images of the task, for instance, were dominated by the goals of comprehension, summary, and simple response, and offered little or no place for critical response, original synthesis, or interpretation for a rhetorical purpose.

The reading-to-write task students imagined for themselves also had a direct effect on performance: it affected the goals they set, the strategies they used, and the ways they solved problems during composing. And it led to differences in teachers' evaluations of the texts—although, this study suggests, these evaluations may confuse the conventions of organization (e.g., use of topic sentences) with the writer's control of ideas. When students began to examine their options and attempt the more demanding task of interpreting for a purpose, certain students, whom we called the Intenders, showed important changes in their writing and thinking process. These changes, however, were not evident in the text nor apparent to teachers. Finally, this study showed how students' images of the task were rooted in the students' histories, the context of schooling, and cultural assumptions about writing they brought to college.

It is not surprising that some of the images students bring with them are at odds with the expectations they encounter at a university. However, when the expectations for "college-level" discourse are presented in oblique and indirect ways, the transition students face may be a *masked* transition. That is, the task has changed, but for a number of reasons, the magnitude and real nature of this change may not be apparent to students, even as they fail to meet the university's expectations.

One of the key implications of this study is that reading-to-write is a task with more faces and a process with more demands than we have realized. We see students thinking hard and doing smart things, even when they misgauge their goals or their written text fails to meet certain standards. This close survey of the cognitive and social landscape of reading-to-write in a college class gives one added respect for the students in this transition and for the complexity and sophistication of the "freshman" task as they face it.

Our heartfelt thanks go to our colleagues John R. Hayes, Karen A. Schriver, Nancy Spivey, Tom Huckin, Christina Haas, Lorraine Higgins, Stuart Greene, Jennie Nelson, Tim Flower, Stephen Witte, Mike Rose, Gerald Rutledge, and Kathy R. Meinzer.

Pittsburgh   L. F.
May 1989

Contents

READING-TO-WRITE

Introduction:
Studying Cognition in Context

LINDA FLOWER

"Interpret and synthesize." What the hell does that mean? Synthesize means to pull together, no, to make something up. Why should I want to make something up?—An M.A. student

Since I was talking out loud, I was very conscious of the fact that I was making connections to what everyone was saying. Using my own—using things that have happened to me to connect to the people talking [in the source text]. . . . And I realize that I actually *do* have strategies to read. I thought I didn't. I thought I was some kind of odd person who didn't have any strategies ever. . . .—A freshman

What I wasn't used to was interjecting my own feelings about the assignment as I went along. And when I think back on that, the fact that I stopped and responded to what the author had just said . . . that is really what kept the paper going and what gave me a lot of ideas. . . . And that was a new experience for me.
—A freshman

This study began as a classroom experiment that surprised both me and my students. Concerned with the task of reading-to-write, we wanted to understand the complex interaction that occurs when students are reading to create texts of their own. As the study took shape through a series of collaborative explorations with students and colleagues, we became impressed with the complexity of this familiar academic task. It surprised students by showing them how they had represented this reading-to-write task to themselves, showing, for instance, how each had negotiated the socially weighted decision to take or relinquish authority over their sources. And against the backdrop of a common assignment, it revealed significant cognitive differences in the ways individual students handled key problems, such as integrating their own ideas with a source text, creating an organizing idea, and constructing a purpose of their own. And, finally, even as this unexpected diversity moved into the spotlight, we began to see a pattern of assumptions and a shared history of reading and writing in school taking shape in the wings.

The goal of the two-part study presented in this book is to understand reading-to-write as the rich cognitive and social phenomenon we observed in that first class—to study it as a task of practical importance, as a window on how students integrate reading and writing, and as a rhetorical act occurring in the charged context of entering college. The study was designed as a collaborative effort to bring a variety of perspectives into close conversation. This initial chapter introduces the study as a whole by sketching these perspectives, with their emphases on cognitive processes, social context, and critical literacy. It then outlines the overall research design, and at the end of the chapter, previews the five key observations that emerged from the study and discusses some of its important limitations.

A second purpose of this introductory chapter is to address, in some small way, the issue of research itself. In tracing the background and collaborative history of the study, I would like to reflect on the process of such research itself and to share some of the problems and issues that arise in attempting to study cognition in context.

READING-TO-WRITE AND CRITICAL LITERACY

Why study reading-to-write? Reading in order to write is inextricably bound up with schooling. In practical terms it is the task we most associated with college-level work whether in English, history, fine arts, or general science. It is a tool used to learn, to test learning, and to push students to build beyond their sources. It is also a gate into that higher literacy in which information from a source text is not only understood on its own terms, but is transformed in the hands of the writer. However, the simple activity of reading and writing does not ensure that this higher literacy will develop. Applebee's 1981 study, *Writing in the Secondary School,* claims that high schools have developed a limited literacy in which writing is merely a tool for testing recall of content. This impoverished form of reading-to-write encourages consumption of information, not the transformation or use of one's knowledge. Richardson, Fisk, and Okun's (1983) critique of junior colleges is also directed at the absence of this higher literacy. In his five-year study Richardson documents a leveling-down effect in which institutions abandoned the goal of critical literacy in favor of the narrower goals of socialization and transferring information.

Various alternative forms of literacy are often defined by looking at the ways people use writing. Literacy, as Richardson, Vygotsky, and others have defined it, is not synonymous with ability to read (decode) or write (transcribe) per se. Rather it is a "goal-directed, context-specific" behavior, which means that a literate person is able to *use* reading and writing in a transactional sense to achieve some purpose in the world at hand (Richardson et al., p. 4). We can think of *critical literacy* as adding further specifications to this definition, in the sense that an act of critical literacy involves carrying out a particularly demanding set of such goals. In college these goals often include the creation of an analysis, synthesis, or original expression in written form. The element of "written form" is important here, since it distinguishes a critically literate performance from critical thinking per se—an ability that does not depend on being literate (Scribner & Cole, 1981). The ability to think with and through written text is a particular art. However, Richardson reminds us, merely practicing the conventional forms of college writing, such as a term paper or essay exam, is not synonymous with an act of critical literacy, even though tradition links the two. One can write a term paper by tying together an endless string of quotes or pass an exam by regurgitating facts. The real test of critical literacy is the kind of thinking a student is able to do in writing and reading. And reading-to-write, we will suggest, is a litmus test that lets us distinguish between the receptive process of basic literacy and the testing/transforming process of critical literacy.

An operational definition of literacy based on what the literate person does should help clarify these distinctions and the notion of critical literacy used in this book. At one level literacy means comprehending the rules, procedures, and instructions that let people function in society, whether they are reading a road sign, filling out an employment application, or following the job specs on a new order as part of their work at the textile mill. This receptive literacy, with its emphasis on getting information, has also traditionally meant being able to read and understand the Bible, the newspaper or union news, or, as in the remarkable Nicaraguan literacy campaign, to comprehend (and by implication accept) a new political or religious ideology.

By contrast, *critical* literacy typically means not simply building on but going beyond reception and understanding. Some aspects of critical literacy have what we might call a *questioning and testing emphasis*. The critically literate person questions sources, looks for assumptions, and reads for intentions, not just facts. For educators with this emphasis, critical literacy may also mean coming into political or social consciousness and questioning both authority and the status quo. And it may even mean rising to a reflexive questioning of one's own assumptions and responses as a reader and one's own assumptions and assertions as a writer.

Another equally important aspect of critical literacy has what I will call a *transforming emphasis*. The critically literate person not only understands information but transforms it for a new purpose. He or she is able to turn facts into concepts, to turn concepts into a policy or a plan, and to see the issue and define the problem within a problematic situation. The National Assessment of Educational Progress emphasizes this transforming process in its list of skills the workplace is coming to require: "Skills in reducing data, interpreting it, packaging it effectively, documenting decisions, explaining complex matter in simple terms, and persuading are highly prized in business, education, and the military and will become more so as the information explosion continues" (1981, p. 5). And from a completely different perspective, educational psychologists see young writers' abilities to transform their knowledge rather than simply relate it on paper as one of the late-blooming but critical skills of writing (Scardamalia & Bereiter, 1987).

Critical literacy, whether it emphasizes a testing/questioning process or a transforming one, is often a highly rhetorical act. It allows a reader to walk into the discourse and have a say; it is the means by which students enter the conversation of their disciplines and learn to talk and think like historians and physicists. We see this social and cognitive process in action when reading-to-write is used to develop an informed critical consciousness, one that gives learners the power to understand others' meaning and to make their own.

In this study we have defined reading-to-write as the goal-directed activity of **reading in order to write**. We have used the hyphenated phrase **reading-to-write** at those points where we want to emphasize this close relationship and its goal-directedness. In taking an operational look at reading-to-write as an intellectual process, we can see why it is a prime area in which to study as well as teach critical literacy. In reading-to-write each process is altered by the other. As the reader slips into the role of writer, the need to test and transform a source text is brought to the fore.

Reading-to-write, in our hyphenated sense of the term, is the process of a person who reads a relevant book, an article, a letter, knowing he or she needs to write. We have chosen to look at those special instances of strong interaction in which each process is actively affecting the other. We can contrast this with many other common situations in which the processes of reading and writing are more weakly linked—for example, a student reads ten books over the term and also writes a paper; a social worker reads letters, agency documents, case reports, and also writes reports. In many of these situations, the reader's process is more distantly constrained by writing if at all; it is guided by a goal of understanding or remembering a text, answering a question, or finding information to fill out a form.

This distinction between reading to compose and reading to do something else matters because different purposes push the reading process into distinctive shapes (Frase, 1976; Frederiksen, 1972; Rothkopf, 1976). Sticht (1977), for example, has shown that people who are reading *to do* something (such as operate a computer or fix an airplane) read much differently from people reading *to learn* something. They use the text to search for information, which they may use and forget, or they try to structure and recall the information they learn around the goals, procedures, or tests that let them carry out the task at hand. In fact, Sticht argues that many instructional texts and manuals fail because they are designed as though people were reading to learn textbook information, when they are in fact trying to act on it.

We can also imagine writing that is only distantly linked to reading, writing that draws heavily on the writer's prior knowledge or current thinking, not on a text at hand. Or writing that is done to explore one's own ideas, to express or to communicate one's knowledge, without the need to deal with another text. For various reasons, most writing research to date has focused on writing that is not directly related to reading or ignored the role reading plays in the construction of a text.

Reading-to-write makes a special demand for critical literacy because (at least in theory) it brings these two processes into strong interaction. The reading process is guided by the need to produce a text of one's own. The reader as writer is expected to manipulate information and transform it to his or her own purposes. And the writing process is complicated by the need to shape one's own goals in response to the ideas or even the purposes of another writer. Without a critical, questioning response, the writer is simply replicating his sources. Without the ability to transform knowledge he cannot synthesize his own knowledge and goals with that of another text. It is possible to bring the testing and transforming stance of critical literacy to any task, but reading-to-write is a good place to see it operate.

On the other hand, reading-to-write is a protean process that *can* be simple and uncritical, depending on the writer's goals. Consider the teacher who quickly summarizes the textbook for his class, the student who tries to piece together several required readings in preparation for a blue book exam, the paper writer who reads a source text to pillage a "good quote" for her argument or even to plagiarize, or the scholar or student who starts an article to learn new ideas but ends up using the source text as a springboard for her own thinking and a paper of her own. These familiar uses do not put a premium on either testing or transforming knowledge. Thus, although reading-to-write is an ideal stage for the performance of critical literacy, the process itself is highly subject to the goals of the writer, the influence of the context in which it occurs, and the abilities of the writer. If we expect reading-to-write to foster critical literacy in school, it appears we will have to create a context for writing that sets such goals and to teach the thinking strategies that can support those goals. The reading-to-write study that follows attempts to observe these goal-directed thinking processes within their academic context.

THE BACKGROUND AND COLLABORATIVE HISTORY
OF THE STUDY

The roots of this inquiry are in the still young but highly diverse tradition of cognitive studies. Sketching these roots may be the best way to explain this study's theoretical foundations and its particular vision of how cognition, context, critical literacy, and classroom research can affect each other. The work in cognitive studies that has influenced us has explored thinking in a variety of situations. It includes studies of "everyday cognition," such as Scribner's observation of men setting up the delivery orders in a milk plant (1984), Chase's look at how cab drivers succeed with incomplete mental maps and visually triggered knowledge (1982), Hayes' discovery of the "ten-year" phenomenon in the musical development of major Western composers (1981), and Larkin's comparative studies of how physicists and freshmen represent and solve physics problems (1983). In the field of reading and writing we have drawn on work such as Brown and Palincsar's demonstration of the dramatic gains poor readers make as they develop the "metaknowledge" to control their own reading process (1989), Scardamalia and Bereiter's descriptive model of young writers' knowledge-telling strategy (1987), Rose's cognitive analysis of students with writing blocks (1980), and my own work with John R. Hayes and our colleagues tracking the shifting structure of the writing plans people make as they compose (Flower & Hayes, 1981c; Flower, Schriver, Carey, Haas, & Hayes, in press). Cognitive studies often use multiple methods that range from naturalistic observation to collecting clinical, structured, and cued recall interviews, to process tracing with think-aloud protocols, to posing experimental tasks, to building computer simulations. (These simulations, as in the Larkin study, are used to test how well the researcher's theory of what people do matches the procedures real people actually use when the simulation or the descriptive theory is used to solve a genuine physics problem.) In its still brief history, this diverse body of work seems characterized by its curiosity about real-world cognition and by the flexible, often inventive research methods it brings to its investigations.

Working in this cognitive tradition, we set the additional goal of conducting *exploratory* empirical research—of understanding the phenomenon itself in greater depth rather than conducting an *experimental* test of a theory about it. This has important implications for both the process of research and the nature and limits of our observations. In the mythos of experimental research (i.e., in the cartoon version) one begins in the morning with a clear-cut hypothesis—a potential answer to a well-defined question. By noon that hypothesis is expressed in an experimental manipulation and set of pre-/posttests. A large pool of subjects known only by number are "run," and once the results come in, the meaning of the study swiftly emerges, expressed as an Anova, or, better yet, a more powerful stepwise regression, in which a set of clear main effects can speak for themselves with little need for interpretation. This caricature of an experimental study would wring a rueful smile from any experimentalist who has wrestled with the imponderable problems of forming a testable hypothesis and the intractable nature of a good design. Nevertheless, these ideals of initial clarity, rigor, and falsifiable hypotheses are central to that mode of discovery and its particular virtues. In contrast to that procedure, the process of much research in composition shows an alternative picture of how knowledge can be developed. The exploratory investigations that go on, particularly in cognitive research, can give us a glimpse into what is possible when rhetoric and composition reclaim the tool of controlled empirical observation and put it to work in the service of their own educational questions about complicated human and rhetorical events.

Like many research projects launched by a surprise, this particular study had its beginnings in a classroom. To encourage the students in an advanced writing class to understand their own cognition and look more closely at their reading and writing processes, I had asked them to take the role of researchers, using observations of themselves as a tool for self-analysis and reflection. As they read a short text, they were to think aloud with a tape recorder, collecting whatever thoughts went through their minds during the process of comprehending the text and writing their own statement on the issue it posed. The transcript or "think-aloud protocol" they created would be only a partial record of their constructive processes, focused on the reader/writer's conscious play of mind. However, this record can be astonishingly rich, and unlike normal retrospection, it makes the surprising and evanescent flow of the writer's thinking available for later reflection.

As students began to articulate and reflect on their own cognition, some meaningful patterns began to emerge. In particular, the transcripts encouraged students to take a thoughtful look at the rapid play of responses, inferences, decisions, and strategies that guided their reading and writing but may have evaporated from consciousness, as so much of our cognition does. The text, reprinted in Appendix IV, was brief—a two-page review of what various researchers and teachers had to say about revision. But it contained covert contradictions and a potpourri of claims and advice that didn't fit into a neat package of received wisdom. One passage noted that experienced writers used revision to "resee" their entire paper, while another passage described how expert business writers did lots of planning but almost no revision. The assignment was a standard, open-ended, and therefore ambiguous invitation to do what college courses typically ask: use the relevant information to interpret, synthesize, and write your own statement about this topic. It allowed students to track a process in action and see how that process was guided by their own assumptions and decisions.

Over the next week the students in the class looked at their think-aloud protocols to do a short, in-class presentation about "an interesting feature" of their own process. We learned more than we bargained for in these presentations. Students discovered goals and strategies used on this task which they began to recognize as part of their "standard operating procedure" for college assignments. For example, as one student reported: "As you read, the idea is to concentrate on a few key words and depend on them to sum up the meaning of the passage for you." For many students these goals and strategies had operated just under the level of conscious awareness. The protocols were letting them step outside of the flow of their composing and comprehension process and see the distinctive patterns and assumptions driving their own cognitive acts. As the talk went around the room, we discovered that students were telling each other how they saw this task and, by implication, many other writing assignments they had done. Yet the perception of what this assignment called for was not shared. We all know that people see problems differently. But the explicitness and individuality of these perceptions, based on seeing the protocol transcript, was striking. Students sitting next to each other were doing radically different things, yet each was assuming that he or she was doing what the assignment called for. While one student was "reading" the situation as a straightforward request for summary—prompting her to use standard summary strategies without a second thought—the student sitting next to her was struggling with a daunting task that dictated, be "creative" but observe a strict use of all the sources.

The students' first reaction to these alternative images of the task was understandable—they began to wonder which was the "right" task. But as we talked it became clear that each of these perceptions of the task had advantages and disadvantages in terms of difficulty, fit or misfit to an instructor's image, potential for learning, personal satisfaction, frustration, and so on. Some representations make the task easy, some lead to a rambling but enjoyable personal reflection, and some lead to a critical engagement with the source texts. Choosing the appropriate task representation meant not only reading the text but also "reading the situation." Through a combination of savvy, close reading of an assignment, asking questions, drawing inferences, and setting their own priorities, students had to interpret the rhetorical situation as a part of their decision about what and how to write.

What this classroom experiment showed was that *representing* a reading-to-write task to oneself is, itself, a critical part of the writing process. It is often an active process in the literal sense of the term: writers devote measurable time and deliberate thought to interpreting an assignment and the rhetorical context that surrounds it, as well as to considering their own goals and strategies. Yet the outcome of this process is a surprisingly individual representation that may carry hidden costs for the writer. (This classroom experiment and some implications of this task representation process are described in Chapter 1. This experience, with the two replications that followed, became the project's phase 1, Exploratory Study.)

In the course of this event, a classroom discovery began to turn into a researchable question: does this normally unseen process of representing a reading-to-write task make a genuine difference? And what if students were more aware of their options? The first set of hypotheses had been constructed by the students. The next step, we felt, was to teach what we had learned more directly to entering students, yet still retain the experience of self-discovery that had seemed so important in the class. The study's second phase therefore took place in a larger, collaborative teaching experiment. In the fall of 1985, the group of teachers represented in this volume, along with Christina Haas, Jennie Nelson, Lorraine Higgins, and Karen

Schriver, began designing an experimental course called Reading-to-Write. Its goal was to link a critical consciousness about the assumptions and strategies people bring to reading with an awareness of one's composing process and problem-solving strategies for writing. The bridge from reading to writing would be the students' awareness of their own reading-to-write repertoire. A second goal of this course was to turn current research into effective, teachable strategies students could use in their ongoing assignments. For example, in one session the freshmen read a short but difficult text on education in order to observe some of their own reading strategies, which they were then able to compare with the strategies we had observed other freshmen and advanced students using. Against this background of options, the freshmen tried out a particular "rhetorical reading" strategy that only the older students in the previous study had used (Haas & Flower, 1988). Some of the fruits of this experimental course are described in *Expanding the Repertoire: An Anthology of Practical Approaches for the Teaching of Writing,* edited by Kathleen McCormick.

As the Reading-to-Write course was being planned, we also began a research collaboration with colleagues at the University of California, Berkeley, as the Center for the Study of Writing at Berkeley and Carnegie Mellon, one of fifteen national centers supported by the Office of Educational Research and Improvement. In creating the research plan for this center, we felt that one of its central missions should be to help construct a theory of *writing as both a social and cognitive process* (Freedman, Dyson, Flower, & Chafe, 1987). And in the next step—designing a specific research agenda—the results of the pilot courses and the new Reading-to-Write course became the foundation for taking such a theoretical look at freshmen. In designing what had now become a formal "study," this social *and* cognitive mission of the center dictated parts of the design and the questions we chose to ask.

This process by which a research plan emerged as a response to multiple goals and influences is, I believe, quite typical. It is one way the "conversation" in a discourse community registers its influence and one way research remains sensitive to needs felt in the field at large. Placed in the context of my own history as a teacher and researcher, this new commitment to understanding *cognition within its context* did not mean a change in that trajectory; rather it expanded the boundaries of the problem I wished to solve. It led us as a group to ask, how can cultural criticism, textual analysis, teachers' responses, the students' histories and perceptions all help us understand the active mind at work in reading-to-write? The work reported here as phase 2, Teaching Study, is an attempt to take different perspectives on a common problem and a shared body of data. This plan made each member of our research groups responsible not only to his or her own data and special perspective, but also to the discoveries of everyone else.

Finally, the results of this research were substantially influenced by another form of collaboration, of the sort usually noted only in acknowledgments. In the fall of 1986, as we began to analyze the data collected in the spring, Nancy Nelson Spivey joined the rhetoric faculty, and Mike Rose came to Carnegie Mellon as a visitor, to teach a seminar on Literacy, Cognition, and the Teaching of Writing. The issues this seminar raised and Mike Rose's own thinking directly addressed the question of how to work within the strengths of a cognitive research paradigm and at the same time open up some new lines of talk with social perspectives on literacy. A key part of the collaboration in a research community is exactly this sort of stimulation and supportive controversy. It changes what you learn. In a more obvious way Nancy Spivey, Mike Rose, and later Stephen Witte became direct parts of this process when we began to struggle with problems of conceptualizing the analysis. They naturally saw problems, for which one is always ruefully grateful. But more important for this discussion, they listened to the data and stayed to talk through alternative interpretations and rival hypotheses. In dealing with the problems of interpretation, they became significant collaborators.

The point of this brief history is not merely to acknowledge the role of individuals and institutions, but to be clear about how research of this sort gets done. This "empirical" study began in teaching and developed in response to some distinctive sorts of collaboration. As Lunsford and Ede (1986), Bazerman (1985), and others are making clear, professional and academic work in many fields depends in part on person-to-person collaboration—the extended hours any two or three people spend planning the design, talking over the data, and defining the key issues. It also depends on the way the field itself not only provides but pressures us all to reintegrate and extend our knowledge. The insights this study hopes to achieve will come from choosing to wrestle with a shared problem. In practice this meant not only working together but trying to create conceptual harmony out of the multiple perspectives we chose to take, each of which spoke with a distinctive voice. We needed to harmonize the many voices of writers speaking from the data itself, with the theoretical background that framed the study, with new ideas and new data from the field and from our colleagues. It was especially when those ideas commanded serious consideration but resisted simple integration that some of our most favored insights were forged.

On the other hand, research does not emerge from a committee or group discussion. Data of this sort is always interpreted by the researcher who has pored over it. Like the voices from the field and ideas said to be "in the air," collaborative input is always mediated by the cognition of the writer doing the research. In that personal constructive process the individual writer/researcher must define the heart of the question as he or she sees it, must draw the inferences that create a pattern of meaning, and must test that meaning against other possible ones. Research and writing of this sort are what an individual mind makes of its context. It is, indeed, this tension and this process by which the individual mind mediates its world and its history that research on cognition in context has to address.

THE INTERACTION OF COGNITION AND CONTEXT

One way a theory of writing as a social *and* cognitive process emerges is not by creating simple dichotomies but by creating shared problems within the field. We can expand the boundaries of our research questions and use research methods normally identified with studying cognition *or* context to look at the interaction *between* them (see Rose, 1984). The focus and methods of the present study, for example, are clearly centered in cognitive research. It did not, for example, attempt to be an ethnographic study. Its purpose, however, was to understand that cognition as it operated in the specific context of a freshman class. One asks, what shape does a given cognitive process take when it is embedded in the historically defined context of entering college, in the social situation of a class, and in the immediate context of a particular assignment? And how does looking at a process from this perspective alter what you attend to?

Let me illustrate this goal of studying "embedded" cognition with our own data. Looking primarily at the cognitive aspects of writing and reading leads one to describe students' thinking at a level of detail that shows up specific differences in how individual writers perform and where they may have trouble. For example, some students regularly elaborate on the text as they read, connecting statements in the text to their prior knowledge or "instantiating" general concepts in the text by supplying their own concrete instances, to clarify or test their understanding (see Chapter 5). Other students use elaboration quite differently, as a way to generate ideas in service of their own writing plan or to test a claim they want to make in their paper. And some students do almost no elaboration at all. On the basis of a process analysis alone, we could predict that these elaborations play an important role in what students write, and we might argue that this cognitive process is also part of what it means for a writer "to make the text her own" or to engage in "critical thinking."

On the other hand, a focus on embedded cognition would assert that this process does not occur in a vacuum. Why do these students who do not elaborate pay so little attention to their own ideas and responses or fail to allot time to questioning and exploring ideas? The social context of writing, we might note, starts with the context students imagine or define for themselves and the goals they set (Herrington, 1988). Those goals and strategies also reflect the social context of a class and myriad assumptions about academic writing that could squelch elaboration, such as: "Don't use I," "Show you have learned the material," "Texts are written by authorities who report facts, while all I can have is an opinion," and so on (Bartholomae, 1985; Nelson & Hayes, 1988). Finally, this context is an even more complex reflection of the culture of school and the cultural community to which the student belongs or aspires (Heath, 1983).

Research in writing needs to recognize both cognition and the context that conditions it. Likewise, teaching may be most effective when it can (1) teach students to understand and expand their own repertoire of strategies for planning, revising, and so on; (2) create a context that supports thinking processes we value; and (3) also help students examine some of the nonsupportive contexts and assumptions they may be carrying in their own heads.

The conceptual diagram in Figure 1 presents a view of embedded cognition in which reading and writing processes are seen as constructive acts and the social, linguistic, and cultural realities are conceptualized as forces acting on cognition. Research whose dominant focus is on those social and cultural forces per se might naturally put the spotlight on a different part of this interaction. But in both cases we could ask the question, how do these large contextual forces spell themselves out in the work and thought of individual writers—especially learning writers?

This conceptual map (see Flower, 1987) highlights certain features of reading and writing as constructive processes:

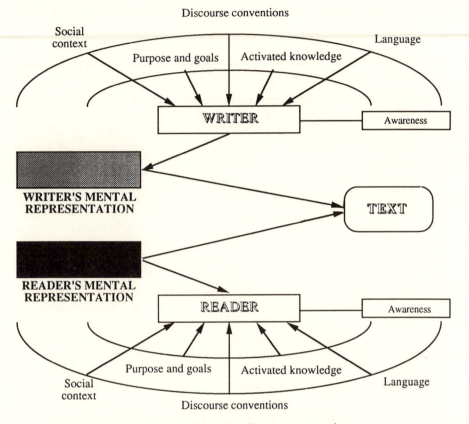

Figure 1. Key elements in discourse construction.

- Writing and reading are acted on by multiple forces: the outer circle in the figure denotes forces such as the social context, discourse conventions, and language, and the inner circle denotes the *activated* knowledge and purposes relevant to this particular act of reading or writing. The two levels let us distinguish between all possible knowledge and contexts known to the writer and those wielding active influence at a given moment.
- Writing and reading lead to the construction of mental representations of meaning—in the minds of reader and writer. These internal representations cannot be equated with the text the writer writes down or the cues to meaning construction the reader perceives or with any one reading of the text itself. We can think of these constructions as two related but different networks of information, which are not necessarily coded in words and sentences or even language. Instead, as the multiple representation hypothesis suggests (Flower & Hayes, 1984), this knowledge may take the form of abstract propositions, code words and pointers to schemas, or even images. Moreover, these representations of meaning are likely to go well beyond the propositional content of

a text and to include both a reader/writer's own web of intentions and those they impute to the other players in the discourse (Flower, 1988).

• Awareness or metaknowledge of one's own representation, of the process that produced it, and of the forces acting on that process appears to be an optional feature—valuable for problem solving but often noted by its absence.

What this conceptual map does not tell us is also interesting, because, unlike a process model, it does not account for how discourse is constructed and how such embedded cognition might operate. For instance, how does social context affect the goal setting of an individual writer? How is it that "meaning," which resides in the minds of readers and writers, not in texts, is negotiated and constructed through texts? How and when do those readers and writers build shared representations— and what do they share? The process models being proposed by Tierney and Pearson (1984), de Beaugrande (1984), and Nystrand (1986) are steps in that direction.

One could argue that research, to date, has achieved tremendous momentum in seeing writing as a cognitive process *and* in illuminating the social context in which people write. But the two ways of knowing—each looking at its own phenomena— do not always talk to one another (Freedman et al., 1987). Nor have we achieved an integrated vision of how cognition and context affect one another in the process of real students' writing (Flower, 1989). To construct a more integrated theory of writing as a social and cognitive process does not mean abandoning strictly cognitive and strictly social inquiry, for each has a valued place. But it will involve seeing this integration as an object of inquiry in itself and finding new, more sensitive ways to study it. A researcher necessarily works within a paradigm, whether it is social, cognitive, or some other type, and every study must have a dominant focus that will be reflected in its methodology—the researchers and the study need to do the things they do best. The goal of a social and cognitive theory is to push to the edges of the envelope—to capture more of the picture where cognition and context interact and to select as an object of study processes in which that interaction matters.

STUDYING A COGNITIVE AND SOCIAL PROCESS

Reading-to-write is a point of just such interaction, and we felt an exploratory, classroom-based design would let us describe the event from multiple perspectives. We did not, therefore, set out to establish expert/novice differences, to test a pedagogical method, or to track the path of development. The results we aimed for are not conclusions in the familiar sense of tested claims. The rigor in this design must come primarily from checks on the reliability of the observations rather than from tests of statistical significance or the power to exclude rival hypotheses. The goal of such a study is to create strong hypotheses—observations that are guided by theory but grounded in detailed empirical evidence.

How then does one observe this cognitive act embedded in a social context? The question, of course, is how to do justice to a complex process. No inquiry is objective in the naive sense of that word, whether it is done by a literary critic doing a "close reading" of the text or by an experimental psychologist recording reaction times. Research and scholarship alike are forcefully shaped by the paradigm from which they spring, by the questions they chose to ask, and by the slice of experience they find compelling to study. This necessary selectivity in research is especially visible in this study because reading-to-write is what some would call an "over-determined" act; that is, multiple forces shape the process, and multiple features of the process affect success. In choosing to concentrate on features such as the organizing plan, the contrast between students' and judges' perceptions, the link between comprehension and planning strategies, the effect of prompts, the context of school, and some cultural assumptions surrounding writing, we were guided by three criteria:

1. We wanted to study aspects of this process that were firmly grounded in a body of theory, whether it was in rhetoric and composition, cognitive psychology, or critical theory; we wanted to make contact with a larger issue.

2. At the same time we wanted to pursue aspects of reading-to-write that could be observed in the experience and performance of real writers. We wanted to pursue those theoretical positions that were not self-referential speculations about metaphorical processes, but rather claims that could be tested, refined, and even radially revised by empirical evidence. In short, we wanted to develop a data-based theory. And this was, in part, a response to our third constraint.

3. We wanted to explore features of this process that are of practical importance to teachers and students. As much as the members of this team value basic research, we felt this exploratory study needed to work close to the bone of experience. Our test was whether we could share our research questions and results directly with students, who in turn would see their own thoughts and processes mirrored in our analysis. More than that, we wanted to study those aspects of the reading-to-write process that are not just significant, but can be taught. We wanted to do research that could make a practical difference.

In a mature, fully developed theory, the links between theory or principles and experience have been forged. Our knowledge of reading-to-write is hardly in that enviable state. So we made a choice to work on two levels in the hope that our top-down journey from theory would connect with our bottom-up journey from data.

This study, then, is organized as two intersecting intellectual journeys. Each chapter is first an attempt to define an issue, a force that shapes performance, or a critical feature of the process—to take a theory-guided, top-down view. We wanted to raise questions we could not answer and to explore issues we are only beginning to fathom. At the same time we wanted to conduct a detailed, close examination of what students in a given situation actually did, to approach large issues in a data-driven, bottom-up fashion. Each chapter in this study therefore also reports on what we observed from the advanced classes and the four sections of Carnegie Mellon freshmen who were part of this study.

The data we collected, as a part of a naturalistic study with one quasi-experimental manipulation, bears this relationship to the theory. It is not itself a generalizable, broad theoretical statement about how students in general perform. Nor does it test the validity of theoretical claims, though it may help set their range of validity. Rather it shows us how a theoretically defined process, such as task representation, *works itself out* in actions of real students on a given task in an actual class. It *instantiates* a theory and concepts with a detailed instance. Data-based observations of a theoretically significant process, we argue, can bring a new level of reality into consciousness. They not only give operational, hence more teachable, definitions to our abstractions, they frequently challenge abstractions and force us to develop a better theory to account for this enlarged picture of the writer's experience. As a theory-guided, data-based exploration, this study attempts to embed empirical methods, where possible, within a broader analysis and interpretation of process.

OVERVIEW OF THE STUDY DESIGN

The research covered in this series of reports was organized into two phases, the Exploratory Study (presented in Chapter 1) and the Teaching Study. Since Chapters 2 through 9 belong to the Teaching phase, we present the design of that study here rather than in each chapter and include those materials that apply to the entire set.

The Exploratory Study

Described in detail in Chapter 1 (and sketched in the Background section of this Introduction), this initial series of classroom experiments and process analyses laid the groundwork for the project. It raised issues and hypotheses that called for more systematic study. By describing the alternative task representations students actually brought to this task, it allowed us to create a tentative "menu of options" against which we could study the actions of freshmen in the study's second, Teaching, phase.

The Teaching Study

An outgrowth of the in-class process experiments, this major phase of the project still involved students in the process of discovery, but at a new starting point, based on what we had learned in the Exploratory Study. The Teaching Study tracks seventy-two freshmen as they do a short reading-to-write assignment, then reflect on their own image of the task, and finally revise that paper to more fully carry out their own purpose. The goals of this second study were to look very closely at how pieces of this complex process were carried out in the specific context of a freshman class. There is no reason to think that Carnegie Mellon freshmen represented those mythical figures, the "typical freshman" or the "common reader," or that the CMU freshman course, with its emphasis on the writing process, is typical of all university composition programs. What this study can yield, however, are sharply delineated reference points for looking at other populations and a concrete instance of how the abstract, complex processes sketched out earlier take on shape and substance in the experience of freshmen.

Students

The study involved four sections totaling seventy-two students in a freshman course called Reading-to-Write, which fulfilled the university writing requirement for these students. Over the term the sections met nine times as a group for a lecture/

presentation on a new topic or approach to writing. The introduction to task representation and resulting assignment was one of these presentations.

Materials

The assignment we used was closely modeled on the task developed in the Exploratory Study. The instructions asked for the range of goals college papers frequently require and included the favored words of such assignments: "read and interpret this data . . . synthesize all the relevant findings . . . [write] your statement about time management based on your interpretation of the data," for example.

The source text the freshmen read was on the topic of time management. It was titled and formatted as a series of notes a student might take. It was designed to contain conflicts, contradictions, relevant information subordinated to other topics, and a set of perspectives that did not fall into a neat package. For example, one authority, Alan Lakein, told people how to "get control of their time and their life" through scheduling; William James advocated renewed concentration in the face of mental fatigue; and a student survey described standard assignment strategies such as "create a crisis." (See Appendix I.)

To help students reflect on their own writing and plans for revision, we scripted a forty-minute lecture on task representation (i.e., on how writers represent rhetorical situations and assignments to themselves). This functioned as a prompt for the self-analysis and the revision task described later. The lecture presented task representation with a metaphoric "menu of options" and described a number of organizing plans and goals students in the pilot study had shown us. The excerpt from this lecture in Appendix II contains detailed definitions of the menu developed from the Exploratory Study, so we recommend it to the reader interested in the features of the task as these students construed it.

A Self-Analysis sheet, which was a condensed version of the task representation lecture, was designed to let students categorize their own performance during the lecture. (See Chapter 3.)

The Revision Assignment took two forms. One reminded students of the task representation lecture and asked them to revise their paper to do an "Interpretation for a Purpose" (if they had not already seen the task that way). The other merely asked students to revise to make their draft "better." Both assignments contained instructions for how to conduct a mini-process interview during revising, in order to look at one's own revising process. (See Chapter 6.)

Subsequent interviews with students followed a script, although interviewers felt free to follow up on issues that seemed important. (See Chapter 8.)

Procedures

The study relied on a battery of interconnected procedures and bodies of data, outlined in Figure 2. We will discuss the procedures in terms of the questions we were hoping they would answer.

Question 1: How will freshmen represent this open-ended reading-to-write task to themselves, in terms of the menu of options observed in the earlier Exploratory Study?

All students in the course were given the Time Management assignment as part of

PROCEDURES   GROUPS OF STUDENTS

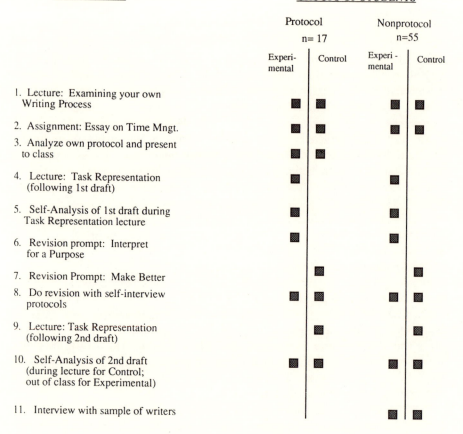

	Protocol n= 17		Nonprotocol n=55	
	Experimental	Control	Experimental	Control
1. Lecture: Examining your own Writing Process	■	■	■	■
2. Assignment: Essay on Time Mngt.	■	■	■	■
3. Analyze own protocol and present to class	■	■		
4. Lecture: Task Representation (following 1st draft)	■		■	
5. Self-Analysis of 1st draft during Task Representation lecture	■		■	
6. Revision prompt: Interpret for a Purpose	■		■	
7. Revision Prompt: Make Better		■		■
8. Do revision with self-interview protocols	■	■	■	■
9. Lecture: Task Representation (following 2nd draft)		■		■
10. Self-Analysis of 2nd draft (during lecture for Control; out of class for Experimental)	■	■	■	■
11. Interview with sample of writers			■	■

Data for Analysis includes think-aloud protocols, texts (drafts 1and 2),
self-analyses (Experimental on draft #1&2; Control on draft 2), revision
protocols, in-class oral presentations, student interviews.

Subjects : Four sections for first-semester freshmen. N=72.

Figure 2. Overview of design and analyses for teaching study.

a unit on Understanding Your Own Writing Process. They were told they would be
using their performance on this assignment to examine their own strategies for
reading and writing. Like certain other assignments in the course, this particular
piece of writing was to be examined and discussed but not given a letter grade. The
assignment came in the third week of college for the protocol section and two weeks
later for the nonprotocol group.

Analysis of students' representations was based on a variety of measures described later: students' own self-analyses, the organizing plan of the text as perceived by judges, and think-aloud protocols during composing and revision. (See
Chapters 2 and 3.)

Question 2: Product measures and self-reports focus on the end result. But how was this representation actually constructed, and how did it affect the strategies students used during the process of reading and writing?

The students from one section of the course did a think-aloud protocol as they read and wrote about Time Management, as students in the earlier Exploratory Study had done. The purpose of the protocol, from their point of view, was to enable them to look more closely at their own thinking and composing process. The papers and tapes from each student were turned in on a Friday, transcribed for them over the weekend, and returned on Monday morning. On the following Wednesday and Friday students in this class gave brief oral presentations on "an interesting feature of my own process" before any further discussion of the task had taken place. They later wrote a short paper on this topic. This assignment was clearly focused on examining one's own writing process on a typical college task. The Time Management paper itself was not graded.

Analysis of these protocols focused on processes of composing and comprehending, including comprehension monitoring, elaborating, structuring information, and creating a writing plan and looked at strategic patterns and problems related to the different tasks students were attempting. (See Chapters 4, 5, 6, and 9.)

Question 3: Would a brief introduction to the menu of alternative representations of this task, combined with a renewed request to "interpret," lead students to a different task when they revised—even without additional instruction in how to do an interpretation?

Second, if this brief introduction and emphasis on "interpreting for a purpose" did have any effect, would the effect be any greater than if students were merely asked to revise and make their papers "better"? Do students interpret these two prompts to revision in different ways?

If students could make significant changes in their papers on the basis of a mere one-hour discussion of options and alternative representations, we could conclude that task representation (rather than some general quality such as "writing ability") was indeed affecting their performance. (Of course, we would still not know whether making such choices was normally under the student's conscious control.) If students fail to change, however, or change in surprising ways, this could point to difficult parts of this academic task for which freshman may need direct instruction or stronger incentive.

To look at within-subject changes, we asked students to revise their original drafts. (It is reasonable, however, to suppose that an introduction to task representation *before* writing might have a different, possibly stronger, effect than asking for revision.) Students were randomly divided into equal-sized experimental and control groups within each class in order to make sure any changes were the effect of the lecture and revision prompt and not a "history" effect of simply revising a draft.

The Experimental students came to the lecture session and heard an introduction to task representation and a review of ways other students had seen this task. At each step in reviewing this "menu of options" students were completing a Self-Analysis of their own representation (based on the draft before them). They turned in a copy of their drafts and left with instructions to revise their paper, this time attempting one of the harder versions of the task, to "interpret with a purpose" (if they had not already done so).

The Control students went to their sections, instead of to this lecture, turned in a copy of their drafts, did an activity unrelated to task representation, and left with the instructions to revise their papers to make them "better." After completing their revisions, these Control students met as a group, heard the Task Representation lecture, and did their Self-Analysis based on the revised draft before them.

As they revised their papers, both Experimental and Control groups were asked to conduct think-aloud self-interviews, on tapes we supplied, at intervals during their revising process, and then to review the tapes for insights into their own process.

Back in the individual section classes later that week, teachers used the split between experimental and control to discuss what effect the revision prompt had on how students saw the task and also to discuss how students perceived revision. Throughout the rest of the term, this common exercise served as a reference point for looking at the useful (and less useful) strategies students already used and to encourage students to examine their own reading and writing processes. This sequence of assignments and self-analysis (in its simpler form without experimental and control sections) appears to be a useful teaching tool that has been continued in subsequent classes.

Analysis of the change in students' task representations was based on (1) judges' blind ratings of the students' original and revised texts, in terms of their Organizing Plan (e.g., was it a summary, a synthesis, etc.?), (2) changes reported in students' own Self-Analyses, and (3) the evidence of the revision protocols that let us distinguish between attempted changes and visible changes in the text. (See Chapters 3 and 6.)

Question 4: How would students perceive their own representation of the task and would teachers/judges reading these papers perceive the Organizing Plan the students intended?

As students heard the Task Representation lecture (before revising for the Experimental students; after revising for the Control group), they followed along with the Self-Analysis sheet based on our earlier study. They were asked to check the features that best fit their performance (or to describe "other"). They were then asked if the strategies they used in this instance were "standard strategies" they normally used in reading-to-write tasks and, finally, to predict what decisions a group of masters' students would make.

We then asked a group of experienced teachers to group the papers according to the Organizing Plan the writer used. This let us compare the Organizing Plans students thought they used with those the teachers thought they saw. An unexpected development in the judging of these essays led us to a further analysis of what teacher/judges look for in judging the complexity of such texts. (See Chapters 2 and 3.)

Question 5: How does the context of writing affect the task students gave themselves on both the original assignment and the revision?

A task in a required freshman course operates in a variety of contexts; we examined a few of these. Looking at the immediate context of the assignment itself, we used protocols to track how students translated instructions into cognitive actions and to trace links between those actions and students' expectations about school writing. In revision, we discovered a range of ways students negotiated the relationship between the prompts, the text at hand, and their priorities outside class.

We conducted interviews with a subset of students whose responses to the assignment had differed. These interviews, in addition to the oral presentations, allowed us to observe some of the shared assumptions about writing students brought to this task and to place certain decisions in the large cultural and institutional context of schooling. (See Chapters 6, 7, 8, and 9.)

PREVIEW OF THEMES AND OBSERVATIONS

In the course of this study, a pattern of observations emerged that crossed individual studies and grew into some themes that recur throughout this book. By previewing these themes we hope to let you, the reader, track how a general observation, such as "task representations differ," played itself out in different keys in the various contexts glimpsed in this study (e.g., in the context of planning, writing, and revising; of English or history classes; or of high school as students remembered it). The key observations that form the leitmotifs for this book are these:

1. Students hold some significantly different, tacit representations of supposedly common academic tasks. Because these multifaceted mental representations are constructed from prior experience, from inferences about the social and rhetorical context, and from writers' own values and desires, students may approach a common reading-to-write assignment with meaningfully different sets of goals, strategies, and criteria.

2. These differences can cause problems. Because these representations are often tacit, students and teachers may be in unspoken disagreement about what constitutes an "appropriate" representation. A student may be struggling in good faith to construct a summary organized by the key terms from the text, carefully relegating his or her own ideas to a tacked-on "response," while the student's instructor may assume that in college writing one would go beyond the source text, would organize the reading around key terms from previous discussions, apply readings to a problem posed by the course, and so on.

Moreover, when a student's written text is used to decide what sort of task (e.g., summary, interpretation) the student was attempting, students and their readers may disagree. It seems fair to conclude that some of these freshmen are still developing their picture of what a complex task such as synthesizing, interpreting, or arguing requires. Their readers are expecting more than the writers deliver. On the other hand, this recurrent observation is also a disturbing indication that the written product can be an inadequate, even misleading, guide to the thinking process that produced it. Our product-based inferences about a student's late-night writing process may radically underestimate the available knowledge, the problem-solving effort, and the unresolved dilemmas that actually exist. When this happens, we may be trying to diagnose and teach a thinking process in the dark.

3. Building an "appropriate" task representation is not enough. Even when goals strategies, criteria, and the constructive process of task representation are brought to the foreground as objects of metacognition and choice, writers are not always able to carry out the plans they intend. Task representation may play a far larger role in a

writer's performance—and success in school—than we have recognized; however, we must not underestimate what is left to learn and to teach. As students confront academic writing in high school and in college, they are entering a discourse community with specialized conventions and expectations that they must learn and a community that expects writers to create and transform knowledge—a task all of us find difficult. Learning to write in college appears to be a mixture of questioning assumptions and building new task representations; of applying to school writing certain broad cognitive and rhetorical capabilities already possessed; and, finally, of learning certain new conventions, strategies, and habits of mind. The teaching problem in helping students through this transition is inferring the appropriate balance—knowing when one needs to challenge the student with a classroom context that calls for those broad capabilities, when one needs to challenge the assumptions and prior images of the task that may confound a student's effort, and when one needs to teach new strategies for thinking and writing.

4. Academic discourse is not a Platonic entity, nor is its community a peaceable kingdom that agrees on its goals and intellectual conventions. This diversity is one part of the writer's problem. At the same time, this study suggests that certain basic intellectual goals or practices, which *do* form a common thread across much academic discourse, can also pose special difficulty for students and may be at the root of other more apparent problems.

Academic discourse, as defined in this classroom study, places special value on two such literate practices. One of these is *integrating one's own ideas and knowledge* into the written conversation with one's sources. The freshmen assumed that more accomplished writers would do this (although they themselves did not). The teachers expected such integration as a move toward critical literacy and toward realizing writing's epistemic potential to transform knowledge rather than to report information. The other valued but problematic practice is *interpreting source texts for a purpose of one's own*—applying or adapting knowledge to solve a problem or to reach one's own goals. Throughout the study we observed students having difficulty with both of these expectations—failing to attempt them, wrestling with confusion over what should be done, or stopped in the attempt by the inherent difficulty of these intellectual acts. These two practices emerged as significant hurdles in these students' full entry into academic discourse.

5. The process of reading-to-write in college is both a cognitive and a social act. That is to say, the performance we observed was a *strategic process* in which students—like all writers—read the context of the rhetorical situation as well as the task at hand, and in doing so constructed their own representation of the task, set their own goals. On the basis of that image and those goals, they drew on the thinking skills, the rhetorical strategies, and the discourse conventions they knew or thought might help. This constructive act not only took place in the immediate social context of a class, it was itself a function of students' history, assumptions, and past experience with writing in school. Cognition and context, goals and strategies were engaged in a complex, interactive performance.

6. Watching writers caught up in this cognitive and social process of negotiating academic discourse makes one increasingly skeptical about trying to specify "what a freshman writer needs to learn." Our data argued against a deficit model that

would point to some missing "cognitive skills" these eighteen-year-old freshmen needed to develop or to generic discourse conventions they needed to master. Nor could we conclude that any given vision of "academic writing" could stand as the ideal toward which we should urge students to aspire. For instance, under some circumstances we place special value on taking a high-effort, purposeful, interpretive stance toward one's reading (see point 4). But our own experience as writers said that one sets that especially demanding task only when the situation and one's own goals call for it. To be an effective writer means being able to read a situation, to weigh the costs and benefits of your own options, and to carry out the goals you set for yourself.

The knowledge writers need, as we came to see it, was best described as *strategic knowledge*. It involves reading a situation and setting appropriate *goals,* having the *knowledge* and *strategies* to meet one's own goals, and finally, having the meta-knowledge or *awareness* to reflect on both goals and strategies. Strategic knowledge is a contextualized form of knowing; it develops over time and out of experience. At the same time it renders that experience and those prior contexts open to reflection. If this characterization proves useful and we choose to teach the reading-to-write process as a strategic, cognitive, and social act, we may find that this final element of metacognitive awareness carries a potential we have only begun to tap.

SOME IMPORTANT LIMITATIONS OF THIS STUDY

Although we feel there are good arguments for the conclusions we reached, this study has a number of important limitations, and trying to articulate these is itself part of understanding what a more adequate cognitive-and-social picture might include. One limitation concerns the definition of context. We have chosen to focus on the individual writer, as a thinker within the context of school; our methods of close analysis, focused on process data, texts, and interviews, are most sensitive to cognition and tend to see context through the eyes of our students. This stands in contrast to a study such as Goodlad's *A Place Called School,* which depended on surveys, interviews, and tallies of behavior to show how the context of school includes far more than students and academic work. Goodlad's broad definition of context includes the function of school, its relevance to students, the way teachers teach and the circumstances in which they do it, the implicit and explicit curriculum, the distribution of resources, and the sense of equity and satisfaction people feel. This broader context clearly impinged on the reading-to-write process as we observed it. For instance, although teachers often talked about student writing in terms of intellectual investment and independent thinking, students also operated in an action context in which time, uncertainty about the rules of the game, and life in the dorm played visible roles in their decisions.

The context in which writing occurs is large; it also includes the history students carry in their heads and the world outside class, which influences what they value and assume about academic work. Our writer-centered investigative stance could reach that world only indirectly; nevertheless, it emphasized points of contact in which a student in the privacy of her dorm and her own mind, in the simple act of crafting a beginning sentence, is both subject to that circle of influence and actively mediating it as she works.

Another limitation is the result of this study's hybrid design. Our observations are based on a limited data set (only seventy-two students, seventeen in the protocol condition), without the benefit of repeated measures (students wrote only one paper and a revision), and without the control of a more rigorous experimental manipulation (only the revision task allowed us to create randomly selected experimental and control groups). In choosing to do an exploratory study in the context of a freshman course, we sacrificed an important measure of certainty for the chance of being surprised. One cannot make strong generalizations based on these data. On the other hand, we do want to use it as a springboard to a more theoretical discussion and a naming of issues. Our goal is to build a conceptual framework that goes beyond the data—to put some generalizations on trial. We have tried to make it clear when we are switching discourse and move from reporting to interpretation. However, Brodkey's (1987b) caution about ethnographic research applies here. It is often difficult to separate perceptions from assumptions in the telling of the story.

Given these goals, the issue one wants to worry about is validity. Here is the story of a handful of students at a possibly unusual university doing a task created for the study. Do the observations this exploratory study let us make constitute good examples of the reading-to-write process, of the demands of academic discourse, or of freshman in transition? Are these data a reasonable foundation for hypotheses about those larger issues? Ultimately the best answer will be a socially constructed one in which other teachers and researchers see consonance or dissonance with their own observations. As an interim measure, we did try to create a form of triangulation in our divided authorship, which brought different theoretical perspectives and methods of analysis to a common body of data and encouraged a dialogue among them. Nevertheless there are real questions, limitations, and rival hypotheses we should consider in interpreting these data.

First, this study cannot be read as a test of students' ability level or capacity for academic work, or as any other examlike measurement. As we discuss at length in Chapter 9, we were not trying to measure what these freshman could do, given well-specified *instructions* and strong motivation. We wanted to see what they would chose to do in the context of multiple options and underspecified expectations—that is, in response to the open *invitations* to academic discourse we believe students often receive. This is a study of task representation, then, not of ability, although we believe the two are often confused when we presume to measure the latter.

A more complex issue of validity involves the relationship between our task and other common academic assignments in other settings. Is there a meaningful overlap? Of the three writing skills English teachers rated most highly in Bridgeman and Carlson's (1984) study, this task asked for two (to organize ideas from several sources and to analyze and criticize) and implicitly invited the third (to argue for a position). However, we should note that the teachers in the Bridgeman and Carlson survey also saw requests for argument or for summary plus analysis as too much to expect from freshmen—a view we do not share. Doyle's (1983) review of research on academic work distinguished four types of tasks based on whether they call for remembering information, using a procedure or routine, giving an opinion, or comprehension and understanding. Because these four types of academic task are embedded in an evaluative context, he argues, they can also be placed on a matrix of ambiguity and risk. Comprehension and understanding tasks combine a high degree of risk (compared to simply giving a opinion) with a high degree of ambiguity (compared to performing a well-learned routine). Our task clearly belongs in this corner of the academic matrix, among the difficult, valued, but typically ill-specified and risky tasks school presents. These demands appear in other studies of academic discourse in specific settings (Herrington, 1985; McCarthy, 1987). On the other hand, the freshman instructors surveyed by Witte, Cherry, and Meyer (1982) do not appear to see themselves as teaching some of the skills we have identified with critical thinking.

The real threat to validity in a study such as this is not in setting higher expectations than some part of the profession, but in failing to communicate to the student one's expectations. The worst-case scenario is what Witte has called the TCT problem in writing evaluation research: You are interested in how well students grow tomatoes; the task, however, asks them to grow carrots, which they do; you then evaluate them on how well they grow tomatoes. Trying to design an ill-defined task that could, like a Rorschach test, tell us more about students' representations than about a given task, carries the risk of creating a task that is simply unrealistic or unfair. If we had given students explicit instructions to discuss contradictions or to make visible use of their own ideas in the paper, we would have probably seen different behavior—at least to some degree. However, the rhetorical situation we wanted to understand was not that of a placement or skills test, but of an open-ended writing assignment in which the whole network of academic expectations is in the air, and in which many options are acceptable and many criteria—too many to spell out—are always in force.

Despite this risk, there are reasons to believe this study is unearthing a repertoire rather than a bunch of carrots. For one thing, although educators may assign precise meaning to their terms of art (e.g., analysis and synthesis), students did not appear to do the same. In some cases the meaning of the assignment appeared to be dictated more by the student's prior experience with writing than by our words:

INTERVIEWER: Do you think your sense of what you should do when you interpret or evaluate an essay is different now from what it was when you took the course?

WRITER: Well, before, "interpreting" in an essay sounded to me like summarize. Maybe clarify some points. But interpret didn't mean to me bringing your own ideas. I've always had difficulty on formal papers bringing my own ideas. I never thought that was right.

In other cases, the writer's representation was created *in the process* of doing the reading, guided opportunistically by ideas that emerged:

And at that point, you start forming your own ideas [about the topic]. . . . Well I found myself comparing my method of time management to how these people said the proper way of doing it was. So, like an image of how I want to set up the paper came to mind. And this was just like sort of automatic.

In the exploratory and teaching phases of the study, students also told us that this task simply called for their "standard strategy." This standard repertoire was probably more influential than the class itself in those first few weeks of college. The course began with a unit on how readers actively construct their own meaning, and it encouraged students to see writing as a similar, goal-directed and constructive process. The context for this assignment then, insofar as teachers controlled it, was designed to validate critical self-consciousness and exploration. Our sense is that the situation invited writers to grow not only tomatoes and carrots but a garden of options. The critical variable was the student making sense of this situation.

Finally, one of the most important limitations of this study involves what should and what should not be expected to generalize to other settings. In Chapter 9 we argue that these students appeared to draw on a "standard repertoire" of those goals and strategies they already controlled with comfort. However, it would be inappropriate to conclude that the standard repertoire other freshman groups might possess would look the same or that the specific set of textual features and organizing plans we noted would be the same for different assignments or for students with different educational backgrounds. The conclusions we wish to draw are at a different level of detail. The argument we propose—which does go beyond our data—is that the process of task representation itself plays a major role in the performance of freshmen writers and that the entry into academic discourse depends on strategic knowledge of the goals and strategies a particular discourse requires rather than on some basic or invariant set of skills or text types or on textual features. If this emphasis on the strategic and constructive nature of this process is correct, it leads us to ask not only what different tasks and contexts invite, but what options students themselves see in those contexts and how they translate those contexts into cognition.

Appendix I: Reading-to-Write Assignment on Time Management

READING AND INTERPRETING DATA

Here are some notes, including research results and observations on time management. Your task is to read and interpret this data to make a brief (1–2 page), comprehensive statement about this subject. Your statement should interpret and synthesize all of the relevant findings in the text. Use approximately ten minutes to read the materials and approximately thirty minutes to rough out what you will say in your statement. Treat this as a draft.

When you hand this assignment in, please include **2** copies of your final essay, and **1** copy of all notes made while doing this task.

THE PASSAGE

Reading Notes on Relevant Research

Time management in professional settings and academic environments has been the subject of extensive research and numerous self-help books.

****

The key to success, according to efficiency expert Alan Lakein in his recent book, *How to Get Control of Your Time and Your Life,* lies in pacing and planning. He notes that planning is decision making, and it is imperative that decisions on using time to best advantage be made. The average worker has two types of "prime time" to plan: external time and internal time. External prime time is the best time to attend to other people. Internal prime time is the period in which one works best. Scheduling large blocks of time in advance helps organize the work day.

****

Noted philosopher and psychologist William James found that most people do not use their mental energies in sufficient depth. He advocated continued concentration in the face of apparent mental fatigue: "The fatigue gets worse up to a certain critical point, when gradually or suddenly it passes away, and we are fresher than before. We have evidently tapped a new level of energy."

****

Cornell University has maintained a major center for research and advising on student skills, directed by Walter Pauk. His work has analyzed the factors that affect academic performance. According to Pauk, the ability to concentrate is an invaluable asset to the college student. Will power alone can't induce concentration. Students may be breaking concentration whenever they remind themselves that they must use will power to concentrate. Nor will motivation alone help students who don't know how to study, don't create a quiet, distraction-free environment, and don't schedule their time carefully. Pauk found that students who schedule as much study time as possible into their days are likely to be better students and suggested that a good daily schedule is the key to quality work.

****

In his guide to intellectual life, Jean Guitton stresses the importance of preparation for peak performance, asserting that it is vital to rest at the least sign of fatigue and to go to work with a relaxed attitude. Preparation for work also includes creating the right environment. Find a place that is at once calm and stimulating. Tolerate nothing that is not useful or beautiful. Steady background sounds, such as music, can mask distracting noise.

****

In a recent survey of private college students, students reported some of the following as their standard strategies for getting through assignments:

- Do what's due; postpone big projects.
- Create a crisis.
- Get all the easy stuff out of the way.
- Do a writing assignment all in one sitting.
- Allow the minimal estimate of time it will take to get a project completed.
- Read material once; don't try to remember it until it's needed.

The students surveyed said they use strategies like these to minimize the debilitating effects of long-range pressures. They assume that they will understand the subject matter sooner or later and that inspiration will be on hand when they need it. Teachers never want as much as they ask for, so overlearning the material will be a waste of time.

#################

Task: Now go ahead and write down on another piece of paper your statement about time management based on your interpretation of this data.

Appendix II: Excerpt from the Task Representation Lecture
REVIEW OF MENU OPTIONS

The assignment: We gave you a very typical college assignment. Normal terms: interpret, use relevant text, own statement. Open ended—to let you see what you did and to see if everyone is doing the same thing on a very common task. (Teachers/bosses usually believe everyone sees the task just as they do when they give these open-ended assignments. Do you think that assumption is right?)

Because we have also asked other people to do this in previous classes for a couple of years now, and asked them about their strategies, we can show you some of the different choices people made. I am going to show you the MENU CHOICES other students make (see p. 43 for an illustration of the menu choices). This will let you build a PROFILE of your own image of the task—the MENU CHOICES YOU MADE.

So we will walk through choices:

You mark down YOUR PERSONAL CHOICES.
Or if Other, tell us what it was.

There is no grade attached to this—no right answer. The game is to see what really happened and let you get some insight into your decisions about this task and to get a chance to privately compare your image to other people's. So be as accurate as you can.

Where I Got My Information—Menu Box

The assigned text
> I tried to stick closely to the text we read. I used quotes, paraphrases, key words, and ideas that came from the material we were asked to read. I tried not to depart very far from the original source information.

The text plus my comments and ideas
> I read the text and used its ideas and key points, but in my essay I *also* included my own response to those ideas, or I included other concepts or information I had read about elsewhere. So the information in my essay is partly from the source text and partly from me.

What I already knew about the topic
> The information in my essay comes from some things I already knew about the topic. I was able to draw on my personal experience and my own opinions.

So I didn't borrow points directly from the text; I used the reading as more of a springboard into my own ideas.

Previous concepts plus this text

The main, organizing idea in my essay was probably unique to my paper. It came from my own knowledge. My main idea was a concept I had learned from another class where I had read about, let's say, decision-making theories or study skills. My main idea, then, came from an issue or problem or theory I already knew about. However, I also made **heavy use** of the assigned reading. Much of the supporting information in my essay comes out of the reading.

Other

If none of these four choices represent the source of your information, specify where you did go as specifically as possible in a complete sentence.

Formal Features and Format—Menu Box
(What does my text look like?)

Notes or a summary paragraph or two

My text looks like notes you might take in class or while reading or a straightforward summary paragraph (or two).

Summary paragraph (or two) plus my opinion

In addition to the straightforward summary paragraphs, I have added a paragraph of my own opinion.

A standard school theme

My text has a formal introduction, a body with a few points, and a concluding paragraph or statement. It is clearly organized around its main points; the paragraphs flow from the introduction and are linked to each other.

Persuasive essay for an academic or a professional audience

My essay starts with a formal introduction, for a public reader who hasn't read this material. In this more formal introduction I raise an issue or indicate the purpose of this essay. The rest of the essay is organized around this argument or my purpose.

Other

If none of these four choices fit your text, describe its formal features as specifically as possible in a complete sentence.

Organizing Plan for Writing—Menu Box

Now let's step back and look at the Organizing Plan you used. How did you pull the information you used into a draft? What Organizing Plan did you use to get started shaping ideas into an essay? What plan did you use to make it hang together? If you switched plans, look at your paper and choose the plan that best describes what you finally did.

Summarize the printed text or Summary + DIALOGUE

I wanted to reduce the reading to its key points and reproduce those points in a clean, orderly way. I didn't want to use additional sources of information.

Respond to/write about the topic

I was more interested in pursuing my own ideas about the topic than in reproducing the main ideas of the text I read. I wanted to draw on my own experience and develop my own insights. I wanted this to be MY statement.

Synthesize/reorganize ideas around a concept

My plan was to start this essay with an organizing concept, some idea that would let me organize and account for the key points in the reading and for my own ideas too. I used that concept as my overview and introduction to the sources in the handout. Finding or inventing this concept was an important part of my process. (*If you used this, circle your synthesizing concept on your draft.*)

Interpret or use ideas for my own purpose

I wanted to do something with this information; to use it for a purpose of my own. That is, although I drew heavily on the reading (and my own ideas), I applied it to a purpose I had in mind. For example, I used it to teach something to a particular audience I had in mind [I used to tutor other students and I wrote this to them].

Or I used it to criticize or support a concept I had learned in another class [e.g., as an example of cost/benefit analysis I learned about in economics]. Or I used it to build an argument [e.g., I wanted to argue that IQ tests aren't good predictors of success in school, and I used this material on time management as one of the reasons IQ doesn't predict what people really do].

Thinking about this purpose or my reader was an important part of my process and the key to my organizing plan.

Other

If you had a different Organizing Plan, describe it in a complete sentence.

Strategies I Used—Menu Box
(Check your Main strategies)

Gist and list

As I read each section I worked with the key words and ideas I found. I wrote to give the gist of what each one meant. I tried to stick to this strategy even when new ideas came to mind, as if I were writing a term paper.
Benefits: efficient, covers all the points.
Costs: no ideas of your own; no new ideas/application.

Gist and list plus my opinion

I used the Gist and List strategy, but then I added my opinion to various sections or at the end. I used my experience as an additional source, but tried to stick with an accurate summary of the readings.

A springboard to thinking

I just sort of took off when I began to write. I used the text as a springboard to write about something I had been thinking about or about some ideas I already had about the topic. The topic triggered something for me, and it let me get a good flow going, so I didn't really need the text much at all.
Benefits: you know what you are talking about; the ideas are sort of organized in your head; can make some good points or write about something that is really interesting.
Costs: the paper may not have much to do with the reading or the assignment.

Skim to interesting points and respond

I like to read along, waiting for the text to trigger good ideas as I read. I use key words or phrases in the text to stimulate my thinking as I read and write about it. So when I write, I write about my responses rather than summarizing or summing up this text.

Benefits: little bursts of inspiration or associations carry you through; the words flow once you hit a place that evokes a response.

Costs: may not deal with the main points or even the ideas of the text; very selective; may not respond to assignment.

Tell it in my own words (or as I understand it)

I stuck pretty close to the key points in the reading, but when I started to write, I put it almost completely in my own words. I really made the points in the readings my own, writing down what I understood they were saying. I wanted to write down what I "took away" from the reading. Or I picked one of the most important points and elaborated on the meaning of that as I understood it. [One version is to learn the material and tell what you learned in your own words. Another is select one of the ideas you relate to in here or understand well and elaborate on the meaning of that point as you understand it.]

Dig out an organizing idea (from the reading)

I tried to find an organizing idea that let me structure the material in the readings. I sometimes have to try out a few ideas to find one that works. These ideas work like topic sentences that let you tuck the key points up underneath and make sense of the reading.

Benefits: pulls the reading together under a new (or found) concept that integrates and gives you an organized plan for writing.

Costs: can be hard to find. What if texts don't all fit?

Divide the ideas into camps or sides

I set up sides as if there were two people arguing about the topic. Each point was either "for or against," or "good idea/bad idea." The sides became the structure for my paper.

Do something for the reader

I spent some time thinking about what I wanted to do for my readers or what the particular reader I had in mind needed. I chose things from the reading and my experience that would let me carry this off. I have a little formula for this: Topic (what I choose to say) = $f(A)$. Topic is a function of the audience.

Use the text for my own purpose

I concentrated on how I could use this information for a purpose I had in mind—this was my own purpose, not the one the original authors had. So I looked to see how I could apply this information or use it to do what I needed to do.

For example, I used it to explain a process or to criticize a theory I learned about in a different course; I used the readings to answer a question that I had or that an instructor had posed. So I read the text carefully, because I wanted to take ideas from it that I needed for my own purpose.

Benefits: good for courses, like the course in economics that asks you to read about cost/benefit analysis and then apply this reading to . . . or discuss XX as an example of . . . ; good for building an argument, like the argument that IQ isn't a good predictor. Use the data on Time Management to show that Time Management can be just as important; good for writing for a reader—Self-Help for college students, teach some techniques.

Costs: harder: (1) have to have a purpose; (2) have to find relevant information and apply it to your purpose; lots more problem-solving and figuring out, compared to the Skim and Respond method, for instance.

I

READING-TO-WRITE:
Understanding the Task

1

The Role of Task Representation in Reading-to-Write

LINDA FLOWER

Academic papers are typically written in the context of a rich rhetorical situation that includes not only the conventions of academic discourse, but the expectations of the instructor, the context of the course, and the terms of the assignment. These requirements can seem so self-evident we are surprised when once again twenty students in a class interpret the same "standard" college writing assignment in strikingly different ways. This chapter is about that act of interpretation. Task representation is an interpretive process that translates the rhetorical situation—as the writer reads it—into the act of composing. As such, it is the major bridge linking the public context of writing with the private process of an individual writer. Therefore, let me introduce this process by sketching three public contexts in which students' task representations make a difference.

In the first context, the freshman composition instructors at my school were in a weekly seminar meeting, trying to understand and diagnose some of the student strategies behind the papers we were reading from the problem analysis assignment. Finding, defining, and analyzing a problem, as we saw the task, was an occasion to struggle with a significant personal or public issue—a problem of the sort that resisted pat answers and called for the extra scrutiny writing allows. In the paper at hand, a young woman had written a polished, coherent essay on the problem posed by a "rainy day" with its awful train of decisions about choosing the right clothes and the dilemma of skipping puddles to class—a mildly clever, discouraging paper. It was not the sort of analysis we had in mind. In the freshman literature course that same week the instructors had spent a class session talking with students about how the response statements due Monday would allow, even demand, students to go beyond the summaries they had written in high school. A response statement, the instructors had discussed, asked students to record and then examine their own response. The first papers were turned in with students claiming they had indeed done this analysis. Fifty percent were plot summaries. Meanwhile, over the bridge at the University of Pittsburgh was a third context we can reconstruct from David Bartholomae's (1985) discussion of a student's freshman placement essay. The reader on the placement committee had come to that point in the essay that would make or break it as acceptable academic discourse—that would place this student in or out of basic writing: "At this point the [student] writer is in a perfect position to speculate, to move from the problem to an analysis of the problem, however. . . . We get neither a technical discussion nor an 'academic' discussion but a Lesson on Life" (p. 137). In failing to make that expected move to analysis, the student had just become a basic writer in the eyes of an institution.

Why, we want to ask, are these students doing what seems to be the "wrong task" in the eyes of their readers, especially on these short assignments to which a grade or even placement is attached? Is it because they are unmotivated, despite the serious looks that suggest they, too, are disappointed if not perplexed by our response? Is standard "academic discourse" a new phenomenon to *all* of these students? Is the assignment not clear, even explicit? If our task involves reading to write, is it that they just have not thought about the assigned readings deeply enough to have something to say? Somehow these answers do not do justice to the real effort made by both students and teachers.

The phenomenon repeats itself in classes outside of English. Teachers ask students to attempt some "standard" form of disciplinary discourse because they want to expand the students' repertoire by teaching a particular way of thinking and writing. Yet the class members seem to be doing a variety of different assignments. Some of these variations are welcome inventions; but others suggest that the student is still confused about what academic discourse calls for. Writing about the problem of a rainy day probably seemed as trivial to the student who did it as it did to the instructor. The purposes of college were not being served for anyone. When writing goes awry in this way, it is as though there were a band of writers each marching to a different drummer in the good faith that he or she was "doing what the assignment called for."

This study looks at one way we might help students to understand and manage the special demands of academic discourse. Part of the problem, we propose, may not lie in the student's ability or even knowledge of the discourse per se, but in the way that student has construed the task. If this is true, students are likely to have many abilities they could use if they prompted themselves to do so. This chapter suggests that we may want to look at *task representation* not as a single, simple decision, but as an extended interpretive process that weaves itself throughout composing. The task, as students represent it to themselves, is the one they perform, but that representation is subject to many influences and may evolve in surprising ways during writing. This process of task representation, we suggest, may be far more involved, unpredictable, and powerful than we have supposed.

This problem of interpretation can be partly described in terms of the implicit requirements of academic discourse students are expected to infer. For instance, if we tell students they need only look into their hearts and write from experience, are we assuming the "personal essay" *our field has in mind* is simply a natural genre the student would discover by consulting those private wellsprings? Pat Bizzell and Bruce Herzberg (1986) have criticized this assumption in textbooks that purport to teach "good" writing when, in fact, they aim to teach a genre-specific form of good writing that has quite explicit, if unarticulated rules. Kathleen McCormick's (1985) critique of a naive use of "response statements" makes a similar point. Response statements, as she describes them, are not pure, untrammeled "responses" to a text. Rather, they are a specialized form of discourse in which students are expected to *use* their personal response to examine their own reading process and assumptions about texts. Charles Bazerman (1981) argues that the discourse conventions of the various disciplines pose a similar problem in writing across the curriculum. The task of student writers is to enter the ongoing intellectual conversation of an established community.

Writing is a move in a discourse game with rules, an action in an intellectual and interpersonal context. Nevertheless, the process of interpreting a task—imagining the action that is called for—is sometimes equated with merely "following an assignment" and, as such, is relegated to remedial workshops on study skills. Teachers want to deal with heady intellectual processes, not with helping students ferret out "what the teacher wants," so they leave it to students to interpret assignments, even though the instructions may be long, imaginative, and complex. Indeed, many teachers hold it as a badge of merit that they refuse to tell the students "what they want" in the desire to foster independent thought. Yet there is sometimes a fine line between maintaining this proper reticence and creating a guessing game in which students who know how to succeed in school do, while those who do not are expected to infer the rules of the game on their own.

We find ourselves in a perplexing position. The genres we hold to be self-evident are not that way to everybody. As Mina Shaughnessy (1977) has suggested, we seem to be urging some students, who do not know the "rituals and ways of winning arguments in academia, . . . into the lion's den of academic disputation with no more than an honest face for protection" (p. 319). But this is not merely a problem of underprepared students. As we become more aware of the interpretive processes of readers and the multiple faces of academic discourse across disciplines, we must face the fact that students do interpret, and often misinterpret, the college writing tasks they set out to do. If, indeed, the process of task representation plays the significant role I am suggesting, our problem is even more interesting. As a field we have almost nothing to say to students or each other about *how* writers represent tasks during composing and about the *features* of alternative representations students bring to any standard task.

TASK REPRESENTATION

Writing starts with a rhetorical situation that poses a need to write (Bitzer, 1968) or, in the terms of this discourse, a task that calls for problem solving. Given that context, the first thing writers must do is define the problem or construct an image of that situation or task for themselves. We can think of this process of representation and problem solving as occurring within a *problem space* (Simon, 1973). This metaphoric space is made up of all the possible goals the solver might consider, all the possible operations, strategies, or moves that might be taken, and all the possible givens, assumptions, or conditions in the world that might constrain the solver's action. The theoretical problem space for even everyday problems is often enormous, but, of course, we work only with those aspects of infinite possibility that we represent to ourselves. We respond to the problems we pose (Freire, 1970). The process of task representation begins when the problem solver begins consciously or unconsciously to represent the givens and constraints of this situation, the goals she would attain, and the strategies or actions she might take, since together these constitute the problem she is solving.

For example, we can imagine two people thinking about the task of "planting beans." One person has a rather simple representation:

THE GIVENS AND CONSTRAINTS: Is it warm out there yet? Did I remember to order that packet of Kentucky Wonders from Park Seed?

THE GOALS: Get 'em in, pick 'em, and eat 'em.

THE STRATEGIES: Make a row with your heel, sprinkle beans, stomp things down, and pray for rain.

We might compare this representation to that of Henry David Thoreau, who also gave some thought to the task:

THE GIVENS AND CONSTRAINTS: Two and a half acres of upland, no equipment, and a plentiful supply of hungry woodchucks were part of this reality. However, Thoreau often seemed to interpret his constraints as sources of value: "As I had little aid from horses or cattle, or hired men or boys, or improved implements of husbandry, I was much slower, and became much more intimate with my beans than usual." (1964, p. 406)

THE STRATEGIES: Thoreau's strategies for growing beans suggest a task of somewhat more heroic dimensions than our first. For instance, his habit is "to go daily to the rescue armed with a hoe, to thin the ranks of the enemy, to fill the trenches with the weedy dead."

THE GOALS: Thoreau's goals also look oddly different. His agenda in planting a field of beans was nothing less than to "live deliberately" and to "know beans." It matters little, he said, to fill the farmer's barn. The goal of the husbandman, in Thoreau's remarkable vision of this task, is not to amass bushels but to "cease from anxiety."

These two visions of planting beans may have little more in common than sunshine and bean seeds. And to a hard-working farmer in 1854 it is likely that neither of these representations would seem sensible. Yet each has a logic and a rightness of its own. The point of this simple example is twofold:

1. A task is something people construct, even when they assume there is a common sense version everyone would hold.
2. These task representations can differ strikingly not only in the information they contain but in how they elaborate and structure that information, in what

they privilege and what they ignore. If this happens with beans, what happens with academic writing? Do students within the same class construct the same task for themselves? Does their image of the task resemble the image constructed by the instructor? And if these various representations differ, as on some level, of course, they must, do those differences really matter? Do they have a real impact on teaching, on learning, or on succeeding in school?

Cross-cultural studies have given us some graphic examples of assignments and tests supposedly designed to test intelligence or cognitive capabilities (such as the power to abstract), but that in fact only describe task representation; that is, they were measuring the testee's assumptions about what a tester might want in posing such a peculiar task. Goodnow's (1976) review of the problems in interpreting cross-cultural research shows how this hidden variable of task representation can crop up in studies that intended to measure how literacy affects cognition.

The "wise man/foolish man" phenomenon is a good example of this hidden influence. Our culture places great value on the ability to abstract and classify in certain ways (Arnheim, 1954), and we often track the development of this ability as a measure of growth in writing ability (Britton, Burgess, Martin, McLeod, & Rosen, 1975; Freedman & Pringle, 1980). Investigators among the Kpelle people asked the Kpelle to classify a set of twenty familiar objects that (to our eyes) belonged in four categories: food, clothing, tools, and cooking utensils (Glick, 1975). The Kpelle persistently grouped them in ten groups of two, based on concrete relations; for example, "the knife goes with the orange because it cuts it." Should we conclude that these people do not carry out formal operations, that they lack these cognitive maneuvers? Glick (1975) noted, however, that subjects at times volunteered

> "that a wise man would do things in the way this was done." When an exasperated experimenter asked finally, "How would a fool do it?" he was given back [groupings] of the type . . . initially expected—four neat piles with foods in one, tools in another. (p. 636; quoted in Goodnow, 1976, p. 171)

Closer to home, these studies have also taught us that certain general tendencies in representing tasks—which we take as a sign of intelligence or commitment—may also reflect culturally induced assumptions about how to handle a school task:

> Within our traditions, for instance, "learning by doing" and "learning from one's mistakes" are often acceptable, and guessing is usually expected. These are the traditions that make an early try feasible. . . . Groups such as the Navaho [by contrast] appear to rely on "prolonged observation, or 'prelearning.' . . . A reluctance to try too soon and the accompanying fear of being 'shamed' if one does not succeed may account for the seemingly passive, uninterested, and unresponsive attitude of Indian students." (Ohannessian, 1967, p. 13; quoted in Goodnow, 1976, p. 181)

Goodnow used this example to show how a "let's have a go at it" attitude toward school tasks can affect test taking. How, we might ask, would this image of school tasks affect students asked to generate tentative plans, notes, or drafts and then to revise them?

Labov came to much the same conclusion in *Language in the Inner City* (1972), in which he attacked the myth that lower-class black children are verbally deprived and unable to deal with abstract, logically complex, or hypothetical questions (p. 220). The source of that myth, he argued, was in what we are calling task representation. Black children placed in settings without normal social support were asked to perform in ways they found mystifying, unmotivated (Why should I tell you, an adult, that this is a space ship you are pointing to?), or unreasonable (You want me to tell you about the fights I get into?). Labov was able to show how changes in the context could elicit striking differences in performance—changes that he attributed to both motivation and the child's interpretation of the task:

> One can view these test stimuli as requests for information, commands for action, threats of punishment, or meaningless sequences of words. They are probably intended [by teachers or experimenters] as something altogether different—as requests for display, but in any case the experimenter is normally unaware of the problem of interpretation. (p. 221)

In these studies of discourse communities, cognition, and language use we can see not only the influence of context, but that that *context is constantly being interpreted by language users*. The special context of school complicates this interpretive process even further. In its evaluative climate certain tasks, including writing, tend to be high in ambiguity (i.e., there is no well-specified procedure) and high in risk (i.e., it is possible to fail) (Doyle, 1983). Moreover, the context students must learn to "read" is constantly changing as they are asked to enter new discourse communities (Bartholomae, 1985), to try on new social roles and ways of using language (Hymes, 1972), and to attempt new ways of telling and transforming knowledge (Bereiter & Scardamalia, 1987). This study tries to add another piece to this picture of cognition in context by looking at the process of task representation itself. In particular, how do students handle this interpretive process on college writing tasks? Are they any more cognizant of this intervening variable than we are as researchers and teachers?

Although task representation may influence all that follows, the process is often carried out with little or no awareness on the part of the writer (Anderson, 1980; Baker & Brown, 1984). For familiar problems the process of representation is likely to be highly automated; it takes little conscious attention and the problem solver may be reluctant to attribute any decision making or selective process to himself. He merely did what the assignment said. This feeling will be especially strong if the task invokes a well-developed schema, such as that for the appropriate response to a short answer exam. Less familiar, more complex tasks, however, can call for extended exploration as a writer considers tentative, alternative ways to imagine the problem. In this process of interpreting a rhetorical situation, imagining what a reader would expect, gauging one's own feelings about a topic, envisioning ways to present a position, and even considering the meaning of terms in an assignment, writers are making critical decisions. They are setting goals and choosing actions that constitute a master plan and set of global instructions for how to approach this task. In an important study of the way social scientists approach problems in history and economics, Voss, Green, Post, and Penner (1983) found that experts created elaborated representations of a problem, which they then tested and argued with as they worked toward a solution. This deliberative process, of course, takes time and effort; one wants to use one's highly automated processes whenever they will do the job. The problem in teaching is to help students learn to invoke conscious choice and evaluative awareness on complex problems that need them. Learning to manage academic discourse seems to be just such a problem.

Task Representation in Reading-to-Write: The Exploratory Study

In the remainder of this chapter we look in depth at the task representation process of students in a series of informal classroom experiments with undergraduate, masters and Ph.D. students, a series we have labeled the Exploratory Study. This initial phase of the reading-to-write project opened up the territory for the more controlled observations of freshmen, labeled the Teaching Study and described in the chapters which follow. The Exploratory Study is interesting for the hypotheses and questions it generated, for the template of alternative representations it provided, and for its rich picture of individual responses. That is where we start.

It is not easy to understand, much less manage, one's own composing process. Our knowledge of how this process operates in real time is often distorted by assumptions and conventional wisdom about how it should work and by the limits of our vocabulary for talking about the process. Because the romantic literary tradition, on which we depend for metaphors about writing, valued inspiration and talent over cognition and effort of mind, we may fail to appreciate the process of sustained thought that goes into normal writing. Even introspection, which is so essential to critical thinking and problem solving, can be a blunt tool for uncovering cognitive processes, since people tend to recognize and remember those acts they expect and know well. Moreover, much of the cognition of writing, like that of any problem-solving act, is fleeting. People perform fascinating intellectual maneuvers, but once those maneuvers accomplish their end, thinkers wipe the mental slate, recalling only the result they struggled toward, and report that "it took a while, but finally it just came to me" (Flower, 1989a).

Process tracing experiments, as a form of classroom research, give students a more vivid and accurate look at their own writing process (see Penrose & Sitko, in preparation). As joint research projects carried out by teachers and students, they not only inform the teacher (as in traditional classroom research), but are an important part of the course content for the students. Both parties have an investment in discovery.

The Exploratory Study began as a classroom experiment designed to look at the process of reading to write. For the junior, senior, and M.A. students involved, reading to write was a process worth examining. It was the mainstay of their college work and it would be as important on the job to the writing majors as to the teachers. So I asked the class to do a small reading-to-write task and to collect a thinking-aloud protocol of themselves doing it. That is, they were asked to think aloud to themselves as they read the source text and planned and wrote their short assignment, making a tape recording of the flow of their thoughts, which they later transcribed (see Appendix III). They could then use the protocol transcription to look more closely at their own process. A week later they returned to class to make a short presentation on "an interesting feature of my own process." (They would later do a short paper in which they applied what they learned to teaching, to professional writing, or to themselves.)

What I did not tell them was that I had, in a sense, stacked the deck. To let them see as much of their own decision process as possible, the assignment was designed to simulate a typical, open-ended, underspecified, and overloaded assignment; it asked for everything: to read, interpret, synthesize, use all the "relevant" data, write their own statement, and be comprehensive. On the other hand, by reciting the sacred words of many college assignments, the assignment tried to invite a wide range of familiar options in order to let students catch a glimpse of how *they were choosing to represent* this Rorschach blot to themselves.

The assignment and source text (shown in Appendix IV) given to the English majors in this study used a series of quotes, notes, and comments on the topic of revision. The goal was to create a short text (manageable in a classroom experiment) that simulated the experience of using one's notes from class and from reading to write a paper of one's own. Each source speaks with its own voice and claims. Some of the authors of the source texts were selected to disagree with one another; others are simply speaking at cross purposes. Some passages bury the relevant information on revision in a subordinate position to distracter topic. Finally, there is no single issue or topic that organizes this set of notes; any ordering principle would have to come from the writer.

Consider, if you will, how you would go about this task, were you a member of the class. In asking this question with various groups of teachers, I found people quite divided as to what the task requires. Some felt that the situation obviously called for summarizing. As a responsible writer, one would want to do justice to all the material here, reducing it to a concise and accurate set of gists organized around a central idea. Other teachers, looking mildly appalled at that prospect, said they would respond to the reading material as a springboard to writing about something they found personally relevant. And there were other responses. If we found this diversity in how experienced teachers construed this reading-to-write task, what would students assume? And how would they go about the process of construing?

As I used versions of this classroom experiment with three different writing and rhetoric classes, it became apparent that writers' top-level, global images of the task regularly differed from one another on certain key features, which are outlined in Figure 3 as a set of implicit options. That is, the tasks students were describing often differed from one another on the Major Source of Information, on the Text Format and Features, and on the Organizing Plan, Strategies, and Goals. Figure 3 should not be read as a generic picture of all academic tasks: it reflects what these students in this class saw as live options. Nevertheless, we can also see here the influence of the larger shared context of school that made this set appear familiar and this task seem typical to the students. These informal classroom experiments were not set up as systematic studies; they were designed to give students a data-based chance to reflect on their own reading and writing. But the spirit of inquiry they fostered led me to a new appreciation of the strategic nature of their process and of the role task representation might be playing. The discussion that follows offers a conceptual

MAJOR SOURCE OF INFORMATION	TEXT FORMAT AND FEATURES
• Text • Text + my comments • What I already knew • Previous concepts +text	• Notes / Summary ¶ • Summary + opinion ¶ • Standard school theme • Persuasive Essay

ORGANIZING PLAN FOR WRITING

To summarize the readings
To respond to the topic
To review and comment
To synthesize with a controlling concept
To interpret for a purpose of my own

STRATEGIES	OTHER GOALS
• Gist and list • Gist and list and comment • Read as a springboard • Tell it in my own words • Skim and respond • Dig out an organizing idea • Divide into camps • Choose for audience needs • Use for a purpose of my own	• Demonstrate understanding • Get a good idea or two • Present what I learned • Come up with something interesting • Do the minimum and do it quickly • Fulfill the page requirement • Test my own experience • Cover all the key points • Be original or creative • Learn something for myself • Influence the reader • Test something I already knew

Figure 3. Some key features of students' task representations.

framework for these observations. It describes what students did, questions some familiar assumptions about reading-to-write tasks, and poses a set of hypotheses that the more controlled Teaching Study and the rest of this book examine. The reader eager to look at the more carefully collected data that will, in part, support and qualify this theoretical statement is referred to the relevant parts of that second phase of the project. This chapter is organized around four issues raised by this picture of surprising diversity within a familiar frame:

1. The power of the organizing plan
2. How a task representation is created
3. Costs, benefits, cognition, and growth
4. Taking metacognitive control: awareness versus standard strategies

The Power of the Organizing Plan

A dominant feature of every writer's vision of this task was the organizing plan (or plans) used to structure what was being read and to structure the writer's own text.

This organizing plan reflects a critical decision for a number of reasons. To begin with, it guides the processes of reading and writing themselves. A plan to synthesize, for example, calls up certain strategies for manipulating ideas and transforming knowledge that a plan to summarize does not generally evoke. The organizing plan is also one of the bridges between process and product, since it may virtually dictate the organization of the written text. The logic of the organizing plan helps writers to create a (to them) coherent text structure and to signal that sense of coherence to the reader in places such as introductory paragraphs, transitions, topic sentences, and conclusions. Because the perception of coherence has such impact on the way instructors evaluate a paper, the organizing plan can influence students' grades. This is especially true if instructors value some organizing plans, such as synthesis or interpretation, as more intellectually significant that others, such as summary. If the choice of an organizing plan has such an impact on the process, product, and social outcomes of writing, what happens when students do not recognize the alternatives among which they are "choosing" or if they do not even realize they have the option of choice? To illustrate the alternative plans this particular task elicited, I draw on the presentations students made as part of the process experiments and on their responses to one another.

THE ORGANIZING PLAN TO *SUMMARIZE*

Martha was a good student in a quiet, dutiful, straightforward sense of the word. She was an engineering student in her junior year, nervous about writing in general and about this class of English majors and M.A.s in particular, but used to succeeding and getting things right. She was also very clear about how to do this task. She used what we later called the *gist and list* strategy. In her view, you read through the text with some care, find the key words in each paragraph, and summarize it trying to capture its main idea. You then write your paper around this string of well-wrought gists. An important caution goes along with this plan: sometimes a new idea might occur to you as you are writing—a different way to organize things or an idea you are interested in. But do not be led astray. If that happens, you must decisively set that idea aside, for it will only confuse you and your paper.

In examining and describing her own process, Martha had uncovered for herself a well-honed strategy that she obviously relied on for other assignments. The task too was familiar, she concluded in her presentation—"just like doing a research paper." If we respond to her organizing plan based on this gist and list strategy as "mere" summary, it is important for us to realize that Martha did not see it as a limited or low-effort choice. She was very serious about her work and serious about this presentation. She was describing the task as she saw it, and as (I believe) she assumed everyone else would see a reading-to-write assignment.

The dynamics of this class are themselves a part of the story of this research. By a stroke of fortune, Martha's presentation had been the very first in the two-day series of talks on what each student discovered. Her well-defined vision of the task, which we called the efficiency expert strategy, created a backdrop against which other representations took shape. In fact, a dialogue began with the very next presentation. That writer, Kate, was an economics major at the beginning of her M.A. in professional writing. Since she seemed to approach everything with Irish energy to spare, it didn't seem surprising when she said that it never occurred to her to use the source text in the way Martha had. In fact, the interesting feature from her protocol was the way the topic of the paper itself had been determined by her sense of an imagined audience. She decided on relevant content information by first imagining an audience of students she had tutored and then deciding what they might want to hear about revision. This was such a standard strategy for her, she told us later, that she even had a mental formula for it: $T = f(A)$; Topic is a function of the audience.

I will return to Kate's vision of this task later. The point of my narrative digression here is simply to convey the impact this sequence of presentations had on all of us. The question of right or wrong was temporarily in abeyance because the point of the experiment was to uncover something interesting about one's own strategies on this small experimental task. What became increasingly clear was that people in the room were holding radically different representations of the task and relying on strategies that would inevitably produce very different papers. Yet each assumed he or she was simply doing the task. Let me briefly sketch the other dominant organizing plans that emerged from these visions of the task.

THE ORGANIZING PLAN TO *RESPOND TO/WRITE ABOUT THE TOPIC*

In sharp contrast to the summarizing plan, some students were not inconvenienced by the assigned text because they choose to talk about what they already knew. They used the reading as a springboard to trigger their own ideas or response to the topic in general. Notice that this is a more freewheeling plan than one that requires direct response to the claims in the source text. This plan for reading and writing can produce excellent themes, which appear well-organized and unusually interesting because they are based on ideas the student has already thought about and is already motivated to consider. In many writing classes, this is exactly the task teachers want writers to give themselves. On the other hand, this plan, like the plan to summarize the sources, sidesteps the process of *integrating* one's own knowledge with that of the source text. It typically simplifies the process of reading-to-write.

Our best insight into this plan came from a student's description of a *skim and respond* strategy she discovered in her protocol and came to recognize as one of her most often used strategies for generating text. The example from her protocol begins with Janet reading a line from the source text (underlined in the following excerpt), briefly thinking, and then composing a sentence (in italics). In Janet's description of this process, the sentence she composed came tumbling out with the energy of a discovery. Notice, however, the relation between the ideas about revision in the source text and those in Janet's claim.

> Good writers check to see if plans have changed midstream. Um, I guess, let's see, your first thoughts are usually muddled or come out like a tidal wave. The tidal wave effect. *The tidal wave effect of a rush of initial ideas or thoughts can be cleaned up and clarified on revision (draft text).*

Janet's strategy was to skim the source text, waiting for those points that would trigger a response and give her something interesting to say. In her example, the term "midstream" (and the notion of change?) seems to have triggered the idea of tidal waves. The link is a lexical rather than propositional one; the two texts are not even talking about the same subject. A series of inferences and associations based on the surface of the source text led Janet to generate her own idea. In her presentation, Janet was intrigued with this discovery because this was the strategy that had gotten her through college. It had been especially good for English courses, she reported; she had once written an entire paper on a word in Shakespeare.

As the course went on, it became clear that Janet relied on this local skim and respond strategy so heavily because she, like a few other students in the class, also depended on the larger plan of Responding to the Topic to organize her reading and writing. In the attempt to find something interesting to say, the substance of the source text served primarily as a springboard for thought or trigger for past associations. And in Janet's version of the strategy, sometimes only the words of the source mattered.

As students talked on, a vision of the costs and benefits associated with these different organizing plans began to emerge. This is one of the critical issues of task representation we will return to, but Janet and Martha illustrate the basic question. Martha's gist and list strategy is highly efficient, a very intelligent plan for many tasks. On the other hand, a strict summarizing plan eliminates the possibility of exploring or expressing one's own ideas. And it is probably not the task instructors have in mind on many college assignments. Janet's plan of Responding to the Topic had apparently stood her in good stead in some undergraduate classes. But in my class she was having genuine difficulty with assignments that asked for a sustained argument and focused analysis of an issue. Our exploration of alternative organizing plans and the strategies that supported them were raising the question: what costs and benefits for the writer do these different representations carry with them?

THE ORGANIZING PLAN TO *REVIEW AND COMMENT*

Many students took a middle ground between summarizing and abandoning the source texts. They carried on what one student called a "dialogue" with their sources in which they would alternate between reviewing or summarizing a source and adding their own comments, criticisms, or associations. A more formal version of this plan was one many students had used in high school in which the writer summarizes a source and then adds an "opinion paragraph" at the end.

This plan not only allowed writers to express their own ideas, it led to an easy and natural way to compose; the text could be structured like a conversation built on the scaffolding of the source text. That is, the writer could simply walk through the source text, reviewing the main points in the order found in the notes, adding occasional comments when he or she has something to say. The ease of composing with this plan also points to its limitation as a plan for thinking or persuading. The review and comment method does not encourage writers to pursue connections or conflicts or to build an integrated picture of a topic. Since this plan assumes major importance when we turn to the work of freshmen, we will return to it later.

By contrast, the final two plans observed in this exploratory work were distinguished by the prominent role they give to integrating ideas.

THE ORGANIZING PLAN TO *SYNTHESIZE IDEAS AROUND A CONTROLLING CONCEPT*

Some writers gave themselves an additional set of goals that went beyond summarizing or reviewing and commenting on the text. They saw their task as organizing information, from both the source and themselves, under a controlling, synthesizing concept. Unlike the summarizers, they read the source text with an eye to uncovering a unifying thread or to creating one, and they tried to organize their own texts around this central concept. And unlike the students who saw the task as responding to the topic, the synthesizers made themselves responsible for at least some of the ideas in the source texts.

Given the wide range of meanings people assign to the term *synthesis,* I want to be precise about the way it is used here. In this study, a text with a "synthesizing plan" is operationally defined as having these features:

1. It offers the reader a clearly articulated "synthesizing concept" that one could actually locate in the text. For example, the following writer used the notion of "mistaken beliefs" to organize his discussion:

   > Teachers of writing find that their students do little revision, if at all, while good writers see revision as a critical part of the writing process. This contrast seems to result from mistaken beliefs about the process of revision.

2. This concept is a substantive, informative idea rather than an immediately obvious inference. For instance, a text which stated that "there are many opinions on revision" and proceeded to summarize the sources was not held to be governed by a unique "synthesizing" concept.

3. Finally, this concept not only appears in the text, it works as a controlling concept that governs the selection of information and the organization of the entire text. The "controlling concept," indeed, has to control the paper's topical structure by being connected to the paragraphs or major units that followed.

To instructors the benefits of this organizing plan may seem particularly striking. To begin with, it encourages thinking processes that learning theorists and reading educators want to foster. It asks the student to read source texts for ideas at the level of gists, not details (Brown & Day, 1983), to generate his or her own macro-level structure of ideas (Meyer, 1982), and to integrate this information into a meaningful, memorable whole (Ausubel, 1963) that assimilates or accommodates itself to one's prior knowledge (Piaget, 1932). The plan to synthesize also has obvious benefits for the writing process, insofar as it would produce a clear organizing idea, a structured integration of various sources, and the opportunity to place one's self in an intellectual discourse, combining one's own ideas with those of other authors (Kaufer, Geisler, & Neuwirth, 1989; Spivey, 1984). (This is not to say all syntheses achieve this, but the plan leads in that direction.)

However, this plan also carries some very real costs. To begin with, it was not clear even to these generally successful college students what synthesis meant when it got down to actually doing it. For one student, this quandary about the task was, in fact, the "interesting feature" of her own process that she chose to talk about. As she found herself saying in the protocol,

> "Interpret and synthesize" [re-reading the assignment]. What the hell does that mean? Synthesize means to pull together, no, to make something up. Why should I want to make something up? [She then re-reads and comments on the wording of the assignment.] Synthesis sounds like I'm making a chemical compound. Hmm. Put together. [re-reads] "All of the relevant findings in the text." How can I do this?

And, concluding that she could not or did not, in fact, want to "make something up," this writer began at this point to summarize:

> Ok, I know everything about these few pieces of writing, about [reading from the assignment] how people revise. Okay, I'll write this down. . . . How people revise.

Other writers set out with the goal of finding the unifying thread in the sources they read. However, we had designed even this short text to replicate the experience of normal reading (outside of textbooks). The source text authors not only disagree but focus on different aspects of the topic so that their main ideas resist falling into neat packages. For instance, how do the rather bare facts about business writers connect to the enthusiastic claims by teachers that good writers do extensive revision? One writer, who spent between two and three hours on the task, found himself caught in an extended struggle with his plan since the sources suggested two major, alternative organizing ideas, yet neither concept was supported enough in the sources to allow a clear choice. The comments here were separated in time; they are numbered to reflect the sequence of points at which this writer encountered the costs of attempting this organizing plan:

1. Uhhh, so what's the contrast here? The contrast seems to be between people who are experienced writers, versus students. Aaahhh, so wait let's see [re-reads text to see if students mentioned in the text were also labeled inexperienced].
2. Essentially the entire passage is oriented toward . . . probably about 75% of it is about editing and revision . . . and the remaining 25% is about planning. Planning is tied into revision because writers review their plans and goals, . . . and then, and then how is that tied into revision?
3a. [Re-reads assignment] Statement about the process of revision.
3b. Well, what have we got? What's the process? Well, revision is part of the process of writing, so maybe we should try and get the big picture.
4a. Well, we have two main axes, two main axes of organization here. . . .
4b. As in my notes we have, uhhh, we have good writers versus bad writers uhhhh [looks at notes], vertically and horizontally. . . .
4c. And various processes of revision in center stage [of his notes].
4d. So . . . there is another potential organization to this paper.

Andrew's solution to this problem is a complex categorization of the research results that builds to what he calls the "willing and systematic" revision process of experts. His taxonomy lets him maintain the precision he cares about, retain the conflicting information he sees, incorporate his own ideas, and still create a clearly organized synthesis of the research.

> When faced with a demanding composition task, almost all writers, skilled and un-skilled alike, go through the familiar stages of planning, writing and editing one or more drafts, and finally producing perfected copy. However, recent research indicates that certain categories of experienced writers differ markedly from novices in the amount and kind of revising they perform.

> Essayists, journalists, academic and creative writers regard revision as an iterative procedure in which, typically, the entire architecture and meaning of a document is transfigured and progressively improved in light of high-level goals and global criteria. Novices, on the other hand, regard revision as a single-pass filtering operation in which the structure of a first (and only) draft is essentially preserved. . . . Expert writers advantageously transform their drafts through a systematic and explicit evaluation procedure [which the writer here describes]. . . .

> These findings do not apply to all composers. Business people differ from academic writers by their medium of expression . . . [and] their composing strategies. . . .

> If future research continues to support and generalize the importance of willing and systematic revision, it could be interpreted as emphasizing the extent to which writing is still an art rather than a mature technology. Enough knowledge has been accumulated about bridge building, for example, so that . . . the construction engineer [can] pro-duce a plan of construction that builders can safely follow; a bridge well-planned should only need to be constructed once! Heuristics for composition, however, are still sufficiently imprecise . . . to oblige even those writers who plan most extensively to expect surprise . . . and to welcome the opportunity to adapt their plans repeatedly in response to discovered discrepancies between what they intended and did, in fact, do.

Andrew's difficulty in planning this synthesis was not unique. The first hurdle for some students was even to recognize that the information offered by the "au-thorities" did not easily resolve itself into convenient, obvious, or even reasonable packages. They had trouble building a meaningful version of the source texts in their own minds. The next hurdle was forging a synthesis. Students who wanted (1) to base this synthesis *entirely* on the text and do justice to most of the sources, and yet (2) to make claims they felt were supported by evidence, found themselves under enormous constraints. They had given themselves a task that was simply undoable without transforming the information the text provided. Although many of these students questioned the assignment, few questioned whether their current represen-tation of the task was a necessary one, the only possible one, or even the best fit to the situation.

Students who attempted to create a synthesis based on a single concept found in the source were far more likely to meet failure and have to revise their plan, even though most did so with some understandable reluctance. As one student said, "I don't like to think of myself as abandoning an idea." But when her attempt to neatly categorize the authorities failed, she felt forced to change the plan and organize the essay around her own impressions. That decision carried its own costs as she moved from *finding,* testing, and using a concept to *generating,* testing, and using one.

The point here is that this plan carries very real intellectual costs. It can be difficult, frustrating, and chancy. The source texts, one's own knowledge, and reality itself may resist synthesis. And there is always the practical question: is "making something up" even called for here; why would I want to do that? Representing the task in this way is a meaningful choice.

THE ORGANIZING PLAN TO *INTERPRET OR USE IDEAS FOR A RHETORICAL PURPOSE*

Synthesis is an intellectually sophisticated endeavor. Because it asks the writer to reorganize and integrate information around a controlling concept, it is one of the mainstays of academic writing, especially of student academic writing. However, a plan to synthesize, as it is defined here, is primarily focused on conveying a body of information; its structure attempts to reflect the structure of that information as the writer sees it. Some writers saw themselves as adding a rhetorical dimension to their task by attempting to interpret or use this information to carry out a rhetorical purpose (in addition to synthesizing). (In using the term *rhetorical purpose* here I want to draw attention to those unique purposes these writers generated that went beyond the conventional purposes of exposition defined as presenting a summary, comment, or synthesis.)

We observed the presence of an active rhetorical purpose or rhetorical goals in three places:

First, during the composing process, some writers spent time attending to the audience or to their own interests and setting goals for what might be interesting or useful to do in this paper. These additional rhetorical goals helped dictate not only what information the writer would use and how it was ordered, but what organizing or synthesizing concept would control the text and why.

Second, in some texts, the essay was organized around a discernible rhetorical purpose, which took the form of making a claim, posing a question, or setting up an issue. For example, one skeptical writer used her essay to ask: "Is there really one good revision process, or does 'good' depend on the kind of writing?" The text functioned as a way to explore that question, to articulate sides of a debate, or to come to a conclusion. As a reader of these texts, one had a sense of being involved in a guided inquiry that had a rhetorical purpose beyond conveying information from the sources. The following writer used a title, a rhetorical question, and a comparison/contrast pattern to signal her intention—to conduct an inquiry into the support for alternative views of revision, a question that may reflect her uncertainties as a new instructor.

> *Research about Revision: What Can We Infer about the Process?*
> Many writers, teachers, and composition theorists believe that the writing process has many parts. The common assumption is that breaking the whole writing process into parts is useful for writers and that good writers do it. Revision is often defined as that part of this process in which writers rethink or resee their texts; or conversely it may be defined more narrowly as editing and proofreading. While theorists disagree about whether revision is defined as a local or global phenomenon, it seems that writers, too, tend to chose one of these ways of looking at revision as they actually revise.
> For instance, Nancy Sommers found. . . .

Faigley and Witte found. . . .

However, Halpern and Liggett found that these distinctions may not hold if the context is not an academic setting. . . .

Textbooks have encouraged. . . . However, based on the results above it seems unlikely that this teaching technique has led to better student revision, possibly because that advice is not operational or readily understood by students. [end of text]

Texts like this clearly make use of the techniques of summary, commentary, and synthesis (in this case, a parallel between theorists and writers' views on the local/global distinction provides an organizing concept). What distinguishes this organizing plan is that the summary, synthesis, and so on are carried out in service of a unique-to-this-text, discernible rhetorical purpose. They are embedded within an apparent plan to determine what we can infer from the research and (an implicit plan?) to apply this to the problem other instructors (the "we" of the subtitle) face. This example also reminds us that "to interpret for a purpose" is to transform, adapt, and reconstruct information. The last paragraph of this text shows how writers can drift away from an announced purpose into a more locally guided commentary on the source texts, or at least fail to make their intended link apparent to readers.

Third, in another group of texts the discernible rhetorical purpose took the form of addressing a particular reader and adapting the writer's knowledge to what that reader might read. These texts were often organized as advice to students or as plans for putting the research on revision to use.

This category of "interpret for a rhetorical purpose" raised some worthwhile problems of definition that might be useful to explore here. To begin with, we need to recognize how a rhetorical purpose, as we define it, differs from other related purposes. A teacher, for example, has an *educational* purpose in asking students to write a synthesis or interpretation—the purpose of the assignment is to teach these valued forms. A given student, on the other hand, may have an equally important purpose quite at odds with that assignment. This writer's *personal* purpose for writing may lead him to summarize as a way of thinking over and remembering what he found intriguing in William James. For that student, summary may have seemed the best personal use to which his writing could be put, regardless of the assignment. Purpose is also inherent in many textual conventions, modes, and genres (e.g., we could say the writer's purpose was to produce a summary, a synthesis, a lab report or some other conventionally defined form, which carries with it an implicit set of purposes). The *rhetorical* purpose to which we refer here is, by contrast, *a set of goals created by the writer, specifically for this text, which functions for the writer (and ideally for the reader too) as an explicit organizing feature of the discourse* (e.g., Kate's purpose was to get the students she had tutored to consider certain revision strategies she thought they did not use). The papers that fell into this final category were adapting, transforming, and integrating information from sources and personal knowledge in order to carry out a discernible rhetorical purpose in a unique piece of discourse.

Looking for a rhetorical purpose (as we have defined it) raised a second problem. Is the text a student produces always an adequate guide to the presence or absence of rhetorical purpose in the writer's own thinking? Later parts of this study (see

Chapters 3, 5, and 6) explore this important issue in some depth. In our observations of the composing process many writers indeed gave *no* apparent attention to matters of audience or purpose, beyond the conventional purpose of conveying information. In this case, the arhetorical, information-centered plan that appeared to organize the texts of these writers seemed to be an accurate reflection of their process and purpose. On the other hand, some students gave a variety of indications during composing, during revising, and in discussion that they did have a rhetorical purpose which influenced their reading and interpretation of the source text. However, in a subset of these cases, even when the protocols revealed an active sense of purpose, the independent raters in the Teaching Study saw little or no indication of interpretive purpose in the student's paper (see Chapter 2). From the reader's point of view no discernible rhetorical purpose controlled the text; the reader had not been brought into the discourse. We wonder if this phenomenon, which Peck describes as the "Intenders," is a common one. As students learn to manage academic discourse, they may be actively engaging in rhetorical thinking and trying new strategies of transforming knowledge before they are able to use that purpose to control a text. The reader may be the last to know. Teachers, it follows, may need to attend to both the process and the text if they want to see a student's development.

Writers' unique rhetorical purposes, by definition, take a variety of forms. Gary initially saw his task as using the research on revision to understand himself and (implicitly) to judge whether he was a good writer or not. He read each section in order to fit it into a private thesis he was building about what a "good writer" should do and at the same time to apply those "shoulds" to himself. Since he normally did not revise at all, this comparison and the conflict it engendered took up a large chunk of his reading and thinking—it invoked strategies for comparing, testing ideas, and evaluating that did not appear in other protocols. However, this effort was apparent only in the protocol transcript, not in the written product, in which he chose to review the sources. The unique purpose he used for private inquiry was not used as an organizing plan for the text, though it is good example of how such a purpose can guide inquiry. Gary's rhetorical purpose was, in a sense, directed to an audience of one. But unlike a freewheeling response to the topic plan, it required him to use the source text, to interpret it in light of a question he posed, and to apply that information to the specific rhetorical purpose of comparing his practice with the "shoulds" he inferred from his sources.

Kate, the writer we referred to earlier, created a rhetorical purpose that involved readers and put even more demands on her reading-to-write process. Like a few other students in the class, Kate apparently assumed that even if an audience was not specified, it made sense to create one. Thus, she approached this material from early in the process, as potential advice for students she had known as a peer tutor. The interesting feature of her own process was the way this plan to advise helped her "bring out meaning." The strategies she described were ones that also turned up in the work of synthesizers: she tried to link the data in the text with her own experience. To select the important ideas to include, she used criteria such as, is this claim supported by lots of points in the source text, does it make a big difference, is it part of a controversy? The task of synthesizing was apparently embedded in her representation (just as the task of summarizing is often embedded in synthesizing). However, the larger plan, which gave direction to her reading and writing process and structure to her text, was guided by her rhetorical purpose. It was this purpose that let her put synthesis to work for a rhetorical end.

I have elaborated on this rhetorical plan because my experience suggests that students entering academic discourse seem less prepared for this rhetorical task than for summary, synthesis, or personal response. They seem, for instance, less prepared to develop their own goals in interaction with a source and often unaware that a text can be a good synthesis but fail to achieve its purpose or adapt information for a reader. Students who do not recognize that rhetorical plans exist as a distinct option in academic discourse might also have trouble interpreting college assignments that call for original thinking or imaginative application of course material to a new problem.

A plan dominated by a rhetorical purpose has an important but unclear status in academic writing. It is clearly risky in doing assigned writing—a student can get off the track and fulfill a purpose that the instructor does not share, especially if the instructor wants students to concentrate on the reading material itself or on learning the formal features of a genre, such as a critical essay or historical analysis. A rhetorical plan can also make the reading process highly selective, since the "relevant data" are those that contribute to the purpose. Although a rhetorical purpose involves using the source text, it may do so in idiosyncratic ways for purposes that the instructor finds surprising or not "relevant" to the purpose of the assignment. Furthermore, to use this plan, one must not only develop a purpose but transform information to fulfill it. Representing a reading-to-write assignment as a highly rhetorical task guided by personal goals can carry both intellectual and political costs.

On the other hand, this vision of one's task has some remarkable benefits. From a pragmatic point of view, it is a good basis for building an argument and for answering questions in college courses that ask you to manipulate ideas rather than just organize and recall them. It also describes the kind of reading-to-write adults often do outside of school when they read reports, instructions, or memos and write the same for their own purposes. In the larger scheme of education, seeing writing as a rhetorical act and the text as an instrument of purpose can be an entry point into the testing and transforming actions of critical literacy. It is a plan that favors guts, maturity, and independence of mind as well as sensitivity to the response of the reader one is talking to. It allows students to treat the ideas and texts of others (including those of "authorities") as well as their own knowledge and texts as open to scrutiny and transformation. Within this vision of the task, facts can be not only tested but interpreted and put to different uses; claims and concepts can be evaluated and transferred to new settings. This is not to say that writers always give themselves the authority this rhetorical representation seems to allow, but it does suggest why, in the context of school, such an image of one's task might carry genuine hazards and costs as well as benefits for student writers.

How a Task Representation Is Created

To represent a task is to imagine a rhetorical situation—to conjure up teachers past and present, their expectations and response, texts one has read and written, conventions, schemas, possible language—as well as one's own knowledge, needs, and desires. Given the contextual, textual, and rhetorical knowledge that could gain a place in the writer's representation, any single feature, such as the writer's organizing plan, is at best only an indicator of that larger image. But despite their limitations, these indicators can show how something as complex as the writer's sense of authority or image of academic writing is in fact translated into action and text on a given assignment. And the specificity of these features allows meaningful comparisons across writers.

The Organizing Plan described previously stood out as a dominant feature of this writing task, but it was not the only important feature on which students differed. As Figure 3 shows, writers on this task made decisions that differed clearly from one another in five areas. They made choices about where their *Information* would come from (i.e., the source text, their own ideas on the subject, both, or concepts and previously structured information imported to this discussion). They made choices about the *Text Format and Features* that seemed appropriate (i.e., informal notes or summary, summary paragraph[s] plus opinion[s] of the sort encouraged in high school; a standard school theme; or the sort of persuasive essay one sees in academic and professional writing). They made, as we have seen, choices about the *Organizing Plan* which guided both the reading/writing process and the plan of the text. In these first three areas—Information, Format, and Organizing Plan—the listed options reflect the major choices we observed. For the last two areas—Strategies and Goals—one can only present a suggestive list of the various strategies students described and of the even wider set of goals they reported, which ranged from being creative to being comprehensive and accurately representing what they had learned.

The set of options in Figure 3 is not the only way to categorize a writing task; it is a reflection of this particular task, and necessarily incomplete at that. What it did for us was function as a backdrop against which we could observe both individual differences and the unfolding process of task representation itself. Given these five areas as important points of decision and difference, when and how are those decisions made?

On the basis of these and later observations, we can propose a tentative theory of *task representation as a constructive process,* organized around three principles:

1. *Writers do not "choose" a representation, they "construct" one, integrating elements from a large set of options and schemas.*

A writer's image of a task is not created de novo, but depends on the schemas, conventions, patterns, and strategies the writer already knows. As we discuss in later chapters, elements of the social, cultural, and immediate academic context are boldly apparent in this process—they are what turn mere options into "live options." In the second phase of the project we were able to collect evidence suggesting the sources of these images which reflect the legacy of school, the context of this class, and broader cultural assumptions about writing.

Given these constraints on what seems possible, what accounts for the equally important diversity? The notion of a constructive process makes a second key point: this repertoire of possible schemas, conventions, and so forth is stored in many independent pockets of knowledge which must be integrated afresh for each new task. To present the notion of choice among options in the teaching phase of this study, we borrowed a metaphor from personal computers in which users must select their commands from a set of options offered by "pull-down menus." For example, Macintosh users make choices from menus for style, format, font, and so on. Pulling down the style allows the user to mix a variety of type styles—

bold, *italic*, shadow, _{subscript,} under_{line,}—

in a range of sizes from 9- to 24-point type. However, if the user does not bother to look at the menu or make a specific choice, the default of "12-point, plain text" is automatically invoked.

This analogy to a computer menu system has important limitations, but it highlights two aspects of a constructive process that are easy to overlook. One is the sheer number of distinct menus from which writers are making choices, whether they realize it or not, as well as the range of choices to be made within each area. Here, we must import a programmer into our metaphor to include the possibility of creating new options as well. Second, the computer analogy shows how using the default option (e.g., using one's "standard" approach to a paper assignment) can be an efficient way to bypass problem solving and leap in with familiar goals, plans, or strategies. However, that happy leap does not eliminate the fact that a real choice, from a much fuller menu, was in fact made. Unexamined decisions made by default are still decisions.

The limitations of this computer metaphor are perhaps equally revealing when we consider how an individual actually constructs a representation. To begin with, the constructive process one observes is not at all systematic or deliberate. There was no composite menu to "pull down" because the choices offered in Figure 3 are a researcher's abstraction across a variety of students and may not represent the repertoire of any one student. Nor was the process particularly self-conscious. Decisions usually rose to awareness only when the writer encountered a problem or conflict, and not always then. Although this study led us to argue for making students more aware of their options and process, it is clear that task representations can be constructed with little deliberate choice.

Writers differ from menu users in yet another way. The package of default selections on a computer represents the standard choices most people will want to use, most of the time. Yet, as we discuss in Chapter 3, there does not appear to be any standard schema or way of packaging even this small set of options we observed. Despite some predictable trends in these patterns (e.g., summarizing paired with gist and list), knowing a writer's organizing plan did not allow a reliable prediction about the Format or the Information source, much less about Strategies and Goals. This constructive process, it appears, cannot be reduced to the simple selection of a standard inclusive schema.

Yet, if no general, shared schemas exist for this task, perhaps individual writers possess their own personal task schemas that they regularly invoke for school tasks. Although this hypothesis found some support, and writers did talk of their "standard" strategies, these students also talked of confusion, uncertainty, and conflicts within their own image of what to do. Students, it appears, may have standard strategies and partial schemas, but still not have an integrated image of the entire task. This is not, we believe, because they are novice writers, but because represent-

ing complex writing tasks is by nature a constructive process. The next two principles attempt to account for the more active constructive process we observed even
on this relatively simple task.

   2. *Because the process of constructing a task representation depends on noticing
cues from the context and evoking relevant memories, it can extend over the course
of composing.*

   Decisions students made about the five features of the task in Figure 3 appeared to
be made at different times and for different reasons. Some decisions came out of
planning or reviewing episodes. But others were the result of an opportunistic
move. For example, some students started with the apparent plan to use the source
text until an interesting idea or inference changed the pool of information. This
choice on the writer's Information "menu" was dictated by a local event, not by an
initial, integrated vision of the task. Nor was it dictated by a conscious decision that
a commentary paper would be more appropriate than a summary. A lucky event in
the reading process determined a piece of the plan.

   The schematic diagram in Figure 4 sketches the cognitive processes that could
account for these observations and predicts some of the problems these writers
encountered. As other research has shown, Planning and Reviewing are both powerfully generative processes (Flower, Schriver, Carey, Haas, & Hayes, in press;
Hayes, Flower, Schriver, Stratman, & Carey, 1987). However, here we wish to
emphasize the role "noticing" and "evoking" can play in shaping the task writers
give themselves. As Doyle (1983) says, "tasks influence learners by directing their
attention to particular aspects of context and by specifying ways of processing
information" (p. 161).

   We read the diagram in Figure 4 as charting a set of possible loops in the process
of constructing a representation. In one loop, the writer's current representation of
the task is about to be changed by the process of noticing or evoking. We begin with
the current TASK REPRESENTATION (located metaphorically in the box on the
right), which at this moment consists of the major goals, constraints, and strategies
currently activated in the writer's thinking. The PROCESS of constructing (in the
center box) is reinitiated in this case when the writer notices the word "synthesize"
in the assignment (from the CONTEXT box). Noticing in turn leads her to search
memory and evoke a little package of relevant information on the subject (she does
not know a lot about synthesis, so this is a small addition). Or, in another loop, it
occurs to her that her current plan to summarize is turning out to be rather boring
(i.e., she "notices" and reflects on her own current task representation), and this
sends her back to the assignment and the Context of writing (i.e., what am I
supposed to do?) or back into Memory and Planning (i.e., what else could I do;
what have I done before?). Or, finally, our writer might make an effort to evoke the
memory of what was said in class or how the instructor typically responds to
original ideas and use this as a clue to what is possible on this task.

   This noticing and evoking process is unlike the act of selecting a more or less
complete schema for a task from memory. It is responsive to cues from the context
of writing, to memory, and to evocative features of the current task itself—cues that
may pop up at any point as more information is assembled or new possibilities open
up (see Simon, 1973). It can go on during reading and writing without the writer's

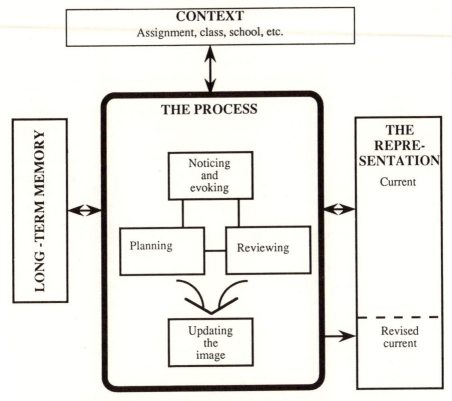

Figure 4. Noticing and evoking within the process of task representation.

conscious control. However, noticing and evoking can also lead to a very goal-directed search of both the context and the writer's knowledge and an active period of Planning or Reviewing.

Noticing does not guarantee a change. The information this process generates can, of course, be lightly considered and ignored, or it can be used to update the current representation into a revised current representation. This act of updating one's image is an interpretive act. For instance, imagine a student who recalls (evokes) her instructor's habit of closely questioning students' claims in class. How will she now translate this cue recalled from the context into a constraint, a goal, or strategy for this task?

The constructive process may continue as a result of this updating if it sends the writer into more planning and setting new goals. A revised representation that now includes "synthesis," for example, may call for a substantial new plan of action from the writer.

This small model lets us describe operationally (1) how the process of noticing and evoking links context, memory, and the writer's representation; (2) how this process, driven by noticing, can run on its own steam throughout composing, so that task representations evolve over time—even after the writer has a plan under-way; and (3) how an interpretive act (the "updating") that stands between noticing and having a revised image can lead to some of the problems we observed. We turn to those now.

3. *Developments and changes in a writer's representation can lead to problems in constructing an integrated task and text.*

As this model suggests, the representation an individual writer constructs over the course of producing the paper is not always stable. Writers in this study tried a variety of strategies: a successful move might suggest an organizing plan; an unsuccessful effort might lead to changes in the plan. This fluidity was not always welcome. Recall the student who "didn't like to think of herself as abandoning an idea" but dropped her initial plan to do a summary with a five-paragraph theme format because she was unable to neatly categorize the "authorities." Abandoning the summary plan and forced to come up with her own ideas for making sense of the sources, but clinging to the theme format, she finally resolved the dilemma by structuring the theme around a comparison of her ideas and those of the authorities. For her, getting the parts of her plan synchronized was the central "interesting" event in her process.

As the noticing and evoking model suggests, a writer's image of the task can change in a piecemeal fashion. A new idea added late in the game may conflict with a goal set earlier, but the lack of integration can remain unseen. This may be one reason writers sometimes end up with texts that appear to have been written by different hands. Looking at their protocols, a number of students discovered to their surprise that they had made dramatic shifts in parts of their representation partway through the task. For instance, one experienced student writer plunged into audience analysis and developed an interesting rhetorical plan focused on her readers—a plan that was elaborated in the protocol and evident in the text. However, in analyzing her own protocol and text, Ruth discovered that near the end of writing she seemed simply to have forgotten this plan to talk to her readers and switched to what she characterized as a standard theme and summary of information. The voice and viewpoint she had been cultivating were dropped, the diction changed, and the paper ended on an unexpectedly lame note. In describing this she was intrigued and mildly embarrassed to discover that her inventive plan for the task had been replaced, without her awareness, by a simpler, doubtless more familiar, plan and practiced strategy, yielding an oddly disjointed text. Yet we might speculate that it passed her own review because each section did fit different *parts* of the plan she had in mind.

A second student illustrates how this ongoing constructive process and its range of options can lead to internal conflicts for a writer. Ann began with the apparently unquestioned assumption that she had to cover all the information in the source texts. As she worked on this goal, an internal critic would burst in and criticize her work for not being original and creative. She wanted to do a thorough synthesis, but became repeatedly disillusioned when the work so far did not also yield an insight that was personally relevant to herself or to the students for whom she wanted to write. The task she represented was not only unmanageable—her internal critic had a low tolerance for anything short of brilliance even during idea generation—but its plan for both inclusive synthesis and marked originality was in conflict with itself.

During her presentation, this writer mentioned that she had never turned a major paper in on time during her college career.

The questions raised by these observations are ones that this study cannot fully answer. However, if the constructive hypothesis is correct, task representation may be both creative and difficult to manage precisely because it is an extended process and because tasks are not simply "selected" in the way old-fashioned textbooks used to tell students to select a thesis. Because this representation is constructed as the process of reading-to-write goes along, the opportunity for choice and revision of choice carries with it the chance of disjointed texts and conflicting plans.

Costs, Benefits, Cognition, and Growth

Because we are educators, any analysis of organizing plans or text types is going to raise questions of value and assumptions about the difficulty or ease, the sophistication or simplicity of different plans. This analysis is no exception, and we would like to consider and question three common assumptions one might use to rank these plans or choose which one to use or teach. Each of these assumptions combines a persuasive element of common sense with a faith that the forms and modes of discourse (in this case, organizing plans) are reliable indicators of sophistication, cognition, or growth. It would be immensely convenient to the educational establishment if this belief were true. The assumptions we wish to question are, first, that synthesis and interpretation are more valuable approaches to a task, second, that they are more cognitively complex, and third, that text types can be arranged on a straightforward development scale.

ASSUMPTION 1: CONCERNING VALUE

Assumption: Synthesis and interpretation are, in general, more valued ways of thinking, more sophisticated, and more typical of mature thinkers. Expert writers on tasks of this sort would, of course, choose a synthesis or interpretation, and students should be encouraged to use syntheses and interpretations when they write.

Alternative View: This study led us to an alternative view of value which is a contextual one. The best organizing plan is the one that fits both the situation (including the assignment) and the writer's goals. "Best" is always a trade-off of costs with benefits.

As this picture of task representation and of critically different images of the task began to unfold in these classes, the students' question turned to which representation is "correct" or, to put it more bluntly, how can I win the lottery and pick the "right representation"?

Educators are likely to pose this same question in more elevated but equally evaluative terms—for example, which representation is better, more intellectually sophisticated, or educationally valuable? Consider the following arguments we could make about the "best" organizing plan: The summary, we could argue, is a foundation skill in reading-to-write. Doing a summary is embedded in most other processes. On the other hand, a summary by itself does not call for the testing and transforming acts of critical literacy. A summary or review with comments can be the basis for critical thought, but it leads to rather limited texts. College writing (at least some of it) calls for a more complex transformation of knowledge and more artful texts (Bridgeman & Carlson, 1984; Schwegler & Shamoon, 1982; Witte & Meyer, 1982).

An organizing plan based on a personal response to the topic has the potential to foster independent thinking, but it can also be an archetypal avoidance strategy that eliminates the need to grapple with a source text and another person's ideas. It is often a substitute for "doing the assignment" even if the paper itself is good. On the other hand, I must admit that my work as a professional often depends on this plan: I begin to read others' work only to find it triggers an idea of my own, and the springboard strategy takes over. I skim, select, follow my own line of thought instead of the author's, and use the text before me to write one of my own.

Synthesis may seem like a safer choice for the "best" plan to teach and encourage. Bloom's (1956) influential effort to rank intellectual skills gives a place of honor to synthesis. It is clearly a powerful and late-developing ability that is regularly invoked in academic writing. Yet, from the perspective of rhetoric and problem solving, I could argue that a rhetorical image of the task is even more valuable, not only for academic work but for reading to write in life after school. A rhetorical, interpretive plan often embeds the acts of synthesis and summary in itself and, it could be argued, might prompt students to a greater transformation of information and/or personal knowledge than would an information-driven synthesis. Furthermore, this rhetorical representation of the task is even more likely to be news to my students, hence more worth teaching. On the other hand, a rhetorical task is a selective process. Students who gave themselves the goal of interpreting for a purpose did not, for example, see many of the contradictions in the source text. They did not necessarily engage in the same sort of critical thinking the synthesizers did. In trying to answer the questions "What task should we do; what should we teach?" there were always "other hands."

I have sketched out this inconclusive line of argument because I think it shows we may be asking the wrong question when we try to create precise value-laden hierarchies of better or more lofty tasks and plans—at least in this context. The question of how to assign value sharpened when our group of instructors faced the issue of how to advise students, after we had helped them to see the power (and necessity) of their own choices. To encourage students to go for broke, to turn everything into a rhetorical task, for instance, or to give themselves the loftiest goals of creativity at every turn seemed, alternatively, naive and hypocritical about the way writing operates in a context. Moreover, it simply did not match the even more interesting reality of how active, professional people appear to operate.

The reality of the task representation process seems to be much better captured by the metaphor of personal costs and benefits than it does by a scale of right or wrong. Writing is a social, political, and strategic act, in the broad sense of the terms. A writer's purpose is a response to the context of writing. If there is little reason to reorganize or transform information, Martha's gist and list strategy is not only efficient but sensible. On the other hand, if a given paper assignment represents a step in the intellectual sequence of an entire course, it makes sense to give oneself the task of adapting the reading to one of the educational purposes of the course or to dealing with an issue that the course raises. Taking on a task of this sort may be more demanding than producing a summary, but the benefits are probably greater. College instructors, for instance, may expect students to carry out a purposeful transformation of ideas even when they do not say so directly.

Reading-to-write is also a personal, intellectual act, and the question of costs and benefits to the writer is just as critical here. Some tasks are more difficult, but they allow writers to go beyond their current understanding, to make something that is meaningful to themselves, or to do something better than they have done before. On the other hand, elevated goals that are out of synchrony with time and occasion can be like the "rigid rules" Mike Rose (1980) described—inflexible demands which ignore that writing is "good" when it serves its purpose for the writer. Ann, for instance, the writer whose internal critic demanded creativity at every turn, did not feel she was in control of her own process or priorities.

Conceptualizing the writer's choice in terms of costs and benefits has an economic ring that may seem odd in this context. However, it is a powerful frame for thinking about processes and decisions that often go unrecognized. Although we have sketched some examples of costs and benefits in this chapter, the value of the concept is probably realized in action when we encourage students to look at their own process. Cost/benefit is a situational concept—it points to the trade-offs people always make in controlling their lives. It also points up a central contradiction in the economics of being a student. Students do not always make the "commercial" choice; they often do not opt for the choice with the lowest cost and the highest short-run benefit. Instead, they plunge into kinds of discourse they have not yet mastered, trying to talk the language, working in the faith that a "good idea" can pull you through and that making a serious attempt is the right thing to do. Our students regularly take on, try out, and plunge in when the costs in uncertainty and difficulty are high, because they are willing to give priority to learning or because good teachers have made the benefits of trying tangible. My point is this: the economic metaphor of trade-offs does not presuppose that a learner will choose the same priorities as a slumlord or low-cost/high-profit manufacturer; but it does recognize the possibility of radical differences in students' and teachers' goals. In fact, it lets us examine these different priorities in terms of what one values, and the costs and risks one is willing to incur. It also lets us recognize the common sense of efficiency.

In response to Assumption 1, then, we would replace a linear scale that assigns intrinsic value to certain text types and tasks with the image of a balance, as in Figure 5. The "right" task representation depends on the way a writer chooses to balance her goals, her reading of the situation, her priorities, the use this text has for her or others, her time, her effort, the risks, her relevant knowledge, and so on.

Consider the following case in point. At the time of the revision and self-analysis assignment, Eileen was a writing major wrapped up in uncertainty about herself as a "creative" writer, which included the depressing awareness that she did not exhibit the persistence and craft she admired in writers like T. S. Eliot. After reading the source text, her protocol starts: "Okay, well this doesn't seem so bad, since I am a

Costs   **Benefits**

Balancing costs and benefits:

Goals
Situation
Time
Difficulty
Priorities

Figure 5. An alternative view of value.

strong believer in revision, even though I don't think I do enough of it. . . . Okay. Well, I think the first thing is to restress what the topic sentence was and then apply it to myself."

Her paper, which a teacher would probably see as a free response to the topic, dives into the question on the top of her mind: "I have found that there lies a distinct difference between what makes a good and a bad writer. In my opinion, that difference does not lie with a person's talent as with patience and ability to stand back from one's work and give an objective evaluation of the piece, something I have been trying to do for years. [Following her discussion of writing as a craft, with a brief reference to Faigley and Witte, the paper ends with an assertion.] If a bad writer could see how a genius such as Eliot agonized over his work and even went so far as to cut out hundreds of lines to make his point and how themes were changed from one draft to the next, they [sic] could see the obvious need for revision."

Eileen's paper let her talk about Eliot and her own personal conflict over the issue of talent and craft (her new values, it seemed, honored craft, but her old self-image and her writing habits had clearly venerated talent). Her text, however, showed only a passing acquaintance with the source material. In the context of this self-reflection assignment, that was a perfectly acceptable decision. But when her next assignment called for a lucid analysis of a specified topic, Eileen's paper showed a similarly breathless glance toward the assigned issue as she continued to unravel her opinions on T. S. Eliot and talent. That paper met few of the grading criteria for the assignment, and over that period Eileen did not appear to be learning much of what that particular course was designed to teach. It is possible that Eileen achieved something valuable for herself by continuing in the "free writing" mode she said she had used in previous classes and found far more comfortable than analysis. It is also possible she believed a "creative" or "talented" departure from the assignment would be rewarded in the end, so dealing with other sources would be unnecessary. What is clear is that this situation involved a pressing set of goals that were in conflict with one another and her decisions were balancing benefits with real costs.

One implication of this cost/benefit view is that task representation, as a social, interpretive act, may involve contradictions and ambiguity. Although "what the teacher wants" may be a legitimate question, it is not the only goal involved. Sometimes the goals of teacher and student are simply in conflict. But even when students wish to operate with shared goals, they must still "read" the situation. Student writers must learn to figure out what different rhetorical contexts call for and, in many cases, to infer their options from limited experience and inconclusive evidence.

A second implication of this view is that the writer is empowered to make decisions about his or her own process and goals. In a sense the writer is unavoidably in control because reading to write is a purposeful process: he or she is making decisions and setting goals even when unaware of the options. On the other hand, this view raises the possibility of genuine empowerment in which writers are not only aware of options but of their own values and their decision processes. The question we raise later in this study is can we help students make this process of negotiating a task a more informed process?

ASSUMPTION 2: CONCERNING COGNITIVE COMPLEXITY

Assumption: Synthesis and interpretation, as we defined them in this study, may not always be the plans of choice, but they are the cognitively complex choice. They are more difficult to do, they require more intellectual maturity, and they lead to more profound or complex transformations of knowledge. They are the hard tasks.

Alternative View: An alternative to this assumption defines cognitive complexity as a feature of the writer's process rather than the text. It says that complexity does not reside only in an organizing scheme, a text type, or genre; complexity is a function of the goals a writer sets within a plan—one can write a very complex, integrative summary as well as a simple-minded synthesis. The complexity of a given task can be measured by the knowledge transformation required to do it. (The term *knowledge* here refers to both a writer's personal or prior knowledge and new information.) The degree of transformation a task requires does not depend on the next type chosen, but on the structure of the writer's current knowledge and the extent to which he or she is willing or able to transform it to meet the demands of a task. Text types and genres have always been convenient pigeonholes for tracking development and accomplishment, but they can be hazardous categories of convenience, *if what we really want to talk about is cognitive complexity.*

Figure 6 represents this alternative view of cognitive complexity as a continuum going from tasks that require low knowledge transformation to those that require a high degree of transformation—for the individual writer on a given task. What makes such transformation necessary or difficult? One key variable is the writer's prior knowledge. If a student comes to research on "revision" with well-organized background knowledge and finds a unifying concept in the text, synthesis will not require extensive transformation of that student's knowledge (see Langer, 1984). Another easy road to synthesis or interpretation is to bring a current *idée fixe,* a dogmatic belief, or a favorite topic, such as Eileen's craft/talent conflict, to bear on whatever one reads. The cognitive task can thus be reduced to selecting and arranging new information in a ready-made schema.

A second variable that raises the demand for transformation is the amount and

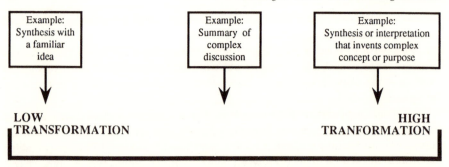

Figure 6. Knowledge transformation continuum affected by prior knowledge, amount and complexity of information, and level of invention.

complexity of the information. For example, a graduate student doing a literature review might find it relatively easy to *synthesize* sources by selecting only the information closely tied to her own research question, but very difficult to accurately *summarize* the gist, key points, and implications of thirty related but internally complex papers in linguistics, psychology, and literary theory. Or imagine trying to create a well-formed summary of a particularly lively two-hour seminar discussion. To do that you might have to wrench ideas from a temporal structure, based on who said what to whom, to create a new thematic structure based on the key issues of the discussion, which you would have to infer in some cases, transforming your memory of comments, implied meanings, and the emotional energy of the speaker into gists, so you could reorganize the whole body of local topics into a meaningful unit. A final example comes from our task in which some students chose to increase complexity by dealing with planted contradictions in the original text; others did not. And some students chose to use their own ideas while others did not. These two decisions affected the cognitive complexity of the task students gave themselves, regardless of whether they did a summary or synthesis. The complexity of their thinking processes was a function of how tightly they chose to integrate the amount of the information they possessed.

The third variable we observed is the demand for invention and the height at which it occurs in a writer's hierarchy of ideas. Writers restructure their knowledge in minor ways all the time at the bottom of the hierarchy when they make local transitions or see that two ideas are parallel or in apposition to each other. They restructure a larger body of information when they draw the inferences that create a sense of gist. When invention occurs at that level, the whole structure of a body of ideas may be involved. Some of the most extensive and most cognitively complex transformations come, as one would predict, when writers are attempting to forge a unique synthesizing concept (that can control the entire text) or when they are attempting to develop a unique rhetorical purpose that does justice to their goals, their knowledge, and their readers. This sort of invention is what gives academic writing its reputation for difficulty, even among experienced writers.

To sum up, it would be convenient if we could measure cognitive complexity or chart cognitive growth by analyzing text features alone, or if we could equate knowledge transformation with certain genres and organizing plans. However, it appears that cognition cannot be easily reduced to the more tangible features of text. As we have tried to suggest in Figure 6, the real measure of cognitive complexity of a given act of composing is knowledge transformation itself. Text types can appear at various places on that continuum. Knowledge transformation happens within the head of the writer, in a given situation. It is a function of prior knowledge, the amount and complexity of the information one is trying to transform, and the level at which invention is going on. For teachers, this means that conceptual difficulty is not simply a feature of the task, but a feature of the writer's process that depends on where the student starts and where he or she is trying to end up.

ASSUMPTION 3: CONCERNING COGNITIVE DEVELOPMENT

Assumption: Our third questionable assumption is that the sequence of tasks students are assigned as they progress through high school and college (from summary [Applebee, 1981] to independent analysis and interpretation) reflects a "natural" pattern of development. That is, students, left to their own devices, would progress through the modes just as our school system now requires them to do. The problem with this assumption of natural sequence is that it seems to go beyond the data. In recent research with kindergarteners, even the shibboleth that children's writing begins with narration has come under question (Dyson, 1986). Based on this presumption that natural development and cognitive capacities are expressed by certain modes, we soon find ourselves using those modes to measure capacity and in the next breath branding students who have not learned a given mode of discourse as cognitively or developmentally handicapped. Such cognitive pigeonholing is especially likely when students are underprepared—just the sort of student who would have lacked much chance to acquire the mode we are calling "natural."

And yet there is an important element of common sense underlying this assumption. I only need to consult my recent memories of student conferences or of my own freshman year to recognize the way students must struggle to move beyond knowledge telling, summary, or review and comment and come to grips with the demands for synthesis, for working at higher levels of abstraction, for using their own knowledge *and* that of authorities, and for putting their knowledge and reading to work in service of a unique rhetorical purpose. Common sense says that freshmen are crossing a threshold that can be roughly equated with attempting more complex syntheses and rhetorical purposes.

Alternative View: Our alternative assumption, then, makes a much more limited and contextualized claim. Students come to college with certain forms of discourse under their control—typically those forms of discourse the school system has asked them to practice for twelve years. Entering academic discourse means encountering new demands, learning how to meet them, and practicing the same. The threshold we see students crossing may in reality be two different thresholds. As Figure 7 suggests, one is created by lack of familiarity and practice, especially for a rhetorical task. If no one has asked you to use your knowledge for a purpose within a community of peers, you will struggle while learning the ropes. The second threshold is created by the fact that writers of academic discourse must often plunge into

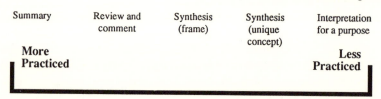

Figure 7. Experience with academic discourse continuum.

knowledge transformation (see Figure 6)—a process that is typically difficult for everyone. Students, for instance, often write about subjects while they are still acquiring knowledge. Scholars and researchers are expected to address problematic topics with unique insights and sensitive adaptation of their knowledge. Academic discourse often values invention that occurs at the top levels of the idea structure, and such writing is often difficult, even with practice.

Our caution, then, applies to confounding development with the effects of practice or the inherent difficulty of knowledge transformation. If students are being asked to represent writing assignments in new ways (to try for a unique, controlling concept rather than a commonplace one) and to learn how to do these new tasks, many of the difficulties freshmen have are not a failure of high school education or a problem of intellectual development. Their difficulties can be a signal that students are in the process of learning to do a new task, which we may need to teach more explicitly than we do. Or they may be attempting a genuinely difficult task of transforming the knowledge they currently possess.

In this discussion we have tried to lay out some of the assumptions we are making about how academic discourse and the tasks it poses are related to value judgments, cognitive complexity, and practice. And we have tried to present three images of those relations that offer alternatives to three more familiar but problematic assumptions. We can use the three elements presented in Figures 5, 6, and 7 to build a composite, if sobering, picture of the task many freshmen face in the transition from high school to college: academic discourse is a game with many rules, many conventions, and many patterns of argument and evidence. Some of the conventions are widely shared, some discipline-specific, but many are new to freshmen. Such discourse typically favors the text plans of synthesis or purposeful interpretation over the plans of summary and comment, although the latter are the plans a freshman is most likely to control. In terms of cognitive complexity, academic discourse often expects not just coherence (e.g., a topical structure linked to an apparent thesis), but the integration of complex material, and it (often) places special value on invention at the top levels of an idea structure. This means that a student's prior knowledge is less likely to do the job and that the most demanding kind of knowledge transformation is required. Finally, because the expectations of a new discourse community are, by definition, unknown, learning to represent this new task—even to recognize that it is in some ways new—is an important step. The benefits of trying to achieve a given set of goals or carry out a plan are uncertain even as the costs of attempting a partly practiced strategy go up.

If this composite picture makes academic discourse sound difficult, it may be realistic. On the other hand, helping students see that any given assignment can be placed on the kind of practice and the knowledge transformation continua sketched in Figures 6 and 7 gives them deserved credit for what they can already do and for the new abilities they are mastering. It suggests that teaching has at least three agendas as well. First, to move students along the continuum of discourse experience, we need to give them experience and practice and a more demystifying insight into the conventions of the discourse before them. Second, to encourage the knowledge transformation we value, we need to teach the thinking strategies that help one to invent and integrate. Finally, to help students make informed images of a task and its costs and benefits, we may need to see task representation itself as a critical part of the process we teach.

Taking Metacognitive Control: Awareness versus Standard Strategies

This Exploratory Study raised a final issue. Is task representation a process that is under students' control? Are their decisions made as a result of awareness of their options? This is a hard but important question to answer.

We begin with a brief description of some of the forms this awareness took, using the four-part model (presented in Figure 4) as a template to ask what happens when writers not only perform an operation or possess knowledge, but also are *aware of their own performance or knowing.* How might awareness affect long-term memory, the current representation, the context, and the process of representing itself? When processes that can be carried out with little conscious thought cross the threshold into conscious attention, or when writers rise to conscious problem solving, we often have an opportunity to see some of the thinking that distinguishes expert from novice. We can also use the much more extensive research on metacognition in reading to help fill in the picture of how this additional level of awareness can affect reading to write. Although much of the reading research looks at younger readers, it helps us isolate those late-developing skills and demanding processes, such as comprehension monitoring, that probably affect adult performance, too. Some problems never seem to go away.

AWARENESS AND LONG-TERM MEMORY

One can imagine some parts of long-term memory as a dimly lit storehouse of oddly filed and poorly cross-indexed information on all sorts of topics (including how to write summaries and syntheses). A great deal of information is there, but without awareness of the contents in general or a system for searching it would be difficult to find and compare different pockets of knowledge. One useful measure of awareness, then, is the ability to conduct a metamemorial search of one's own knowledge, directing attention to memory itself. When Scardamalia, Bereiter, and Woodruff (reported in Bereiter & Scardamalia, 1987) asked fourth and sixth graders to generate lists of topics on which they had either high or low knowledge, the children found the task itself difficult; they could not compare their own pockets of knowledge in that abstract way. Moreover, the texts they wrote on high-knowledge and low-knowledge topics were indistinguishable. Knowing about your knowledge at a meta level and carrying out a metamemorial search appear to be late-developing skills.

Some writers in this study clearly had some distance on and a conceptual grasp of their own bodies of knowledge. Like Kate, they were aware that summaries and purposeful essays posed meaningful options and that "relevant" topic information was a quality they defined rather than found in the task. For this task we could define one critical form of awareness as possessing one's own version of a menu of options, like that in Figure 3, and being able to consider and compare those entities as alternatives.

AWARENESS AND THE CURRENT REPRESENTATION

If being able to search and reflect on one's own stable store of knowledge is difficult, monitoring the changing contents of working memory in the heat of writing can be more so. Writers need to be aware of the changing configuration of their own image of the task. The protocols show us places where writers did, indeed, rise to problem solving and reflection when they encountered a conflict among their own goals or between the task they had embarked on and the assignment (as they read it). However, the oral presentations also registered the surprise writers felt at looking at the shifting sands of their own planning in these protocols and discovering internal conflicts that they had not recognized as problems at the time. That is, although Ann, the writer mentioned before, had responded in various ways to the conflict between her internal critic saying "be creative" and her other goal to "be comprehensive," she had not been aware of this as a pattern or conflict until the protocol and presentation gave her the opportunity to reflect on it.

AWARENESS AND CONTEXT

Writers inevitably write in a context, which like language can be said to partially "write the writer" (McCormick & Waller, 1987). That interaction with one's context, whether it is the context of culture, the classroom, or the current assignment, can be automatic, reactive, and unexamined, or it can be self-conscious and open to self-control. Critical literacy and critical consciousness are states of heightened awareness—knowing the covert messages the context is sending and your own assumptions and habits of response (see Chapter 8). In the initiation to academic discourse, Bartholomae (1985) argues, writers move from imitating and internalizing the conventions of a discourse to innovating within it. Awareness means the ability to invent/infer context even when it is not given. In one study of expert and novice readers (Haas & Flower, 1988), this awareness took the form of an active strategy. When experienced adult readers were asked to comprehend a difficult passage out of context, they used a rhetorical reading strategy in which they inferred a context, purpose, and author as an aid to making the text meaningfully coherent. This strategy was entirely missing from the performance of freshmen.

College writing assignments have many levels of context one could be aware of: the expectations of the class and course, the social and intellectual context of college, one's own personal history as a writer, the cultural assumptions and conditions that affect doing assignments, generating ideas, and so on. However, looking at the assignment as a small and local instance of context reveals a principle that may hold for other contexts: awareness, like any cognitive process, is an act of selective attention. Even when writers were explicitly aware of the assignment as a context, they often chose different aspects of it to promote awareness. Here are thinking-aloud comments from three students made immediately after re-reading the assignment:

Writer A
1. OK. Now let's see if we can put this together into a [reads] comprehensive statement.
2. OK. [reads] The process of revision.
3. Topic sentence [and writer goes on to summarize].

Writer B
1. OKAY. Let's go.
2. Two pages she wants.
3. Let's get a lead [and writer goes on to synthesize in a breezy journalistic manner].

Writer C
1. [reads] Interpret and synthesize.
2. What the hell does that mean?
3. Synthesize means to pull together.
4. Not to make something up.
5. Why should I want to make something up? [and writer goes on to summarize].

Writer A apparently reads this context as an invitation to the familiar conventions of a comprehensive summary guided by its topic sentence, while writer B attends to the page requirement as a personal request from me ("Two pages she wants"), and sees the task as a journalist (which he had been) might. Writer C turns her confusion into a self-conscious negotiation with the assignment. Awareness alone may not be enough to help writers deal with a problematic context. In a study of audience awareness of expert and novice writers, only the experienced writers went beyond recognizing features of the readers to setting goals to affect those readers (Flower & Hayes, 1980). In the second phase of the study, which allowed us to see the role of context more closely (Chapters 7 and 8), and in the examples that follow, we can see how awareness of context takes on special power when it allows writers to translate their knowledge into action.

AWARENESS AND PROCESS

Awareness of one's own process operates at a number of levels. The burst of recent research on metacognition in reading distinguishes between the statable knowledge people have about their own thinking (including the late-developing capacity to reflect on that process as it is happening) and the active "regulatory" knowledge that lets people guide their own process and employ strategies such as monitoring comprehension, planning the next move, and evaluating the effect of a strategy for learning (Baker & Brown, 1984). This research, reviewed by Baker and Brown (1984), has found that inexperienced and young readers bring surprising theories about the goals of comprehension to the process of reading (e.g., understanding a text means recognizing all the words, even if they seem unrelated). When it comes to monitoring comprehension, they fail to detect problems in their understanding and planted inconsistencies—a finding that Baker (1979) has described in college students as well. Finally, even when readers detect breakdowns in their comprehension process, they may or may not be able to invoke strategies for repairing the problem. This research suggests that the process of monitoring and repairing gaps in comprehension is difficult for us all, child or adult. However, proficient college readers observed in process-tracing studies were distinguished by three features: their ability to talk about reading problems and strategies, the quantity of their comprehension monitoring comments during reading, and the number and kinds of strategies they used (Hare, 1981; reviewed in Wagoner, 1983).

We can see parallel kinds of awareness in the writers in this study:

a. At the lowest level of process awareness (and highest level of simple efficiency), we see writers *using strategies* they *invoke by name* or category (e.g., "Let's get a lead") but do not examine.

b. At a little greater expense of metacognitive attention, writers also *monitor their own process,* noticing what they are thinking and what they have done so far, reflecting on whether it is working, or simply musing on their own experience. In this example, the writer is monitoring the associative path her own memory has taken, her own performance, and her current plan.

1. This is making me think of, one of the things I read was that inexperienced writers jumped into their writing and experienced writers, um, would take a little more time to plan.
2. I guess if I want to fall in the category of experienced writer, I should make a little more of a plan myself.
3. Um . . . the plan that I have made so far is simply to write down either what I know or what I remember from reading this piece about revision.

c. Awareness at the level of monitoring sometimes leads to frustration if it does no more than confirm that the writer is indeed in a pickle. Awareness takes on new power when the writer can rise to conscious problem solving and use this awareness to actually guide the process of reading and writing. In studies of the ways writers conduct the processes of planning (Flower et al., in press) and revision (Carey, & Hayes, 1986; Flower, Hayes, Carey, Schriver, & Stratman, 1986; Hayes et al., 1987), this ability to rise to problem solving to resolve planning conflicts and diagnose and plan solutions to problems in text was a distinctive feature of experienced writers. Under these circumstances the writer's goals, constraints, and possible strategies themselves become the objects of thought as writers engage in what Bereiter and Scardamalia (1983) have called "intentional cognition." The writer in the following example combines a lively awareness of her own interests and options (her habit of "giving a purpose" to things in comment 1), with the context and constraints set up by the assignment. Notice that in comment 2 she chooses the closing phrase as the instruction of interest, that is, the purpose is to say what you think. In comment 3 she considers another potential plan (to adapt to students) and continues in 4 and 5 with a reflective monitoring of her own reading process, followed by an apparent decision to go with the initial goal (to make it interesting to myself) while the second goal (adapt this for my students) is left to percolate gently on a back burner.

1. Hmmm. I kind of like to give a purpose to, to the reason why I'm writing this other than just to write this.
2. [Rereads part of assignment] It just says we're interested in what you think.
3. Hmm . . . I'm wondering if I could write this in a way that it could be used for my students. [Writer is a beginning instructor.]
4. That's one of the things I was thinking about when I read this was how could I adapt this to be helpful to them.
5. And one of the things that I do when I write is I have to get some overall goal or purpose to write.
6. Right now I'm doing it just to make it interesting to myself.

HOW AWARE ARE STUDENTS OF THEIR CHOICES AND PROCESS?

The Exploratory Study showed us that individual students possessed many kinds of awareness about their own task representations at many levels. But as educators we want to ask if most of the students were operating at a level of self-awareness in all four areas proposed by our model. Awareness is clearly a hard quality to measure, and as teachers hoping to open new doors, we may be pleased to overestimate the novelty of what we teach. However, the net effect of the protocols, the presentations, and group discussions was to suggest that metacognitive awareness of the writing process and of task representation in particular is not a well-established part of the repertory of these students. Although they appeared clearly capable of and in possession of such awareness in isolated parts of their writing, they were not, it appears, engaging in active metacognition about writing.

Support for this tentative conclusion came from various quarters. To begin with, the sharp diversity in representations that emerged from the presentations came as an initial surprise to all of us. Yet as the goals students were giving themselves began to form a pattern, there was a general sense that important and familiar decisions were being made explicit through this process of data-based reflections. In their presentations many students registered surprise at the confusions, the contradictions, the inventions, and the strategies they saw in their protocols. Some were features of their process that they had not registered at all in the heat of composing. Others were strategies they now realized were unacknowledged mainstays—and in some cases mainstays that could not support the more demanding work they were trying to do in college.

In a questionnaire completed by one class in this exploratory study, 50 percent of the students said they had not even considered the written assignment closely (despite all the artfulness we had put into its design), but, had simply invoked their "standard strategy." That decision was clearly a move for efficiency; since students' operational definitions of this all-purpose "standard" strategy varied so much, however, one wonders how good that strategy was at pleasing many and pleasing long, given the varied demands of college writing. Finally, what does that move say about the writer's awareness of his or her own options, about the need to "read" the rhetorical context, and about the writer's control of her own cognition? The vision of a rich but unexamined process that emerged from this Exploratory Study led us to ask, what effect does task representation have on the reading-to-write process of freshmen—writers on the threshold of college-level academic discourse? This question led to the second phase of the project, the Teaching Study. The design and materials for the Teaching Study were presented in the Introduction, "Studying Cognition in Context." The results of that study are analyzed from various perspectives in the chapters that follow.

Appendix III: Protocol Instructions

The following instructions were part of the practice session that trained students to collect their own thinking-aloud protocols. They were designed to help clarify the dual roles of the writer and the protocol collector, although the use of a second person was optional.

THINKING ALOUD WHILE YOU WRITE

Instructions for the Writer

In the process of writing, people think and say many things to themselves that are quickly forgotten. Yet these thoughts are interesting and important parts of the writer's problem-solving process.

We are interested in the thoughts that go through your head as you work on this problem. We are asking you to do three things:

1. Work on the task as you **normally** would: read, think, jot notes, or just write. (However, don't erase. Simply cross through anything you don't intend to use.)

2. While you are reading, thinking to yourself, or writing—please **read and think aloud,** even as you are writing something down.

3. We are NOT asking you to **talk about** your process or to explain or justify what you are doing. We want you to focus all your attention on doing the task. Simply think out loud, as if you were **talking to yourself** as you solved the problem.

Instructions for the Protocol Collector

1. Find a place that will be free from interruptions. (Put a sign on the door.) Have paper, pens, tape, and everything ready before the writer gets the assignment. (Coffee and tea are fine; no gum.)

2. Before the writer begins, prepare the tape recorder by reading the subject's name, the date, and the name of the task onto the tape. Then **test the tape** by playing your introduction back. Put the mike on a towel or quiet surface and test for

good volume and placement of the mike. Cue the tape to start at the end of your intro.

3. Ask the writer to do a short warm-up session (3–4 minutes) thinking aloud on a practice task, then listening for where you had to prompt before trying again. During the practice session **prompt the writer by simply saying "What are you thinking now?" whenever the writer falls silent for more than 3 or 5 seconds.**

4. Make sure the writer knows when the first side of the tape will be full and can turn the tape over if you will not be there.

5. Turn the tape on. Stay with the writer for the first part of the session to prompt the writer whenever he or she falls silent. If the writer mumbles, turn up the recorder and ask the writer to speak up.

6. When the session is over, **collect all the materials**—notes, drafts, text. Make sure the writer's full name, phone number, and address are written on the text. Make sure notes and pages are numbered in the order in which they were written. You may need the writer's help to figure this out.

7. Finally, protocols are typed double spaced, no paragraphs, with name and date, and with dots (. . .) for short pauses and underlined spaces (_____) for unintelligible fragments.

Appendix IV: Reading-to-Write Assignment on Revision
READING AND INTERPRETING DATA

Here is a short passage, including research results and observations, on the performance of experienced writers. Your task is to read and interpret these data in order to make a brief (1–2 page), comprehensive statement about *the process of revision* in writing. Your statement should interpret and synthesize all of the relevant findings in the text. As you read, please read out loud, and when anything crosses your mind, say out loud whatever you are thinking, even if it seems irrelevant or incomplete. Do whatever you would normally do, except say aloud whatever you notice or think to yourself as you read and make your statement. People think and do many different things while they are reading: we are interested in how you do it.

THE PASSAGE
Some Recent Findings on Writing

Recent research has found a number of differences between the writing processes of good writers and weak writers. When Pianko (1979), for example, timed the various actions of college student writers, she found that students enrolled in the remedial writing course (the weak writers) began writing about forty seconds after they were given a topic. Students enrolled in the standard freshman writing course, on the other hand, waited for over a minute before they began to write. Pianko assumed that the students were using the time before they began writing to plan their essays and concluded that the stronger writers did more planning than the weaker writers did.

Writers who approach writing as a problem-solving activity tend to treat editing and revising as useful steps in composing because these activities break the process up, making it easier to handle. They find that many of the problems that block writing can be solved when they return to the work as editors, and that editing is an inexpensive method (in terms of time and effort) for making dramatic improvements in writing. These writers feel that editing lets them concentrate on **communicating** with a reader.

Sommers (1980) interviewed a number of people who said they were experienced writers and like to write. She found that when they wrote, they normally did more than one draft and that they talked about revision as if it were re-vision, that is, a chance to resee their whole paper and possibly rethink and reorganize the whole thing. The students she interviewed described revision as cutting and "slashing out" unnecessary words, weak parts, and errors. They usually didn't revise their papers.

Many textbook writers say that effective writers are rewriters. A first version, they often feel, is never as good as a second version, a second one as good as a third, and so on, **so long as the changes from version to version are made for good reasons.** But how do good writers arrive at good reasons? They evaluate their writing in three ways:

1. They set standards or criteria by which it can be judged.
2. They relate their subject to the criteria.
3. They draw the conclusions that follow.

Halpern and Liggett (1984) studied the writing of a number of business people who regularly dictated their letters, memos, and reports. These people did a good deal of planning, but they did very little revision, especially of the spoken "draft." These researchers also found that when textbook writers and other researchers talk about the writing process, they are often thinking of the writing process of a certain limited group of writers—essayists, journalists, academic, and creative writers—but not business people.

Good writers review their goals for their papers and the plans they used to implement these goals. Then they study their papers with those high-level goals in mind. They test to see not only if the papers fit their goals and plans, but also to see if their plans changed in midstream. Faigley and Witte (1981) found that when the experienced writers and journalists they studied revised a text, they made changes that affected the *meaning* of the text, not just the wording. Even when they changed only single words those changes would have altered a summary of the piece. The inexperienced student writers in their study stuck to finding errors and altering individual words, but their changes did not alter the meaning.

Revising often produces shorter words and shorter sentences. Witte (1983) asked a large group of students to read and revise a long paragraph from a textbook. After judges had sorted the revisions into "good" and "poor" ones, Witte found that everyone had made the paragraph shorter and used simpler words. However, the successful revisers had made deletions that emphasized the "gist," meaning, or main point of the original text; they had connected and subordinated the other sentences to it. The unsuccessful revisers did not seem to use the gist of the original to organize their revision, and their paragraphs had no single, clear focus.

Task: Now go ahead and write down (on another piece of paper, please) your statement about the *process of revision* in writing based on your interpretation of these data.

Please think out loud as you do this. Be sure to tell the tape recorder if you are doing any rereading and what you are looking at. Make any notes, marks, or changes you want to, but please do not erase anything if you change your mind; just cross things out. And try to say everything that crosses your mind, even fragments and stray thoughts.

Thank you. We are interested in what you think.

2

Promises of Coherence, Weak Content, and Strong Organization: An Analysis of the Students' Texts

MARGARET J. KANTZ

It is a fact of life that students interpret writing tasks in different ways. These task representations matter because they affect the written products. Differences in task representation lead to marked differences in papers that may, in turn, determine whether individual papers fulfill a teacher's expectations and how they are evaluated. Sometimes, however, students appear to think about a task in one way but do it in another way, producing papers that send conflicting textual signals that confuse the teachers who read them. In the study being reported in this chapter, teachers who operated on the basis of seemingly reasonable expectations for structure and coherence found themselves temporarily unable to agree about the differences in particular papers—and, hence, unable to agree on how the writers had interpreted the assignment. In the papers that caused this difficulty, for example, the introductions might announce a plan to argue or discuss information, but the bodies of the papers would use coherence-building strategies that matched a quite different task interpretation, such as summarizing the information. We identified half a dozen strategies for announcing or building coherence. In some essays, readers felt that the discussion of the Time Management material matched the strategy; in others— the papers that they found difficult—the discussion did not match the strategy. We feel that discussion of the seemingly inconsistent task representations embodied in these papers, a phenomenon not clearly predicted by the literature, may shed light on a common problem teachers have in reading student papers—namely, judging whether or not the textual signals that students use to indicate persuasive analyses of source material are enacted in their discussions.

This chapter first describes the ways that readers saw the structures in a set of freshman papers, giving the results of the Teaching Study described in Chapter 1. The readers' analysis was motivated by the question, "Given the alternative organizing plans this task elicited in the Exploratory Study, what choices would the students in the Teaching Study make?" The second half of the chapter discusses the problem that the judges encountered when they applied the initial taxonomy of organizing plans, developed in the Exploratory Study, to these freshman papers. This problem, involving mismatches between content and structural cues, led to the development of a somewhat elaborated taxonomy of task representations. This elaborated taxonomy (the new subcategories are indented) is summarized here and was used to code the essays, as reported in Figures 8 and 9. (See Chapter 1 for definitions of the five major categories; instructions to judges are found in Appendix V.)

Summary
States gist or selected ideas from the source text.
Review and comment
Combines a summary or selective review of material from the source text with commentary or additions by the writer.

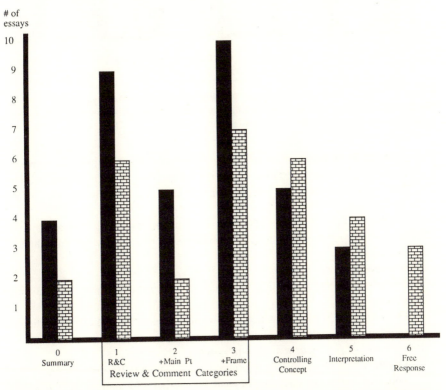

Figure 8. Choices students made about organizing plans for original essays. Graph shows the distribution of original essays across coding categories. $N = 69$. Black bars indicate control group; bricked bars indicate experimental group.

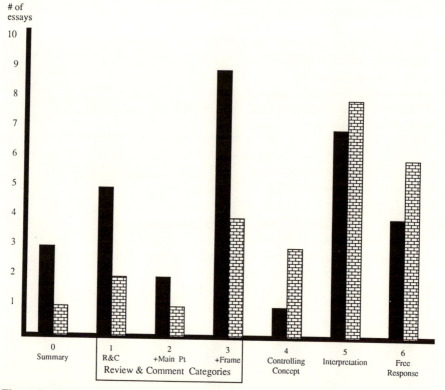

Figure 9. Choices students made about organizing plans for revised essays. Graph shows the distribution of original essays across coding categories. $N = 57$. Black bars indicate control group; bricked bars indicate experimental group.

Isolated main point or conclusion. A subcategory of review and comment containing a statement that is signaled as main point or a conclusion but does not appear to control the structure or selection of content in the body of the text.

Frame. A subcategory of review and comment containing a statement that frames the review with a vague, highly general, or obvious introductory statement.

Free response to the topic
Discusses the topic with little reference to information from the source texts.

Synthesis
Organizes a discussion (which draws on source materials) around a unique (nonobvious) controlling concept.

Interpretation for a purpose of one's own
Organizes a discussion (which draws on source materials) around a unique and apparent rhetorical purpose (beyond the purpose to summarize, comment, synthesize, etc.). (See Appendix VI for examples.)

Figures 8 and 9 show the organizing plans that students used on their original and revised essays, as the readers saw those plans using the elaborated taxonomy. (See

Appendix VII for interrater reliability.) Out of the seventy-two students originally enrolled in the four sections of the freshman course, three did not hand in either an original or a revised essay and were dropped from the study, bringing the number of subjects observed to sixty-nine. Of these students, all of whom handed in an original essay, thirty-six were in the Control group and thirty-three were in the Experimental group. Fifty-seven of these students (82 percent) later handed in revised versions of their essays. Of these fifty-seven students, thirty-two were in the Control group and twenty-five were in the Experimental group.

Figure 8 shows the choices students made on the original assignment; Figure 9 shows their choices when they revised the essay. The figures show clear differences in the types of plans used in the original and revised essays; in particular, students in both the Experimental and Control groups moved from using Review-and-Comment plans to using controlling concepts that actually did control their discussions. This result suggests that, in this study, the act of revision apparently stimulated the students in both the Experimental and Control groups to rethink their interpretation of the writing task. Students in the Experimental section were alerted to their own choices and asked to attempt the task of interpreting for a purpose. They heard a lecture on the options we had observed to date (see Appendix II in the Introduction), worked through a personal checklist (see Chapter 3, Appendix VIII), and revised their discussions using directions to choose a rhetorical purpose. The Control group, randomly selected within each section of the course, were asked to revise their text "to make it better." They did not hear the lecture or use a personal checklist until after they completed the revision. Although the original essays in both groups are distributed across all the categories, 68 percent are clumped in the knowledge-telling group that includes Summary plus the various forms of Review and Comment; the Review-and-Comment-with-Frame category alone accounts for nearly a quarter of the papers. Among the revised essays of both groups, more students wrote essays using a controlling concept.

The experimental manipulation did appear to have an effect, however. More students in the Experimental group wrote revised papers with rhetorical interpretations of the source than did students in the Control group. A chi-square test was used to determine whether the number of essays coded as transforming knowledge (i.e., controlling concept or interpretation) differed significantly between the original and revised groups. The obtained result was significant at the .01 level ($x^2 = 7.6$, $df = 1$). To understand the nature of and the rationale for these shifts, however, we need a more detailed analysis of what individual writers did. An analysis of the revision process that students brought to this task and a detailed comparison of the two groups will be found in Chapter 6.

Rationale for the Two Taxonomies

Before we can understand why certain essays seemed to embody inconsistent representations of the assigned task, we need to examine the essays, especially those that caused the readers' difficulties, in order to learn what characteristics produced the confusion. But first it is necessary to understand how the essays were identified as deserving special scrutiny.

We began our study by developing a five-element taxonomy (Figure 3) describing ways that students might approach our writing task. This taxonomy is not a theoretical description of academic writing tasks in general; it was designed in the context of our task. Nor is it intended for use in a testing situation. Performance testing requires a highly explicit writing prompt (task) that produces clean, reliably coded responses to be used in discriminating levels of ability. When writing is used for assessment, as Ruth and Murphy (1984) have shown, a prompt that is open to multiple interpretations can (and they argue, often does) lead to disastrous consequences for some students. In a testing situation one wants to design a prompt that will not only have a uniform interpretation and cue a specific response (that can be described by a primary trait rubric, for instance), and also to create enough difficulty to "weed out" weak writers or discriminate between a good and average performance (Ruth and Murphy, 1984; Smith et al., 1985). In this setting, differences in interpretation of the task are defined as "response errors," that is, as failure to design a good prompt.

By contrast, we wanted to study a situation that invited multiple task interpretations in order to observe a range of possible interpretations. Our prompt was thus designed to invite a range of responses rather than specify a particular response. Using this prompt, we expected to study the process of task representation. We thus needed (1) an open-ended prompt from which the writers had to construct their own plans, (2) the context of a class, so that the web of expectations associated with academic writing was implicit but too conditional or too complex to be spelled out in the assignment, and (3) a taxonomy that described the students' texts without evaluating relative levels of quality. We therefore developed the first taxonomy, a tool that named some of the most distinctive (to us) options that writers took on this task and created a continuum of approaches going from least manipulative (summaries) to most manipulative (interpretations for a persuasive rhetorical purpose). We planned to use the taxonomy as a way to talk to the students about their choices of task interpretations.

In designing this taxonomy, of course, we faced the problem of how to avoid deciding in advance what we would see, that is, of distorting our understanding of the data by prescribing its interpretation. To avoid this error, we designed the initial taxonomy from three kinds of information. First, we used the organizing plans that seemed most apparent and most distinctive from one another, based on our reading of texts from the three pilot classes of junior–senior undergraduates and M.A. and Ph.D. students. Second, we brought some preconceptions about common text types that teachers encounter (summary, synthesis, free response). Third, we brought two theoretical questions we wanted the textual analysis to comment on: "How do students integrate (or do they integrate) ideas from a source text with their own ideas?" and "To what extent do students carry out any sort of purposeful, rhetorical transformation of their information, as might be reflected in both a synthesis and an interpretation?" Although we expected the resulting five-item taxonomy to oversimplify the possibilities, we decided it was at least conditionally usable because it met our goals of starting with the categories observed in the pilot work, of maintaining descriptive simplicity, and of achieving some sensitivity to two theoretically interesting features of these texts. It offered a workable tool for analyzing the freshmen texts, or at least the basis for developing such a tool.

The second (final) taxonomy presented in this chapter contains two new categories that describe variations on the Review and Comment plan: texts marked by an isolated main point or conclusion and texts marked by what we call a frame. The process that led to this elaboration is in some ways typical of any attempt to build a coding scheme. However, the process is also worth reporting because the conflict between the structural cues and the information structure in the texts, which our judges encountered, may reflect a problem that other teachers face in trying to evaluate similar freshmen essays. The problem is this: If the raters read closely for content, they risked failing to recognize attempts to organize the material, and if they read closely for organization, they risked overlooking weak content. Moreover, if the readers read strictly, refusing to admit essays into categories that they might not belong in because of content/structure mismatches, they risked overlooking genuine achievements in the papers. If, however, they read generously and admitted the papers into categories to which they did not quite belong, they risked making invalid assumptions about what the writers had tried to do. Before we could make decisions about how the writers had interpreted the task based on their essays, we had to agree on what the essays did. The new taxonomy describes characteristics of student papers we suspect occur commonly in other papers written for other classroom assignments, and which we believe deserve discussion because they confuse readers.

Promises of Coherence: What Were Those Essays Doing?

When we created the initial taxonomy, we assumed, incorrectly, that the structural cues the students had created about how the ideas in their texts were related would indicate whether the writers had actually restructured or transformed the information from the sources. For instance, one writer might cue readers to expect a synthesis by making an evaluative statement about the material in the first paragraph, such as "This material on time management seems very useful." Another writer might cue readers to expect a summary by announcing a plan to discuss three main aspects of the material, such as "The most important ways to manage time are planning when to do tasks, managing one's energy level, and creating a good study environment." Readers usually expect the signaled structure of a text (the cues it sets up) to serve the content—to indicate reliably the internal logic of the information presented. This link between content logic and structural conventions is one of the important traits teachers consider when they evaluate papers (Freedman 1979a, 1979b, 1982), and it gives a convenient means of talking about whether students have goals of telling knowledge or goals of transforming knowledge, for example, paraphrasing sources or using source material to build an original argument, especially an argument that is adapted to a rhetorical purpose. As the thought develops, the structure shifts to accommodate it; so goes the conventional wisdom. When Freedman (1979b), for example, described her study for which she rewrote thirty-two student essays so that they would be weak or strong in content, organization, sentence structure, and mechanics, she explained that all possible combinations of variables were used except that weak content was never combined with strong organization: "It would have been *an exercise in absurdity* [our italics] to try to order illogical ideas logically or to order and transition appropriately a group of inherently unrelated ideas" (p. 162).

The essays in the pilot studies appeared to confirm the conventional wisdom. These essays had typically fallen into clear organizational patterns that coincided with the ways the writers had manipulated their information. Summaries, with or without authorial comment, used the order of sources in the time management text. Essays built around an original synthesizing concept typically foregrounded that concept and did not depend on the organization of the original text; instead they used a structure that complemented the controlling concept, such as problem–solution or comparison–contrast. Essays that reinterpreted the assignment for a rhetorical purpose—that is, talking to a particular audience about time management for a particular reason—also used a structure that complemented their controlling idea. Organizing plans as signaled by structural cues, then, seemed a convenient and logical basis for categorizing papers.

Yet when we applied these categories to the undergraduate essays, Freedman's "absurdity" is what we sometimes found: when we tried to place the essays on a continuum of idea-transformation, from those that summarize (tell ideas) to those that transform for an original rhetorical purpose (transform and use ideas), we found a group of essays in the middle of the continuum in which structural signals did not match the treatment of ideas. We found, for instance, apparent summaries sprinkled with comments and evaluations of the source text, arranged in an implied chronological order. We also found texts in which unrelated pieces of source material were arranged as a list and presented with other cues that were apparently meant to suggest a logical sequence. These oddly linked summaries were often framed in the introduction and conclusion by a larger idea that had an implicit topical relationship to the essay content but that did not in any way control the discussion or presentation of the content. These mismatched textual signals made it very difficult for the raters to decide what approach to the task the writers had been trying to use.

Using the first taxonomy to categorize these texts produced an interrater reliability that was significant but too low to be acceptable. The three raters for the next analysis were experienced teachers and highly motivated members of the research team who, after two training sessions and a refinement of the category descriptions, had achieved a high degree of agreement on training materials (a random sample of papers written for the Time Management assignment). The problem, it appeared, was not in the raters, but in the ability of the taxonomy to account for a subset of the texts for which we could not get unanimous judgments. Here is an example of such a text:

> *Essay 066: Extensive research has produced many books on the subject of Time Management in professional and educational settings. Experts agree that to work effectively, one must set aside time for a particular purpose. A noted efficiency expert, Alan Lake [sic], says that the secret to success is the pacing and planning of one's "external and internal prime time." External prime time is the time that one extends to helping others. Internal prime time is the time in which one does the best work. It helps to block out this time in advance.*
>
> > *Once this time has been put aside it must be employed well, that is, concentration must be maintained for its duration. This is perhaps the greatest challenge with an even*

more personal solution than the dilemma of simply setting aside the external or internal prime time. A distraction-free atmosphere is needed for concentration so that one's thoughts may be directed towards a particular project. This means no disturbing sounds, from music to background conversations, should steal your attention. Another nemesis of concentration is mental fatigue. Psychologist, William James states the answer lies in overcoming mental fatigue when it appears. He says that this is done by pushing for continued concentration until a "second wind" is acquired. Another expert, Jean Guitton, believes that when one feels the slightest sign of fatigue it is vital to rest immediately and that one should always approach work with a restful attitude. This is in sharp contrast with James's theory. Concentration is achieved through different means by different individuals. It may take years for one to learn to do so.

Utilization of the time set aside for work requires an answer on the part of every individual. Another problem is how much time to set aside for a particular project. A recent survey of college students revealed that they manage their time in a manner designed to alleviate pressure. They put off long-range projects and finish the easier assignment first in order for them to have fewer projects and therefore fewer distractions. Having one of a number of projects finished seems to take away more pressure than working on many simultaneously.

Time management is much more than simply writing a weekly schedule of work hours. It requires knowing when and where to find quality time, and what to attend to first. This knowledge is gained through experience. Like any other skill, one must practice time management to be successful using it.

This essay was variously scored as a summary, a summary plus comment, and a synthesis. Clearly, it contains summary, some comment, and a conclusion of some kind. One reader argued that the summary develops into an argument that is specifically stated in the final paragraph (Review and Comment); another reader felt that the argument, though not stated clearly until the end, could be said to integrate the discussion throughout (Synthesis). In other words, our readers, who like all good readers were trying to build a coherent text, could (1) find clear cues that this was summary, or (2) could give more attention to the last paragraph and perceive the selection of statements as an argument/commentary, or (3) could, by making an even greater constructive effort, see the conclusion, with its broad organizing truism, as a source of coherence for the entire text. Since coherence is something readers construct, the organizing plan they perceive is affected by those structural cues to which they choose to attend and by the significance they give those cues. These texts sent out mixed signals not only about their structure but also about their conceptual depth and the degree to which the information in them was adapted or transformed according to a central plan. Our readers could not decide from the essay how the writer had interpreted the task.

Essay 066, for example, starts off with two sentences that might introduce a controlling concept but instead lead to a summary of one person's ideas. The second paragraph develops another idea, the effective use of one's time, but the potentially interesting conflicts in the experts' advice are simply presented with the moral, "What works for X may not work for Y." The third idea, deciding how much time to allocate, is stated without reference to the previous ideas and introduces another paragraph of summary. The final paragraph summarizes the essay and adds a moral. Although the essay has an overall topical coherence, and the individual paragraphs cohere, as a whole it cannot be said to develop any original idea about time management, and the three paragraph topic ideas do not treat the topic in a logical order. Indeed, since the essay uses the order of the source text, one could argue that the writer presented its ideas as paragraph topics and just tacked the concluding sentences on to what is basically a summary. Although the pattern of general statements and specific statements is that of the classic five-paragraph theme, in this case the pattern has not produced a logically developed essay. A teacher reading this essay might conclude that it is disorganized, incoherent, and incompetent, and that the writer, far from interpreting the task, simply misunderstood it.

On the other hand, given a combination of good will and constructive effort on the part of the reader, the paper can be read as if it were coherent, as if an intention of overall coherence were implicitly present throughout, finally emerging in the conclusion. "After all," another teacher might say, "paragraph one sets up an approach, based on the process of studying, which controls the order of the discussion. The process moves from setting aside time to using the time, including finding a good place to work and then concentrating on the work. So-and-so is a good student and always tries hard; this may not be her best paper, but I'll give her the benefit of the doubt." The conflicting scores (summary, summary plus comment, and synthesis) given to the essay by raters indicate that such a sympathetic reading is indeed possible.

We believe that the reasons for the lack of unanimity among our raters are interesting because we believe that other teachers have struggled with mixed messages such as those in essay 066. In such essays, coherence building strategies seem to be used independently of logical relations within the information itself. Such coherence cues include the use of repeated key words, the causal, chronological, or additive phrases that link adjacent paragraphs, and the presence of an idea raised in one paragraph that becomes in some way associated with an idea in the next paragraph. These structure-building cues lead one to expect that the information in the text has been transformed into an argument, a synthesis, or a commentary that will lead to new ideas; yet the substance of the text fails to live up to these promises of coherence and transformation.

Thus, in deciding what should receive priority in their interpretation of the text, the readers were apparently often forced to choose between these two elements— "strong" structure and "weak" content. To provide more information on what the raters were attending to, we asked them to jot comments about their basis for judging these problematic essays. One rater said about a particular essay, "This is a pretty sleazy concept, but there *is* a concept so this must be a synthesis"; another, however, called a spade a spade: "Never mind the decorations; I know a summary when I see one." The raters were not even consistent in their own readings of such essays: They not only disagreed with each other, but on subsequent readings they sometimes disagreed with themselves, depending, it seemed, on whether they gave priority to structure or to content. (It should be noted here that conflicts between "strict" and "interpretive" readings did not necessarily reflect consistent tendencies to read one way or the other; rather, each rater read sometimes one way and sometimes the other.)

The reasons for this indecision became clear when we sorted the essays according to the categories in conflict (e.g., Summary/Review + Comment, Summary/Synthesis, Summary/Rhetorical Reinterpretation). The largest areas of disagreement occurred between the categories of Review-and-Comment and Synthesis. Since we had defined Synthesis as a paper with a controlling concept (a large idea that governed the presentation of material in the essay), this confusion of categories meant that our raters could not agree whether our student writers were thinking for themselves (transforming knowledge) or reproducing their sources (telling knowledge). The essays appeared to mix summary with original thought, and the raters could not agree which purpose predominated.

The following excerpt, for example, is not a synthesis, but it is more than a summary or a review with comments. The summary is subordinated to the concept of the various aspects of Time Management, and that concept controls the summary. On the other hand, the controlling idea is so loose that it allows the writer to say almost anything.

> *Essay 005: Something that affects us all, at different times and in different situations, is the problem of time management. Time management is an involved process that can be broken down into many different aspects.*
>
> *Pacing and planning, according to efficiency expert Alan Lake [sic], are two very important aspects in time management.* [A summary of Lakein follows, then a summary of the rest of the text. Sample paragraph topic sentences include:]
>
> *Environment is vital in one's preparation to work efficiently. . . .*
>
> *Certain strategies are used by students that help reduce pressure caused by upcoming assignments. . . .*
>
> [The essay concludes:] *After taking into account the planning and preparations, the ability to concentrate, a good environment and certain standard strategies, the subject of time management is basically an individual process. Its usage is unique for every individual, whether at home, on the job or at school.*

As another example, essay 100 is not a summary or a summary with comments. Although it seems relatively free from the stimulus text, it cannot be considered a free response to the topic. But the list order for presenting ideas might exclude it from being considered a synthesis governed by a controlling concept. One reader might say, "Except for the first sentence, this is a pretty coherent comparison—contrast of two approaches to time management, so I'll call it a synthesis"; another reader might say, "Announcing that 'different views exist' is not my idea of a real concept; this may not be a summary, but it sure isn't a synthesis either! I don't know what it is, and I have no idea what this writer thought he was trying to do."

> *Essay 100: The first and foremost observation about this packet is that is [sic] a poor source of information on time management. Only the first section is about the topic and only some of the others mention it at all. The next observation is the different views on time management given by people in a situation to apply it and those advising people to apply it.*
>
> *People in a work situation, in this case students, manage time on the assumption that there isn't enough time to do everything. Difficult tasks are scheduled last and work is thought to be better under rushed conditions. Time is precious and never use more than absolutely necessary is the recurring theme along those in the position to actually manage time.*

> *Researchers and others detached from the actual places where time management is employed suggest the opposite theory. Pauk, the researcher, and Lakein, the efficiency expert give a perspective from above and outside the place of work. Their studies suggest scheduling. Assume that you have plenty of time and allow large blocks of time for each individual task. Their strategies seem nowhere near as specific as those of the students.*
>
> *In general, those involved in time management personally assume there is very little time and they must rush. Those observing and advising say there is lots of time and the slower you go the better. Perhaps if these two views could be integrated better, a full understanding of time management would result.*

When the structural cues and promises of coherence were not supported by the substance, some raters still sometimes found themselves led by the promises of such coherence to credit these papers with achieving an integration and transformation of information that other readers were certain they had not achieved. The raters' sense of this conflict was reflected in comments which noted that such papers were "poor" syntheses (a value category our scheme had not provided). Apparently, even experienced readers could be led to conflate superficial coherence (i.e., the lavish use of conventional coherence-building cues) with conceptual integration, even when the promised connections or integrating concept were not fully realized in the text.

This variation may, of course, be what one expects from normal constructive readers. Although we saw this conflict as a striking feature of some freshmen papers, it may have been equally present but unnoticed in the pilot texts, since those papers were not categorized by multiple readers. On the other hand, this tendency to unwittingly conflate the superstructure of coherence with the content structure may occur in other evaluative situations in which teachers must decide whether or not, as readers, to "construct" a coherent student text on the basis of weak cues. For instance, Spivey (1984) found that the discourse syntheses written by less able comprehenders scored lower on "connectivity for the reader" than those by more able college-age readers. "Low connectivity" in this case was a measure of how often readers felt that the "flow of reading would be interrupted because of an unusual burden of constructive processing" in which they were forced to reorder, to disambiguate, or to infer plausible connections (p. 16). When Applebee, Durst, and Newell (1984), focusing on the text structure rather than the reader, compared passages from published textbooks with comparable analytical essays written by ninth-grade students, they found that the students were "more likely to produce an essay with two parallel and unintegrated content structures," that is, a "mixed" structure that might contain islands of narrative, and thesis/support, question/answer, or other organizing patterns (p. 68). Applebee et al. suggest that such mixed and unconnected structures are not unusual: "This pattern of relying on familiar structures in the transition to more complicated forms is common as students extend their writing skills" (p. 71).

How do teachers categorize (and evaluate) such papers? In the context of our study, teachers reading such papers may face two dangers: (1) in attending to the underlying summary structure, they might fail to give credit for good intentions or for a conceptual structure that is "present" but buried in a first draft, or (2) by responding to these superficially coherent papers as if they were "genuine" arguments or syntheses or interpretations (as our rates sometimes did), they would be failing to tell students that these more complex organizing plans call for *both* structural signals *and* a substantive transformation of information. A response that refused to fill in the gaps might send a more accurate message to students by saying that, for academic readers, coherence must be more than skin deep.

Looking at this experience, at the students' own self-evaluations (see Chapter 3), and at the confusion that terms such as "synthesis" and "interpretation" caused in the protocols, we came to a disturbing, if tentative, conclusion. The freshmen in this study did not seem fully aware of the difference between building coherence through the use of local or superficial cues and building coherence by adapting, restructuring, or even generating information. Their texts promised one thing and did another. Moreover, our judges had difficulty making consistent judgments, depending on which of these powerful but unstated criteria took priority. Neither we nor the teachers nor the students had a ready vocabulary for making this distinction.

Our solution to this problem was, in essence, to provide a vocabulary in the elaborated version of the taxonomy to distinguish between coherence-building techniques and a more thoroughgoing transformation of information. With the help of Thomas Huckin, we first gave these texts a "generous reading," actively looking for the many ways these writers helped the reader construct a coherent text. Such a reading makes one appreciate the large repertoire of such techniques these students possess, even when the techniques are used independently of the knowledge-transforming process that interested us. These promises, with the forms that the essays took, can be described as follows:

Limited promises

For example, of summarizing, as in "Different experts say different things about time management." Such promises were usually fulfilled, sometimes with comments added, such as "I like Lakein's distinction between pacing and planning because I hadn't really thought of that way before."

Framework promises

For example, "There are three major aspects of time management." These promises were usually fulfilled in the form of a series of capsule summaries within the structural framework (see essay 005).

Common sense concept

For example, "Time management is important for everyone." These concepts were sometimes developed, sometimes ignored in favor of more local concepts (see essay 100), and sometimes developed for a while and then abandoned for other local concepts or summary.

Moral at the end

Usually a belated promise that the time management advice does, indeed, add up to something that everyone can learn from (see essay 066); this strategy was difficult to evaluate. Sometimes the moral looked like an insight arrived at during writing; in other papers it seemed to be a general technique for rounding off what was basically a summary. Its organic relationship to the text varied widely. In some papers it took the form of a comment on the next-to-last paragraph of material, whereas in others it related to the source text as a whole or the writer's response to the topic, rather than to the essay.

Unique concept

When this promise was offered, the concept was often signaled by a formal or "sermon" voice (e.g., "We must all learn and practice time management") or by a "written-to-the-examiner" voice, as if to demonstrate mastery of the material (e.g., "Although experts on time management agree on certain basic points, they disagree about the need for rest."). In the problematic papers, the unique concept frequently deteriorated into a summary of the source text.

Interpretation for an original purpose

When the writer focused on a group of readers, the text often promised to show struggling students that they would be better off using time management techniques. Other writers used their paper to show how expert advice confirmed "what I've always thought and tried to practice" or for some other purpose of interest to them. Such papers usually carried out the announced purpose, except when they drifted into summary.

Disguised summary

For example, the summary in essay 066, which closely follows the structure of the source text but is presented as a process, with the ideas seemingly addressing the problems that a student would encounter as they would occur. With some notable exceptions, writers usually added little to these descriptions by way of evaluation or personal experience; that is, they typically did not blend source material with original material and they did not create an original process structure with the source material embedded in it.

On the basis of these observations we developed two new categories—the Isolated Main Point/Conclusion and the Frame—that described some of the hybrid essay structures we were seeing. Essays in the category of Isolated Main Point/Conclusion typically began with what looked like a controlling idea and then lapsed into summary or, like essay 100, began informally and then used the summary as the basis for a main idea that was stated in the final paragraph. Essay 066 (which was also marked as a synthesis) offers a slightly more sophisticated version of this pattern: it begins with two generalizations, the second introducing the summary of Lakein, and concludes with a summary statement about learning to manage time that is unrelated to the topic of the first sentence ("Extensive research has produced many books on the subject of Time Management in professional and educational settings."). Essays in this category relied on local coherence strategies; the larger idea, whether at the beginning or end of the essay, seemed tacked on to what was basically a summary or a summary with comments.

Essays in the Frame category, by contrast, began and ended with the same generalization, for example, that planning one's time and using it effectively are the two major aspects of time management. The discussion usually developed the framing concept, but the concept was subordinated to a summary of the sources. These categories let us accurately distinguish essays that seemed to the judges to have a predominately review-and-comment structure plus signals for other sorts of coherence. Because these papers give relatively consistent coherence cues, they may reflect a step on the path of a writer's development. Nevertheless, the attempt did not produce a thoroughgoing transformation of ideas that supported a sense of conceptual coherence.

This conflict between promise and delivery will always make categorizing such essays difficult. Coordinating the signals and the substance may, indeed, be an important skill that freshmen writers are trying to learn. However, if these papers are at all representative of college-level work elsewhere, one can conclude that our freshmen had learned the value of coherence and the wisdom of offering their readers promises of coherence. Most of the papers written for the Time Management task made some such promises. The problem for teachers is to decide to what extent the promises are performed.

The existence of the textual inconsistencies discussed in this chapter suggests that composing with a written source text was difficult for our students. Even when they had an idea that could seemingly give them enough momentum to reinterpret the source material for a clear-cut purpose (e.g., helping their fellow students), the sheer presence of the source text seemed to create a barrier between the students and the paper they wanted to write. This impression was strengthened by the interviews and self-analyses, which indicated that many students thought they had written quite different kinds of papers than the readers saw. Chapter 3 presents the students' side of the story—how they saw the task and the real difficulties they faced by sometimes failed to meet.

Appendix V: Essay Categories and Instructions to Judges
CATEGORY 0: SUMMARIZE

USUALLY,
> the summary consists mostly of gist statements, and possibly a stray sentence or two of authorial comment that may reduce the entire text to one or two sentences.

HOWEVER,
> it need not include each main point from the text and
> it need not follow the plan of the text.

IN ITS LOWEST FORM,
> the "summary" can be a short group of sentences that relate to the topic but don't say much.

CATEGORY 1: REVIEW AND COMMENT

These papers show some (limited) independence of the text.

OFTEN,
> they read like a free-writing response statement.
> When comments and summary appear throughout the essay, the summarizing purpose controls the paper (comments are subordinated to it).

ALTERNATIVELY,

comments may appear in only the first or last paragraph, or
may focus on the writer's response to only one or two ideas in the text.

IN RARE CASES (the most sophisticated form of this category),

the essay has a controlling idea or theme that emerges during the summary but
is never stated as being relevant for the entire paper.
These papers read like nicely focused summaries.

CATEGORY 2: ISOLATED MAIN POINT AND/OR CONCLUSION

USUALLY,

the opening contains what could be called a controlling concept;
essay then reviews, summarizes, or reviews/comments on the sources *without
reference to the original main point:*
the ending may have a conclusion or a moral.

ALTERNATIVELY,   .

the opening doesn't say much;
the essay reviews, summarizes, or reviews/comments on the sources;
the ending has an original conclusion or opinion.

IN ANY CASE,

the body does not contain links that tie the review/comment to the concept in
the beginning/end.

CATEGORY 3: SETTING UP A FRAME

USUALLY,

the opening sets up a frame, then uses the structure of the text for summary
and/or comment.
The frame can be very open and simple, such as "time management has three
important aspects—planning, environment, and stamina"; "Time management produces better quality work"; "Some of this advice could help
students."

ALTERNATIVELY,

the framing concept may emerge during the discussion and be stated in the
final paragraph.
The frame can be stated in the first person, such as, "I don't entirely agree
with this advice."

TYPICALLY,

the frame creates an expectation of a focused discussion that may occur in a
loose (review and comment) manner.

HOWEVER,

the focus may get lost or become implicit by the end of the paper
As a controlling concept, the frame is so vague that it can hardly be called
unique.

CATEGORY 4: FREE RESPONSE TO THE TOPIC

This type of paper is written with little or no reference to the Time Management text.

CATEGORY 5: CONTROLLING CONCEPT

ESSAYS IN THIS CATEGORY
   contain a stated organizing concept which controls the discussion.
   Even if the "discussion" is just a glorified summary, *it is subordinated to the concept.*
HOWEVER,
   the text may thematize authors rather than concepts. (Watch out for this misleading cue.)
   The organizing concept appears throughout the essay and should be clearly identifiable, even when it is diffused.
RHETORICALLY,
   the implied purpose is usually to discuss and demonstrate understanding of the text material.
HOWEVER,
   the beginning may set up an ostensible rhetorical purpose that is not carried out in the body of the essay.

CATEGORY 6: INTERPRETATIONS FOR A PURPOSE

The discussion is subordinated to the writer's purpose, which may be to help the writer herself.

The "discussion" may be a rhetorically presented summary or a summary with comments.

IN ALL CASES,
   the purpose, whether stated or implied, is clearly identifiable
   and is carried out in the body of the essay.

DECISION PATH FOR JUDGING:

1. Is the essay a summary, with little or no other comment?
   If YES, choose Category 0.
   If NO, choose Category 1, 2, 3, 5, or 6.
2. Does the discussion contain something that looks like a controlling concept or frame?
   If NO, choose Category 1 (sometimes 2).
   If MAYBE or YES, choose Category 2, 3, 5, or 6.
3. Does the concept or frame actually control the discussion?

If NO, choose Category 2.

If YES, choose Category 3, 5, or 6.

4. Is the concept a FRAME? That is, does it set up an open structure for discussion that lets the writer (a) discuss aspects of the topic and (b) use a review structure for the rest of the essay?

   If YES, choose Category 3.

5. Is the concept a "real" CONCEPT? That is, does it commit the writer to a focused discussion and control the focus of the paragraphs that follow?

   If YES, choose Category 5 or 6.

   If the concept is a "real" concept but does not control the focus of the paragraphs that follow, choose Category 1.

6. Does the essay reinterpret the assignment for an original purpose and write to a particular audience?

   If YES, choose Category 6.

   If NO, choose Category 5.

Appendix VI: Essays Using the Interpret-for-a-Purpose Organizing Plan

This organizing plan took two somewhat different forms which are best illustrated with examples from the freshman texts. In essays such as 115, the apparent organizing purpose is to explore a question, think through a conflict, or solve a problem. The papers present an issue-based intellectual purpose stimulated by a conflict, quandary, or need. In other essays the writer's purpose was expressed as an attempt to address or instruct the reader in some particular way. These papers seem motivated more by an audience-based, pragmatic purpose reflecting an awareness of the special needs of the reader. Essay 045, which follows, is an interesting hybrid in that it is clearly addressed to a particular reader but also tries to involve that reader by raising a question and potential conflict.

> *Essay 115. One of the most important and least discussed issues facing students is time management. Based on a number of research and self-help books, I feel that the solution to the problem of time management is a compromise of many of the opinions of professionals whose arguments are similar in some ways, but still disagree overall. Many of their "helpful hints" are actually obstacles to many students whose work habits are similar to mine.*
>
> *Of those recommendations from research conducted on time management, I feel that the most hindering of these concerns students scheduling large blocks of time in advance in order to organize the work day. Alan Lakein, author of* How To Get Control of Your Time and Your Life, *is in agreement with Walter Pauk of Cornell University. Both men advocate the use of scheduling work throughout the day in order to subdivide what might appear as a large task. In theory I agree with them, however, when a student attempts to accomplish this scheduling, he finds that plans do not usually go as expected. There are various types of interruptions and complications that occur in everyday life; obviously there are too many to be listed here. In case there are no*

interruptions, many students, who are like myself, will create their own interruptions in the form of procrastination. . . .

There is a paradox resulting from Pauk's suggestion in that when put in a "distraction-free" room, a student will seek out a distraction, either consciously or unconsciously, and thus not concentrate fully on his task. . . . [Approximately a page of the essay reviewing and evaluating the source ideas follows.]

My argument with James' theory is based on what economists call the Law of Diminishing Returns, . . . For example, if a French student were studying the new vocabulary for a quiz, he might learn thirty new words in the first hour, twenty in the second, and ten in the third. He keeps learning, but less efficiently as he continues. . . .

After studying some of the research on time management, I have formed my own formula for time management. First of all I agree with the majority of the students who want to "get the easy stuff out of the way," but once that is accomplished, there should be some time left over to work on the long-term projects. It comforts me to think that if I work on the project in advance, I can relax near the time it is due; in this case I agree with the "create a crisis theory." When I am ready to begin an assignment, I am alert and have the radio on. If, at some point in the assignment, I feel fatigued, or that further study will not result in more knowledge, I take a rest break. By following these few simple guidelines, I and others with similar study habits should be able to effectively manage our time.

Essay 045. Have you ever felt you had too much to do in too little time? Have you ever wondered how you are going to get all your work done? Have you ever stayed up all night long to finish a project or cram for a test? As college students, we've all felt bowled over by our workloads at one time or another. It's unavoidable. There simply are not enough hours in a day. Or is that really the case?

It is no lie that the college-level workload puts extreme pressures on a student's time. To escape the time burden, college students try to do the maximum amount of work in a minimum amount of time. We've all got all sorts of tricks to decrease our work time. We do the "easy" stuff first and rush through projects at the last minute. We try to complete writing assignments in one sitting. We gloss over things we don't have to turn in, if we bother to do them at all. We use these and other strategies constantly. But that's how you play the game. It's the only way to do all that is expected of us. Right?

Let's take a good look at ourselves. Sure, we're getting the work done, but it is really as good as it could be? We often sacrifice quality for quantity. Our cute time-saving strategies may decrease the pressure of large assignments, but our overall performance is not up to par. We've got a problem. What can we do? As college students, we need to learn better strategies that not only permit us to use time wisely but to also do our best work.

This key is time-management. [The rest of the paragraph discusses planning time.]

Okay, so now we've found enough study time and scheduled it into our days. That's not enough. We need to use the newfound time effectively. Here's where concentration comes into play. A good student working environment is quiet and free of distractions. This may mean turning off the stereo or unplugging the phone. Groan . . . moan. . . . but aren't your grades worth it? Another key to concentration is avoiding fatigue. . . .

Time management, when practiced properly, can be a tremendous asset to college students. By learning to use time wisely, we can get maximum performance in minimum time. And that's what we're all looking for.

Appendix VII: Inter-rater Agreement on Elaborated Taxonomy

Rater Pairs[a]	Kappa	SG
LN/KB	.10	.11
LN/XR	.39	.13*
LN/RJ	.25	.09*
KB/XR	.46	.15*
KB/RJ	.27	.11**
XR/RJ	.65	.12*
All raters	.37	.05*

Percentage of essays agreed on in each set (range): low = .78; high = 1.00; mean = .90.

Percentage of unanimous agreement in each set (range): low = .26; high = .56; mean = .40.

$*p < .01$.

$**p < .05$.

[a]Because we originally used three raters, the essays were divided into six sets, so that each possible pairing of raters would occur. After the revised taxonomy was developed, a fourth rater was added who read all of the essays. We thus ended up with six possible pairings of raters. Although agreement on the revised taxonomy was taken to mean that two out of any group of three raters agreed, in fact the raters were often unanimous.

DISCUSSION OF COHEN'S KAPPA

Cohen's kappa (Cohen, 1960) is a statistical procedure developed for measuring agreement among judges when the data involves independent subjects, independent ratings by judges, and a nominal scale with categories that are independent, exhaustive, and mutually exclusive. Unlike the better-known r values, the kappa does not simply measure a relative proportion of agreement/disagreement. The number of an r value represents a proportion of agreement or disagreement that is greater than chance (0.00), such that when the r value is subtracted from ± 1.00 (representing absolute agreement or disagreement), the remainder is understood to mean a proportion of noise (i.e., chance, bad data, etc.). Thus, a high r number indicates a large proportion of agreement/disagreement and a small proportion of noise. Cohen's kappa is a one-tailed procedure that involves calculating the frequency of chance-expected agreement and subtracting it from the observed agreement. A kappa states the proportion of nonchance agreement.

Unlike an r value, however, a kappa does not stand on its own as a meaningful measure of agreement because the proportion of chance-expected agreement varies depending on the distribution (variance) of the data. If the raters' agreements are spread out over all of the categories in the nominal scale, the chance-expected frequency of agreement will be small and the kappa will be large. If, however, the data are skewed, so that the raters' agreements involve few categories, the chance-expected number will be large and the resulting kappa small. In both cases, the actual number of agreements might be the same. As an extreme example, this researcher encountered an instance in which judges agreed on 48 out of 48 items, an agreement that an r value would express as 1.00. Yet because 47 of the 48 agreements were located in a single category, the chance-expected frequency of agreement was so high that the kappa was .00.

Therefore, the relative size of the kappa cannot be taken by itself as a measure of agreement. Instead, the value of the kappa must be considered in the context of data distribution. This context is provided by the standard gamma, which gives the size of the standard deviation (the variance of the data). A small standard gamma indicates narrow standard deviations; a large standard gamma indicates wide standard deviations. The ideal is thus to have a relatively large kappa and a relatively small standard gamma, as is the case with the overall interrater reliability shown earlier. A kappa that is ±1.96 of its standard gamma is significant at the .05 level; a kappa that is ±2.58 of its standard gamma is significant at the .01 level, and so on. Thus a kappa of .50 might reflect a very high nonchance frequency of interrater agreement, no agreement, or any level of agreement in between, depending on the size of the standard gamma. In contrast to r values, for which significance probabilities are not normally given, the kappa requires a standard gamma and a significance probability to be correctly interpreted.

3

Students' Self-Analyses and Judges' Perceptions: Where Do They Agree?

JOHN ACKERMAN

The task of forming a clear representation of an assignment is a challenge for both teachers and students of writing. From the standpoint of the teacher, assignments constitute the heart of the writing course in which theories of learning, semester objectives, and target skills are translated into an occasion for practice and assimilation (Bartholomae, 1983). For the student a writing assignment is an exercise in pragmatics. Each student must decide how to represent the information before her, mediating the teachers' explicit and implicit requirements while at the same time reconciling what is possible and desirable. These decisions appear at times to come quickly, with little evaluation, the product of years of schooling. Yet, for a given assignment, students surprise us with their diversity and inventiveness when they face a range of choices and consequences.

It is not surprising, then, that in many cases the assignment given by an instructor and the assignment taken by a student are not a reciprocal fit. Giving and responding to an assignment is an act of negotiation that depends on a number of variables, including the following:

- The feasibility of teacher expectations (Is the assignment doable as it is presented?)
- The clarity with which an assignment is presented
- A given teacher's willingness and ability to alter or tailor an assignment
- The student's history with the whatever genre or type of writing is sought
- The student's familiarity with a topic and facility with the preferred language

- A student's stature in class and the personal circumstances that surround an act of writing
- Practical constraints resulting from other assignments in school and out

This formidable list could mean that assignments have so many variables that reasonable agreement between teachers and students is impossible. This, of course, is not the case—diversity and complexity do not prohibit the successful completion of assignments. Instead, the list of variables illustrates the multiplicity of contributing factors involved in representing and responding to an assigned piece of writing.

In Chapter 1, Linda Flower argued that, first, a task is something people construct even when they assume there is a common sense version everyone would hold and, second, the level of complexity for a given task can vary enormously. In other words, although we gave our students a writing assignment that involved reading from sources—a common academic assignment—we expected a variety of approaches. But on a practical level what does it mean for students to represent a task differently? Do varied representations bring noticeably different results, in this case, in the type and quality of a draft? And how does the range of student representations match their instructors' perceptions, a critical question if for no other reason than an instructor's perceptions eventually translate into an evaluation and a grade?

The study of task representation presented here explores how students and teachers perceive the same assignment. We compared the reported representations of the reading-to-write task from our freshman writers with the essay evaluations from trained judges. We did not assume that a trained judge simulates the evaluation procedures of a teacher, who often (and wisely) tailors a text evaluation to a given student's progress or to shifting demands in an academic writing situation. Yet we wanted to know how the consensus of three judges (teachers who designed and taught the course) compared with student perceptions. We found that teachers who served as judges and students who composed the essays disagreed (67 percent of the time) far more than they agreed on features in the final products. However, we also discovered that these rival perceptions could be tempered somewhat by prompting and instructing students to "interpret with a purpose" when they revised a first draft. As mentioned in the Introduction, one class period was devoted to listing and describing the categories of information and decisions that accomplished writers often address when they write from sources. The students who received this instruction tended to revise their essays to incorporate more complex and sophisticated rhetorical plans, and the gap between teacher and student perceptions was lessened.

We also learned that the bases for the different perceptions and expectations are the more interesting and practical findings from this study. By looking closer at the range of decisions the students faced and their responses as they wrote, we can understand better how students negotiate our assignments and how we can best intervene. This report begins with a summary of the student accounts of how they composed a first draft. Tallies and comparisons of their reports provide a basis for contrasting how students and teachers evaluated the same essays. Conclusions from these comparisons point toward commonalities in student task representations and toward ways teachers can predict students' initial responses to a writing assignment and guide revision.

The Study

The analysis reported here centers on a Self-Analysis Checklist, one component in the "Teaching Study," which also includes the reading-to-write assignment, the lecture on the concept of task representation as described in Chapter 1, and a procedure for independently rating the student essays. During a regularly scheduled class lecture, students were given the Self-Analysis Checklist (S-AC), which briefly described five major decisions that a range of writers made working through the same assignment:

- *Major sources of topic information*—ranging from text-based ideas to the student's own experience with the topic.
- *Text format*—the image a writer has of the type of prose desired, from summaries to persuasive essays.
- *Organizing or rhetorical plan for writing*—within the text, the way a writer arranges and presents information.
- *Strategies*—nine practical concerns and approaches to finding and shaping ideas for a draft.
- *Goals*—twelve general purposes and objectives that appear to guide composing.

The forty-minute lecture detailed the range of options that accompany each of the five decision categories, with examples and as much time for questions as possible. These options also appeared on the S-AC (Appendix VIII).

At the beginning of the lecture, each student was handed the S-AC. While they listened and referred to their drafts, they selected the decision options that best represented how they had composed the paper. In this way the checklist augmented the lecture by asking students to make links between the lecture and their own writing. The checklist also provided an outline, summarizing and illustrating key points in the lecture. For example, while the students listened to a description of a major consideration for a writer, the Source of Topic Information, the checklist offered four common options: assigned texts (readings), a mix of text ideas and personal commentary, prior experience related to the topic, and previously learned concepts that could be applied to the writing. In addition, each option was accompanied by descriptions and definitions written in short, personal, and complete sentences. Students also had the option to present and describe their own option for this decision and the four decisions that followed. Throughout the lecture, then, with their drafts and the checklist before them, the students recalled and recorded the decisions they made as they composed.

The S-AC was central to our exploration of how our students represent their assigned writing, since it eventually captured the reports of seventy-two students across four sections of freshman writing. These guided reports do not provide the detail found in a protocol analysis or other forms of cued recall. The checklist does, however, indicate in a balanced, consistent way how four sections of freshman writing, using our framework, perceived their composing. A guiding premise in this study was that the *representation* of an act of composing matters at least as much as the decision processes and circumstances inferred from final products or coded in a "think-aloud" transcript. Since one of our general goals as researchers was to surmise how writers and readers construct and reconstruct the same text differently, our students' personal representation of an academic writing task became an object of research worthy of time and interest.

Besides offering a relatively accurate and consistent means by which to recollect how a writing assignment was perceived, the S-AC, we hoped, would serve as a tool for inquiry. It might help students evaluate future pieces of writing, anticipate a useful approach to a draft, or provide a vocabulary for talking about writing in college. In class discussion following the task representation lecture, we learned that many students were surprised and encouraged to discover that their decisions and strategies are common and therefore acceptable, creating for some students a currency in what they normally do. For other students, the checklist was also an organizing tool for sorting through at least some of the myriad of decisions they normally face in writing.

To restate, both groups, Experimental and Control received a follow-up assignment to revise their first draft of the time management essay. As the Experimental group received instruction in "organizing plans" and an introduction to writerly issues in task representation, they completed the S-AC. One week later, when the second draft of the assignment was due, both groups received the checklist. The Experimental group, of course, completed the S-AC on their revisions while the Control group received the lecture (minus the revision assignment) and the introduction to the self-analysis procedure. This system gave us two major comparisons. The perceptions of the Experimental group could be compared over two drafts of the same assignment, and the two groups of students could be compared according to their revisions.

The final component in the study, an independent rating of the first and second drafts, adds another perspective to the students' reported perceptions. Three instructors were trained and asked to blind rate the student essays according to the four "organizing plan" options introduced in lecture and listed on the S-AC. The raters' decisions resembled those of a teacher who must evaluate a paper largely on explicit text features. These ratings and eventually the comparisons between student and teacher perceptions are limited to organizing plans because we assumed that rhetorical plans would dominate how students finally composed and would appear in their final products (Meyer, 1982).

To clarify their judgments, the raters refined the four options listed for the students under organizing plans (see Chapter 2). The student category of Summary was expanded to include the following categories: Summary, Review and Comment, Main Idea, and Frame. This extension was not inconsistent with what the students heard in lecture. As students filled out the checklist they were told to select Summary if their plan had been to summarize (or review) and comment. For this analysis "Summary" includes both summary and its variants.

What Our Students Reported

The presentation of the study findings begins with how students reported their task representation using the S-AC. We must interpret these findings with caution because the checklist data depend in part on recollection and because we could not monitor influences such as the lecture environment (pacing, distance from speaker), much less attitude or proximity to friends. Our impression, however, from administering the checklist and from talking with students in class following the lecture, was that students took this exercise seriously like any other classroom exercise in the semester (which is what it was meant to be). The data created both a context for exploring why and how the students composed two versions of the time management essay and a basis for comparing the students' perceptions and those of the independent judges. The S-AC presented five major decisions in task representation. Beginning with the first three decisions—Source of Information, Format, and Organizing Plan—students could choose only one option, which allowed us to compile the frequencies reported in the following section. For the remaining two decisions—Strategies and Goals—students were encouraged to select more than one option, creating more of a cumulative measure and allowing the checklist to account for more idiosyncrasies between students, as is discussed later in this chapter.

THREE DECISIONS: SOURCE OF INFORMATION, FORMAT, ORGANIZING PLAN

Table 1 compares for drafts one and two the Experimental group's declared sources, formats, and plans. To simplify the table and focus discussion, the only options listed are those that received the most attention from students (highest frequencies). A complete listing of the selections and frequencies from the Self-Analysis Checklist can be found in Appendix IX. We wanted to know if the lecture and revision instructions led to a shift in student perception and helped them revise their drafts. As Table 1 illustrates, on the first draft the Experimental group reported primarily drawing upon Text (32 percent) and Text + Comment (54 percent) as sources of information for their essays, accounting for 86 percent of all selected options in this category. These students also tended to prefer, a Standard Theme format (50 per-

Table 1. The Task Representation Options Selected by the Experimental Group for Drafts 1 and 2

		Draft 1 (%)	Draft 2 (%)
Source	Text	32	06
	Text + Comments	54	41
	Prior Knowledge[a]	15	53
Format	Standard Theme	50	24
	Summary + Opinion	25	24
	Persuasive Essay	07	47
Plan	Summary	43	18
	Synthesis	25	12
	Interpret with a Purpose	11	59

[a]For brevity in Tables 1 and 2, "What I already knew" and "Prior concepts" from the checklist are collapsed under one heading, "Prior knowledge," to focus the comparison between text-based and experience-based ideas.

cent), and plans to Summarize (43 percent). This set of options all decreased in the revision, sometimes dramatically. For a revision, students reported depending on Prior Knowledge as a source of information (53 percent), a Persuasive Essay as a format, and the assigned plan to Interpret (59 percent).

This shift suggests that the lecture and assignment led to a change in representation, a change toward the explicit goal of the assignment to "interpret with a purpose." We do not ignore the normative influences of a public lecture or our students' own eagerness to be seen as "good students"—they could have been telling us what they thought we wanted to hear. Evidence to the contrary, however, comes with the number of students reporting what *was not* assigned (41 percent chose options other than Interpret). The checklist also was introduced as a personal exploration into the students' representations of how they composed. Through the Reading-to-Write course their teachers had encouraged self-reflection and an awareness of reading and writing as a social and cognitive process. And, as mentioned earlier, when the students made their selections, they were reminded to refer to their drafts as an aid to memory. Therefore, we read this self-analysis, with due reservations, as a meaningful indicator of what students *thought* they were doing. The Experimental group perceived their first drafts as text-based, standard theme, and primarily summaries; their revisions tended to be seen more as depending on prior knowledge to construct persuasive interpretations.

Table 2 lists the reported options for the same three decisions, cast this time according to the second major comparison in the study, the revisions of the Experimental and Control groups. Did the different revision instructions lead to different self-perceptions? Apparently so; the reported representations for the two groups differ at each option shown here. The Control group's revision decisions look much like those associated with the Experimental group's first draft (66 versus 54 percent for Text and Comments, 58 versus 50 percent for Standard Theme) listed in Table 1. The exception to this trend is the high percentage of plans to Synthesize for the Control group. For this group, the instruction to "make better" led some students to change from Summary to Synthesis. The similarity between draft 1 (Experimental) and the revision (Control), coupled with the Experimental group's preference for Prior Knowledge as a source, Persuasion as a format, and Interpretation as a plan, support the claim that representations did vary between groups, following the lec-

Table 2. The Task Representation Options Selected by the Experimental and Control Groups When They Revised to Produce Draft 2

		Experimental (%)	Control (%)
Source	Text + Comments	41	66
	Prior Knowledge	53	18
Format	Summary + Opinion	24	21
	Standard Theme	24	58
	Persuasive Essay	47	18
Plan	Synthesis	12	58
	Interpret with a Purpose	59	15

ture on task representation. As noted, the difference in organizing plans is striking. Random sampling should have guaranteed that the two groups had equivalent abilities, and both groups revised under roughly the same circumstances. The Experimental group saw themselves as writing a more "purposeful" statement on time management, one that integrates more personal knowledge of the topic and attempts to engage an audience. This perception will be tested later against the scores of the trained raters.

If stock is taken in the highest percentages from the data, a generic student for each group begins to emerge. Although correlations between options are difficult to infer from the frequencies listed in Tables 1 and 2, the percentages imply certain patterns of behavior. For example, a Synthesis written in a Standard Theme format using Text ideas plus Comments is a plausible schema for writing a typical freshman essay involving sources. In reality, none of our students exactly fit the profile of the "generic student." Not one of seventy-two students participating in the study chose each of the six most popular options. This fact matches our intuition and early prediction that students have diverse and complex representations of a reading-to-write task. The value of seeing the patterns of task representation lies in understanding the assumptions and habits that students bring to a piece of writing. If we can draw a bead on those assumptions and familiar strategies, even hypothetically, we can more accurately offer guidance to students and alternative ways to progress.

Within the general trends evidenced thus far, there appear to be correlations among reported perceptions by both groups that are worthy of attention. The options most often selected by students are illustrated in Figure 10. The figure is read by beginning with the highest number in a row. For example, in the first row, of the eleven students who chose Text selections, eight also chose Standard Theme, and of

Source	Format	Plan	Group
11 Text	8 Standard Theme	7 Summary	E & C
15 Text and Comments	(no more than 5 of any of the formats)	7 Summary	E & C
14 Text and Comments		14 Summary	E & C
	13 Standard Theme	14 Summary	E & C
	10 Persuasive Essay	10 Interpret	E
	10 Standard Theme	17 Synthesis	C

Figure 10. Interrelationships among source, format, and plan.

those, seven chose Summary. And in the last row, of the seventeen control students who wrote Standard Themes, ten reported reliance on a Standard Theme format. Shaded areas correspond with categories where no clear trend was apparent, and thus there is no correlation to consider.

Figure 10 shows that the connections are higher among pairs of decisions. For example, the Text option under source correlates fairly highly with a Standard Theme format and Summary plan. In fact, the only plan that connects with source options is a Summary. This implies that if a student chooses a Synthesis or Interpret plan, the information for those papers will come from a variety of sources. A strong relationship appears to exist between Summary plans and Standard Theme formats for both groups, as we might predict. After all, the utilitarian Standard Theme is often characterized as consisting of stock arrangements of generally recognizable ideas (Bartholomae, 1985). A strong relationship also appears between the Interpret plan and the Persuasion format (Experimental group). The relationship between dominant formats and plans does not appear to carry for a Synthesis (Control), which poses the questions: Do syntheses invoke a wider range of formats (the opposite seems likely)? Or is the difference a perceptual issue, perhaps tied to the difference in tasks? To sum up, students seem to create clusters or pairs of options such as plans to summarize and standard theme format and persuasive formats and plans to interpret. However, the correlations suggested by these data are tentative at best, and we are skeptical that such simple patterns exist, given the complex nature of the task representation phenomenon.

STRATEGIES AND GOALS

So far the data have shown that there are patterns in how the groups, using the S-AC, responded to an explicit request to interpret their decision processes and final products. We found differences between first and second drafts for the Experimental group and differences between Experimental and Control groups. The patterns illustrated previously show that, although no generic student exists, meaningful couplets provide insights into the thinking patterns that lead to certain types of student drafts. The last two decisions presented in the lecture on task representation and on the checklist, strategies and goals, should be seen as supplementary information. The students could select one or more options under each decision to try to paint a clearer picture of their task representation. In addition, we asked each student to "predict" what strategies and goals a "graduate student" would bring to a similar piece of academic writing. Table 3, like Tables 1 and 2, lists only those selections that received the most attention from the students. (See Appendix VIII for a complete listing.)

The table's clearest message is that one strategy or goal does not dominate the field. The variety of options selected indicates the complexity of the students' decision processes in contrast with patterns or trends. Student choices varied widely, and all of the twenty-one options in both categories drew responses (and no student wrote in "other" options). Interesting differences appear between the first and second draft for the Experimental group. These students paid more attention to an Organizing Idea (23 percent) and writing for your Own Purpose (17 percent) as

Table 3. Strategies and Goals[a]

		Experimental		Control
		Draft 1 (%)	Draft 2 (%)	Draft 2 (%)
Strategies	Gist and List	16	03	02
	Skim and Respond	16	06	11
	Organizing Idea	18	23	20
	Audience Needs	02	11	11
	Own Purpose	06	17	07
Goals	Present Learning	20	06	09
	Do the Minimum	13	04	07
	Page Requirement	12	00	03
	Influence Reader	00	20	05
	Cover Key Points	18	08	14
	Originality	00	10	11

[a]These percentages are calculated from the total number of selections, not the total number of students making selections.

strategies and to the goal of Influencing a Reader (20 percent) in the revision, though the latter two of these selections were not prominent in the selections made by the Control group.

In the preceding section of this chapter, the possibility of patterns among decisions was explored. A similar question would be whether any of the goals and strategies appear to cluster around, for example, a plan to interpret or synthesize. When strategy and goal options were compared with plans, we found that a given plan elicited the full range of strategies and goals with no clear trends in the proposed connections between decisions. The strategies and goals freshmen predicted for the older students, however, did reveal a trend. Both groups were remarkably consistent in their prediction (± 2 percent on all but "audience needs"). Collectively, on the checklist and later in class, the students predicted that older students would be more concerned with "originality" (represented by the Springboard strategy for their own ideas and Originality as a goal) and "audience." Graduate students were thought to have more time and control over their work, since they wrote to peers and mentors who appreciated the creation of a personal frame addressing a reader. This revelation helped to focus discussion later in class. We explored why many students saw their roles as academic writers limited in comparison to those of older students, and in doing so we began to examine several of the assumptions underlying our students' notions of authority and originality in school.

The number of common perceptions, patterns between decisions, and even the diversity of options students reported choosing raise the thorny issue of what to do with this description of student thinking, beyond puzzling over it. Should discrete decisions or patterns of representation be taught? We think not. There is no evidence so far that one representation leads safely to a successful final draft. One virtue in this whole enterprise was the added ammunition to show students that a safe route to an "A" paper does not exist. At best, the trends and shifts in student perceptions do suggest ways to anticipate and predict reasonable behavior for a writer in a given situation. For example, from the students' vantage point, an exclusive investment in Text material as a source of information for a draft probably will not lead efficiently to an Interpretation as sources that tap Prior Knowledge. The true mettle of these perceptions, however, will appear when they are tested against the judgments of others. After all, if a piece of writing goes public, its worth is largely defined by the reader's perception of its message.

ORGANIZING PLANS

To compare the students' perception of their papers, specifically the organizing plans, with the rhetorical plan readers might respond to in the texts, both versions of the essays were submitted to a rating by three independent judges. The judges were asked to sort the papers on the basis of seven essay categories. Because the categories used extended the categories on the students' checklists, the judges were allowed to make finer distinctions between drafts. Figure 11 shows both the students' options for organizing plans and the judges' elaborated categories.

Before looking at how judges' and students' perceptions compared, it would be helpful to characterize any trends or patterns in the judges' scoring. In contrast to the student selections, listed and categorized earlier, the raters showed relative balance across all seven categories for both drafts. For example, the students labeled 72 percent of their revised papers as either a Synthesis or an Interpret with a Purpose plan. The raters, in turn, used these categories more conservatively to account for only 42 percent of the organizing plans. The conservative nature of the judges' scoring may be a result of their training, their experience as readers of academic writing, or refinements in the coding scheme. At any rate, this difference forecasts the categories on which students and judges disagreed.

AGREEMENT BETWEEN STUDENTS AND RATERS

Of the seventy-two comparisons between the Experimental and Control students and the judges' evaluations, sixty-seven comparisons were made. The loss of five comparisons resulted from students who failed to attend lecture, complete the second checklist, or turn in a revised essay. The percentage of comparisons remained

Students	Judges
•Summary	•Summary
	•Review & Comment
	•Isolated Main Point
•Response	•Response
•Synthesis	•Synthesis
•Interpret	•Interpret

Figure 11. Categories of essay plans.

consistent across both versions of the essay and across groups. As stated in the Introduction of this report, students and judges agreed on all organizing plans for both drafts 37 percent of the time. This low agreement suggests that they saw different texts, brought different criteria to the judgment process, or both. Looking closer at specific agreement and disagreement, the raters and students agreed more often with the more complex organizing plans, Syntheses (five of twenty-five) and Interpretations (four of twenty-five), although the individual rates of agreement for plan are not strong (no higher than 20 percent). No pattern of disagreement appeared, save the disproportionately high number of mismatches for Response plans. Only one student labeled any draft a Response while the judges found seven. This judgment may have been affected by the lower value placed in the classes or during the lecture on a "personal response" to the topic (versus the readings) in the context of an assignment in which critical reading of outside authorities is stressed.

Agreement shifts noticeably from the first draft to revision, but not from one group of students to the next. In the first draft comparisons (all with the Experimental group), agreement was higher at 48 percent than the overall average of 37 percent. In the second draft, agreement for both groups with the judges dropped to around 33 percent (30 percent for Control and 35 percent for Experimental). Two reasons for the across-the-board drop are possible. First, students in the Experimental group, who were attempting a more complex task, may have had more difficulty either recognizing or carrying out such plans. The instruction in task representation may have successfully led to a more accurate but complicated picture of the task. Predictably this complexity would hinder their ability to label and carry out text plans, since they were asked to rethink text features and their assumptions about essay writing. Or second, concentration simply may have dropped when the students were asked to judge their writing after they had revised and were preparing to move along to other assignments in the course.

To understand further where students and judges agreed, signal detection analysis was used to separate and plot the number of student decisions for a given plan against those of the raters. A signal detection analysis of the checklists and ratings presents not only the instances that students and judges agree or "hit," it also scores "misses" and "false alarms." The latter two measures help us understand the nature of the disagreement between students and judges. Since signal detection analysis depends on a standard, fixed score, the judges' expertise and decisions were taken as our assumed standard for assigning hits, misses, and false alarms. A "miss" in this case occurs when a student says "yes" to a plan when the text has been rated something else, and a false alarm occurs when a student fails to recognize a given plan.

To say that our judges have the final word made intuitive sense in that a teacher must decide and act on some standard for evaluating papers, however arbitrary. In using signal detection analysis, we do not ignore the opening claim of this chapter—that what is possible and acceptable in a writing assignment is practically and finally negotiated between teachers and students. Nor do we forget that trained raters do not proceed in the manner of a teacher evaluating a class's performance or a writer's self-evaluation of a draft. To compare teacher and student perceptions, a standard must be assumed, and we chose the consensus reached by three teacher-evaluators. Figure 12 portrays the four possible comparisons inherent in signal detection analysis.

The signal detection analysis required that the judges' extended Summary categories were collapsed so we could score all four student options. For Summary, this meant that a student judgment was scored a hit if it matched any of the judges' first four categories. Figure 13 lists the scores for each of the four student text plans. These scores are included in this report to show the reader how the judges labeled the essays in the sixty-seven comparisons and where students agreed with those labels.

The sixty-seven possible comparisons become the total number of possible hits or chances for complete agreement. The four totals for the "yes" column (bottom left corner) illustrate how the judges used the four categories of text plans to label the student essays. Judges found most often Summaries (thirty-nine) and Syntheses (thirteen), as the collapsed categories might predict. The thirty-seven percent agreement for students' and judges' perceptions across all plans can also be checked by dividing the number of hits (e.g., 14 for Summary, 6 for Synthesis . . .) by the judges' total "yes" for all plans (or 67). The probability of student "hits" and "false alarms" is listed in Figure 14 and shown in the accompanying graph. Plotting hits against false alarms makes it easier to see the relative power of the hits in a given category of text plan. The ideal location on the graph would be high along the vertical axis and to the left along the horizontal, meaning that hits would far exceed the probability of false alarms.

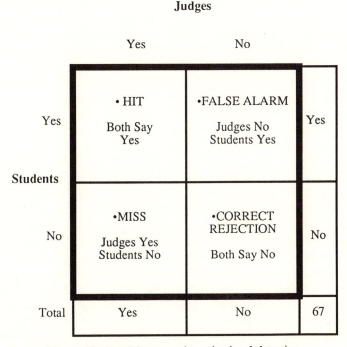

Figure 12. Possible comparisons in signal detection.

Summary		
14	1	15
25	27	52
39	28	67

Synthesis		
6	17	23
7	37	44
13	54	67

Interpret		
4	14	18
4	45	49
4	59	67

Response		
1	5	6
6	55	49
7	60	67

Figure 13. Scores from signal detection for four text types.

Signal detection analysis shows us that students are fairly accurate in judging a Summary insofar as they rarely label their texts a summary when they are something else (probability of a false alarm = .03). The low hit rate (.37), however, means they often thought texts had a more complex organizing plan than the judges did. Since students almost completely avoided the Response plan, when judges were categorizing texts as Summaries, Review and Comment, Main Ideas and Frames, students were seeing themes as Syntheses and Interpretations. With these latter plans, the students had a higher hit rate (.54 and .50, respectively), with a higher false alarm rate as well (.29 and .24). Generally, they saw complexity when to a reader's eyes complexity was not there.

Conclusions with Implications for Teaching

This report opened with the twin premises that forming a clear, practical representation of a writing assignment is a challenge for both teachers and students and that the level of complexity between one representation and another can vary enormously. Certainly if we look at the wide range of Goals and Strategies reported by both student groups alone, complexity and individuality are the norm. Even though trends and patterns in student perceptions appeared in the summarized totals from the Self-Analysis Checklists (Tables 1, 2, and 5), a "generic student" does not exist. The checklist presented five major decision areas with more than thirty options, and students took advantage of the entire corpus to describe their essays. The data can

	Hits	False Alarms
Summary	.37	.03
Response	.14	.08
Synthesis	.54	.29
Interpret	.50	.24

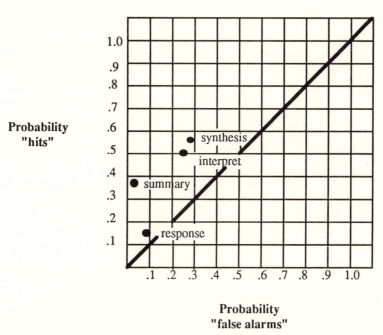

Probability
"hits"

Probability
"false alarms"

Figure 14. Probability of students making hits and false alarms.

be read, then, as evidence for the high number of contributing factors involved in representing a writing assignment.

Any further conclusions from these data must be considered against the problematic nature of inquiry into teachers', students', or anyone's perception of a complex task. For our analysis we chose to assume that judges' perceptions approximated teachers' perceptions, that our self-analysis instrument tapped, in a consistent way, important considerations in the students' composing, that our judges' basis for evaluating essays was reasonably comparable to the students' application of the text-plan categories. Tracking perceptions is messy, yet the compiled frequencies of student selections did illustrate shifts in reported perceptions and patterns or connections among task decisions and options. At the very minimum these shifts and patterns help the teacher-researchers in this study to understand, in the context of this reading-to-write assignment, what it means to represent a task differently. The lecture on task representation and directions to revise to "Interpret with a Purpose" appeared to lead to shifts in perceptions: for the experimental group Prior Knowledge as a source of information, Persuasion as a format, and Interpretation as an organizing plan all increased following the lecture with specific revision directions. From another angle, the Control group who revised without specific instructions produced a second version of the time management essay similar to the Experimental group's first draft, except for the proportionately high number of Synthesis plans. Assignment directions and instruction in the five major decisions at least contributed to the contrasting perceptions in the two groups.

Shifts in perception, however, do not equate with finished products. Student perceptions of text plans tended not to match those of the judges and the signal detection analysis revealed that students found complexity (synthesis and interpret plans) in drafts when readers did not. Perhaps a more telling contrast is the fact that the shifts and difference in perceptions between groups did not result in any significant difference in final products. Though the Experimental and Control groups saw their revised text as more complex (fifteen "Interpretations" and sixteen "Syntheses"), judges agreed with these perceptions less than 10 percent of the time. Also, the judges saw no difference in the number of complex text plans (Syntheses and Interpretations) for both groups (eleven for the experimental, ten for the control).

The students' perceptions, then, could have been influenced by the goal to revise toward complexity, embedded in the lecture and revision directions, rather than actual refinements they saw in their texts. This mismatch between writer and reader perceptions helps to build a case for instruction and practice in evaluating both emerging and target text plans and the corresponding decisions in generating them. In this light, the gap between student perceptions and the judges' evaluations mirrors the traditional distance between the image writers have of their own drafts, a reasonable and predictable egocentricity, and a reader's often rival interpretation of the same text (Flower, 1981; Kroll, 1978). Practice in recognizing text plans and exploring the decision processes behind them could narrow the perceptual distance between writers and readers so that the two can begin to build a comparable vocabulary to refer to academic genres and conventions.

Casting the specific points of misperception in terms of a dialogue—how writers negotiate an assignment and a reader's perception of their texts—places a value on recognizing the patterns and connections that emerged from the student reports. Both student groups appear to associate Text sources with Standard Theme formats and Summary plans, a pattern that reflects "schooling" in summarizing explicit information in reading material (Applebee, 1984b). The commonality of this and other associations (Persuasion format and Interpret plan) is supported by an auxiliary question on the Self-Analysis Checklist. Students were asked if they saw their decisions on the task as representing their "standard" strategies or goals. We explained that a standard strategy (or goal) would be typical or especially familiar, one that has been used to complete a number of academic writing assignments. They reported that half of their options for these two decisions were standard, meaning they were common and somewhat comfortable. Practice in recognizing decision patterns and alternative strategies, such as the consideration of Prior Knowledge as a source of information, could help students to reexamine standard strategies and goals and other habits and commonplaces. If students consciously attend to assumed standards and perceived risks in a writing assignment, the negotiations among teachers, students, and assignments may become more explicit and, thus, open for discussion and critique. From a cognitive perspective, students may then sharpen their regulatory mechanisms (Brown, 1985; Palincsar & Brown, 1983), which help to predict and monitor progress with a draft. From a social perspective, the negotiation of expectations and perceptions can strengthen the collaborative nature of a writing classroom. We want to underscore the positive contribution that the Self-Analysis Checklist made to the Reading-to-Write class. It helped students to be aware of an existing repertoire of thinking strategies and of the gains and losses that one approach can bring in a given situation. And importantly, for some students it raised the possibility of extending and enriching this repertoire, an issue that surfaced repeatedly in classroom discussion through the semester.

Practice in recognizing text plans, relationships within decision processes, and the interplay between decisions and final products may, in turn, nudge students toward a perception of writing closer to that of older, more advanced students. Awareness and an increased repertoire of strategies is a reasonable step one might take to acquire more flexibility, authority, and "originality" in the writing of academic essays, where students both have a reason to write for readers and possess more means to do so. Writing for critical readers remains an act of negotiation, but added awareness and control over composing strategies and text features are a form of "ownership"—a step, we would argue, toward reader-sensitive composing in the context of college-level writing class.

Appendix VIII: Self-Analysis Checklist

MAJOR SOURCE OF INFORMATION   CHECK ONE

ASSIGNED TEXT
• I stuck to the key words, sentences, and ideas from the readings
• I didn't import additional information

TEXT + MY COMMENTS
•I used the text's key ideas with support from my experience and the readings
•I partly used my thinking and partly the assigned readings

WHAT I ALREADY KNEW ABOUT THE TOPIC
•I used my personal experience and opinions on Time Management
•The readings served as a springboard: I didn't have to borrow printed information

PREVIOUS CONCEPTS + TEXT
•I used my own knowledge to provide a unique main idea
•I supported this idea with examples from the readings

OTHER: Write a detailed description of your information in full sentences

---

TEXT FORMAT   CHECK   ONE

NOTES OR A SUMMARY PARAGRAPH OR TWO

SUMMARY PARAGRAPH WITH AN OPINION PARAGRAPH

STANDARD SCHOOL THEME FOR ANY READER
•I wrote an introduction, a body with several paragraphs and maybe a conclusion
•I used a thesis statement and topic sentences

PERSUASIVE ESSAY FOR ACADEMIC OR PROFESSIONAL PUBLICATION
•In my formal introduction I raised an issue or indicated the purpose of the essay
•I organized the body paragraphs around an argument

OTHER: Describe the format of your paper in conplete sentences

---

ORGANIZING PLAN FOR WRITING   CHECK ONE

SUMMARIZE THE READINGS
•I reduced each paragraph in the readings to key points
•I reviewed the key points in an orderly way, adding nothing extra

RESPOND TO THE TOPIC
•I pursued my own ideas about the topic
•I didn't repeat the specific points made in the readings
•I made the piece mine, not the stated authorities'

ORGANIZE AROUND A SYNTHESIZING CONCEPT
•I paid attention to the ideas in the readings
•I found or invented a specific concept to account for these ideas
•I used a synthesizing conept to organize my paper

INTERPRET FOR A PURPOSE OF MY OWN
•I used information sources to do something for a specific reader or purpose
•I selected only ideas from the readings or my experience that fit this goal
•I organized the essay around my own outside purpose

OTHER: If your plan is different, describe it in detail and complete sentences

```
STRATEGIES                              IF   NECESSARY,
                                 CHECK MORE THAN ONE.

GIST AND LIST

GIST AND LIST + OPINIONS

READ AS A SPRINGBOARD FOR THINKING

TELL IT IN MY OWN WORDS

SKIM TO INTERESTING POINTS AND RESPOND

DIG OUT AN ORGANIZING IDEA

DIVIDE THE IDEAS INTO CAMPS OR SIDES

CHOOSE WHAT MY AUDIENCE NEEDS TO KNOW

USE THE TEXT FOR MY OWN PURPOSE

OTHER? Describe your strategy in complete sentences
```

```
GOALS                        CHECK   THOSE   THAT   APPLY

TO DEMONSTRATE THAT I UNDERSTAND THE MATERIAL

TO GET A GOOD IDEA OR TWO OUT OF THE ASSIGNMENT

TO PRESENT WHAT I LEARNED

TO COME UP WITH SOMETHING INTERESTING TO SAY

TO DO THE MINIMUM AND DO IT QUICKLY

TO FULFILL A PAGE REQUIREMENT

TO TEST MY OWN EXPERIENCE

TO COVER ALL THE KEY POINTS IN THE READINGS

TO BE ORIGINAL OR CREATIVE

TO LEARN SOMETHING FOR MYSELF

TO INFLUENCE MY READER

TO TEST THE READING TO TEST SOMETHING I ALREADY KNEW
```

Appendix IX: Total Number of Selections with Percentages from the Self-Analysis Checklist

	Experimental				Control, Draft 2	
	Draft 2		Draft 1			
Source	$N = 28$	(%)	$N = 23$	(%)	$N = 33$	(%)
Text	9	(32)	1	(06)	5	(15)
Text + comments	15	(54)	11	(48)	22	(66)
Prior knowledge	1	(04)	5	(22)	1	(03)
Previous concept	3	(11)	5	(22)	5	(15)
Other	0	(00)	1	(04)	0	(00)
Format	$N = 28$	(%)	$N = 33$	(%)	$N = 23$	(%)
Notes/summary	3	(11)	1	(03)	1	(04)
Summary paragraph/opinion	7	(25)	7	(21)	4	(17)
Standard theme	14	(50)	19	(58)	6	(26)
Persuasive essay	2	(07)	6	(18)	12	(52)
Other	2	(07)	0	(00)	0	(00)
Plan	$N = 28$	(%)	$N = 33$	(%)	$N = 23$	(%)
Summarize texts	12	(43)	5	(15)	3	(13)
Respond to topic	5	(18)	2	(06)	1	(04)
Synthesizing	7	(2)	19	(58)	3	(13)
Interpret	3	(11)	5	(15)	15	(65)
Other	1	(04)	2	(06)	1	(06)

			Draft 2				Prediction			
	Experimental		Experimental		Control		Experimental		Control	
Strategies	$N = 49$	(%)	$N = 46$	(%)	$N = 91$	(%)	$N = 62$	(%)	$N = 49$	(%)
Gist and list	8	(16)	2	(04)	2	(02)	0	(00)	1	(02)
G and 1 plus opinion	8	(16)	6	(13)	12	(13)	3	(05)	2	(04)
Springboard	2	(04)	1	(02)	6	(07)	10	(16)	7	(14)
Tell it in own words	4	(08)	5	(11)	14	(15)	2	(03)	2	(04)
Skim and respond	8	(16)	2	(04)	10	(11)	5	(08)	3	(06)
Organizing idea	9	(18)	10	(22)	18	(20)	10	(16)	8	(16)
Take sides	6	(12)	5	(11)	13	(14)	8	(13)	6	(12)
Audience needs	1	(02)	5	(11)	10	(11)	15	(24)	14	(28)
Own purpose	3	(06)	10	(22)	6	(07)	9	(15)	7	(14)
Other	0	(00)	0	(00)	0	(00)	0	(00)	0	(00)

			Revision				Prediction			
	Experimental		Experimental		Control		Experimental		Control	
Goals	$N = 60$	(%)	$N = 57$	(%)	$N = 100$	(%)	$N = 71$	(%)	$N = 65$	(%)
Understanding	6	(10)	5	(09)	9	(09)	6	(0)	3	(05)
Get good idea	4	(07)	4	(07)	8	(08)	2	(03)	2	(03)

(*continued*)

Appendix IX (Continued)

	Experimental		Revision				Prediction			
			Experimental		Control		Experimental		Control	
Present learning	12	(20)	3	(05)	9	(09)	5	(07)	6	(10)
Interesting to say	7	(12)	9	(16)	18	(18)	6	(09)	7	(11)
Do the minimum	8	(13)	3	(05)	7	(07)	1	(01)	0	(00)
Page requirement	7	(12)	0	(00)	3	(03)	1	(01)	0	(00)
Test experience	3	(05)	1	(02)	4	(0)	2	(03)	3	(05)
Cover key points	11	(18)	4	(07)	14	(14)	6	(09)	12	(20)
Originality	0	(00)	6	(11)	11	(11)	16	(23)	12	(20)
Learn something	4	(07)	7	(12)	7	(07)	1	(01)	1	(02)
Influence reader	0	(00)	13	(23)	5	(05)	22	(32)	18	(30)
Test my knowledge	4	(07)	2	(04)	4	(04)	2	(03)	1	(02)

II

READING-TO-WRITE:
Cognitive Perspectives

4

Exploring the Cognition of Reading-to-Write

VICTORIA STEIN

In previous chapters we have explored the complex and highly variable nature of the reading-to-write task. Students may have differing representations of this task that in turn may affect the processes they bring to bear on performing it. Similarly, teachers' representations of the task may differ from those of their students, yet because they may be unaware of this difference, they may not be giving students the kind of instruction they need to do more highly valued forms of the task.

Since reading-to-write tasks are frequently assigned at all grade levels, the average college freshman has had a great deal of experience with them, the kind of extensive practice that often leads to the development of strategies and procedures for getting the job done (see Chapter 7). As part of our investigation into the nature of reading-to-write tasks, we wanted, first, to find out what kinds of cognitive processes students routinely brought to bear on this task. We also wanted to discover more about the ways in which the cognitive systems of reading and writing (often explored independently of each other) interact during such a task. Would reading strategies affect the writing process? Would writing goals affect the way students read source texts?

To learn more about the cognitive acts underlying the process of reading to write, we examined protocols of two groups of subjects performing the Time Management task described in Chapter 1. One group consisted of seventeen of the freshmen who participated in the teaching phase of this study. The second group was composed of nineteen junior and senior writing majors and graduate students enrolled in Carnegie-Mellon's Master of Professional Writing program. This group had acted as pilot subjects for the Time Management materials. The text they received had one additional paragraph, deleted in the freshman version to reduce length. Both groups were asked to think aloud from the time they began reading the instructions for the task through completion of a first draft. Their comments were recorded and transcribed verbatim. These protocol transcripts are the basis for the study described in this chapter.

While the two groups vary in age and writing experience, their protocols share some important features. With four exceptions, the overall patterns of processing are the same: the students read through the instructions and source text a first time, making minimal, brief comments (an average of 2.2 lines of protocol transcript). These comments either indicate comprehension work in the form of gisting or questions or contained off-the-cuff responses to the text. More often than not, they merely indicate agreement or disagreement with the source text ideas. Sandy's protocol provides some examples. In these excerpts, sentences from the source text are in italics; notes and writing appear in boldface; the actual comments appear in plain type:

> *The average worker has two kinds of "prime time" to plan: external time and internal time. External prime time is the best time to attend to other people. Internal prime time is the period in which one works best. Scheduling large blocks of time in advance helps organize the work day.* That's true. I do that—try to do that anyway. . . .

> *He advocated continued concentration in the face of apparent mental fatigue: 'The fatigue gets worse up to a certain critical point, when gradually or suddenly it passes away, and we are fresher than before. We have evidently tapped a new level of energy.'* All right, wait a minute. So in other words, you get energy from putting away a sufficient amount of time. Let me go back. . . .

These students then went back and read the source text a second time. In this second-pass reading, comments become more frequent and much longer (more than twice as long, an average of 5.7 lines of text compared to 2.2 lines in the first-pass reading). The function of the comments changes as well. Students began testing the assertions of the source text more carefully, comparing them with their own experiences in similar situations, conditionalizing them, stating reasons for agreement or disagreement at greater length. Here, for example, is Jack during his second-pass reading:

> *The students surveyed said they use strategies like these to minimize the debilitating effects of long range pressures. They assume that they will understand the subject matter sooner or later and that inspiration will be on hand when they need it.* I don't . . . that doesn't make sense to me. If you have . . . what's the difference between long range pressure and many, many short range pressures? I think that's definitely worse. If you have a long range pressure you can work it out . . . you've a lot longer time. If you just put it off, you'll never get it done. And assuming you've got inspiration, that's a very bad strategy. . . .

Following this second reading, these students then engaged in some planning for their papers. Such plans could include rough outlines of key points to include, search for an organizing idea, and more rarely, discussion of the audience for the paper. Here is Toshi, working out his major premise:

> Now what's the main point of this? What should I try to do? Well, basically, what is the main theme? What should I say in my statement? Well I suppose I could say **many of these suggestions seem sensible.** Well, yes, they do seem sensible. Every one except the last one tends to . . . or give good advice. However, accomplishing these is a problem, so I guess . . . **accomplishment is not always possible.** That **should be manageable.** So I think that's basically what I would say. . . .

Following such planning, students then began to write their papers, either working from notes or referring back to the source text, or both.

Four students, one graduate and three undergraduates, followed a somewhat different path. These students generally read the source text through only once, with longer comments, many of which became actual text. Only one of these students engaged in any planning and revision of text written after that one reading.

The thirty-six protocols we gathered went through several analyses. First, we identified four categories of cognitive processing that supported both reading and writing behavior: monitoring, elaborating, structuring, and planning. Then we looked at the way students applied those processes in some important areas within the task:

1. As they built representations of meaning of the source text and then of their own texts
2. As they brought prior knowledge into the reading process
3. As they applied automated processes and practiced strategies to the task
4. As they tried to balance the development of ideas and opinions with constraints of the task

These qualitative analyses had two goals: to see what cognitive processes students used to realize their representations of the task, and to explore the relationship of cognition to context, as manifested in the expectations and knowledge they brought with them and in the current task. Finally, we performed a quantitative analysis to investigate possible correlations between use of certain cognitive processes and the types and quality of papers our students produced.

An Examination of Cognitive Processes

The four categories of cognitive processing we established derived from two sources: (1) the literature on cognitive processing in reading and writing and (2) examination of pilot protocols. We sought, first, to establish broad categories that would delineate the major patterns of activity. These included the following:

- Monitoring
- Elaborating
- Structuring
- Planning

MONITORING

Experts monitor either comprehension during reading or progress with a task overall because it enables them to identify problems with processing (see Baker & Brown, 1984; Newell & Simon, 1972). We believed that monitoring plays an especially important role in reading-to-write because it allows us to see how students took exigencies of various contexts into account. For example, instances of task monitoring would enable us to see how conflicting contextual goals (e.g., "synthesize relevant findings" versus "finding something interesting/new to say") are handled. Instances of comprehension monitoring (e.g., paraphrasing, restating gists) would show not only how representations of the meaning of the source text are handled, but also the way in which students imported propositions from the source text into the text they were writing.

ELABORATING

Elaboration—that is, production of meaning-enhancing additions (Levin, 1987)—is the principle means by which students bring what they already know into the reading (Hamilton, 1987; Reder, 1980) and writing (Benton, Glover, & Plake, 1984) processes. In fact, it is through the process of elaboration that we see the clearest indication of how the constructive processes of reading and writing interact, as prior knowledge combines with source text propositions to create new ideas and critical perspectives (see Kucer, 1985; Spivey, 1987; see also Chapter 5).

STRUCTURING

How students shape and reshape material gleaned from source texts is a significant part of the process of moving from reading to writing (Kintsch & Van Dijk, 1978; Langer, 1984; Meyer, Brand, & Bluth, 1980). We hypothesized that when students had to deal with multiple, perhaps only partially connected, source text propositions, structuring activities would play an even more important role in creating a new text. In this category, we looked for any activity in which a subject began to manipulate propositions in a source text to begin forming a new text. Such activities include looking for instances of agreement and disagreement between propositions in source texts or between a proposition in the source text and the student's prior topic knowledge, looking for superordinate categories under which to subsume items in the source text, arranging text into high-level and low-level propositions, and discovering relations between ideas in the text that may not have been apparent on reading alone.

PLANNING

Planning plays a central role in moving from reading to constructing a text of one's own. However, experienced writers performing tasks like ours rely much more heavily on planning than inexperienced writers (Burtis, Bereiter, Scardamalia, & Tetroe, 1983) and they construct more fully elaborated and integrated plans (Flower,

Hayes, Carey, Schriver, & Stratman, 1986). In the context of this task, we wanted to see how students went about constructing a text of their own. We looked to see how they dealt with content, that is, ideas from the source text or from memory; how they dealt with text features, from single sentences to whole paragraphs; how they developed organizing ideas to guide the construction of the text; and how they developed a sense of rhetorical purpose of their own.

Clearly there is some overlap in these categories. For example, a student may need to elaborate in order to discover connections between ideas in the source text; monitoring comprehension in the form of restating gists from the source text may be an integral part of dealing with content while planning. In such cases, double coding was used to account for the overlap.

Figure 15 shows the results of this coding. The coding categories run across the top of the grid. The paper type (using the categories outlined in Chapter 2) run down the left side. The protocols were first parsed to differentiate between reading, rereading, writing, and commenting. Comments were then marked off as episodes, ranging from a single sentence to over two pages of transcript. In earlier research on the internal structure of the writing process, we found that although these goal-directed episodes are complex units of thought, they are reliably visible to judges and they account for underlying logic and structure and timing of the composing process in a way that other patterns such as paragraphs or the topoi do not (Flower & Hayes, 1981b). We defined an episode as an instance in which a student was primarily engaged in one activity, such as planning.

As the chart indicates, these students devoted most of their time (43 percent of all

	Monitoring	Elaborating	Structuring	Planning	Total # Episodes	Total # Students
Summary	27	34	9	10	80	2
Review & Comment	148	205	52	99	505	11
R&C +Frame	31	65	22	40	158	5
R&C +Main Pt.	145	236	55	98	534	12
Controlling Concept	13	21	14	16	64	2
Interpretation	36	42	7	17	102	2
Free Response	23	53	3	4	83	2
Totals	423	656	162	284	1525	36

Figure 15. Distribution of process categories across paper categories.

episodes) to elaborating, that is, comparing source text ideas to their own knowledge of time management. Twenty-seven percent of the remaining episodes were devoted to monitoring comprehension, 19 percent to planning, and only 11 percent to structuring the information at hand. This trend does not change noticeably with paper type. Those students who construed the task as knowledge-telling (summary/response categories 1–4) divide their processing time by precisely the same percentages. Those invested in knowledge transformation (synthesis and interpretation) vary slightly, with 38 percent of their episodes devoted to elaboration, 30 percent to monitoring, 20 percent to planning, and 13 percent to structuring. Those who wrote free responses, which rely less heavily on source text ideas and more on prior knowledge, spent fully 64 percent of their time elaborating, 27 percent monitoring comprehension, 5 percent planning, and 4 percent structuring.

These trends suggest that elaboration played an important role in performance of this task. A more detailed exploration of the impact of this kind of processing can be found in Chapter 5. It should be noted, however, that these students were writing on a topic they had a fair bit of knowledge about, which may account for the reliance on personal experience. Also, the source text purposely lacked certain conventions of coherence, so students may have turned to structured memories and experiences as a source of coherence. Even so, these students also paid close attention to the source text. All in all, a total of 60 percent of all episodes were dedicated to gathering information from the source text and from memory. Those involved in knowledge transformation spent a little more time on planning and structuring.

It would be difficult to say whether the distribution of effort over these categories represents an unusual reliance on information gathering. To be sure, for the reasons stated earlier, this particular task invited more elaboration and comprehension monitoring. It may also be that, in general, proportionately less planning and structuring is the norm. At the present time, not enough data exist on the way writers use these four processes in reading-to-write to compare these figures to.

To what end would students use these four major processes? One hypothesis that we could draw from expert/novice studies is that variables such as the quality of writing and the type of paper written (e.g., summary, synthesis, interpretation) can be predicted by the frequency with which students use certain strategies that reflect these processes. In other words, the students who perform tasks more successfully are more likely to use these strategies more often. Later in this chapter, we report on our attempts to investigate such connections. On the other hand, reading-to-write assignments are complex tasks, in which students juggle myriad goals and constraints as the processes of reading, writing, and task representation impinge on one another. Our analysis, therefore, was designed to also consider a rival hypothesis: that strategy use would be context-bound. That is to say, the frequency with which a student used a given strategy would not depend on reading or writing expertise alone; rather, how a student defined a task and chose to solve a problem, the nature of a student's plans and goals, and the constraints created by the way in which the student pulled information together all affect where, when, and how often a student would apply a strategy (see Flower et al., 1986). The case studies that follow illustrate the contextual and strategic processes we observed.

The Cognition of Reading-to-Write: A Case Study Perspective

It seems clear that reading-to-write tasks make a unique set of demands on students. A typical reading-to-write task requires a student to be able to read and comprehend a number of different materials on a given topic, materials that may have different orientations and different information on the topic. The student must then be able to sort out the similarities and differences in the source materials, figure out how to apply her own prior knowledge, decide what she feels is important to write about, determine what kind of paper will best suit her approach to the topic and materials, and then attend to the usual set of demands that any writing task makes.

The reading-to-write assignment therefore constitutes an enormously complex task environment, which incorporates a plethora of smaller tasks and goals, each of which changes with context. Changing contexts and goals often lead to differences in the way people use basic processes, as well as in the kinds of papers they write. Such a view suggests that as students perform this kind of task, they make choices about which cognitive processes to use and when to use them. That is, contextual constraints may require students to use different strategies for monitoring, elaborating, structuring, and planning at different times, tailoring their use to the immediate needs of the task. In effect, then, students must "manage" (Schoenfeld, 1979) the application of strategic knowledge, making decisions about which strategies to use when.

The following case histories are intended to shed some light on how students manage or fail to manage this process in four different areas of the reading-to-write process:

- Moving from the source text to new text
- Applying prior knowledge
- Using practiced strategies
- Balancing creativity with contextual constraints

These four areas call for strategic choice, and within them, we found that students handled decision making quite differently, although the extent to which students were aware of the choices available to them varied. They put the processes of monitoring, elaborating, structuring, and planning to use under very different goal structures, creating very distinctive process histories in the ways they used their own cognitive resources. A case study perspective highlights the interplay between strategic decision-making processes and reading and writing processes.

MOVING FROM TEXT TO TEXT

Students had trouble generating coherent texts of their own when they could not first assemble source materials into a unified coherent whole during the constructive process of reading. In other words, they needed to build a representation of the texts they were reading in order to build a representation of their own text. The complexity, difficulty, and importance of this process can be seen in the protocols of Darnell, Claudia, and Darlene.

Darnell

Darnell's protocol is short, only eight pages (as opposed to an average length of thirteen pages for most of our subjects). As he begins the task, he does what almost everyone else does—he reads the text on time management, interjecting evaluative comments on specific sentences, and working out small comprehension problems. His evaluative comments are not unlike comments made by others, assessing the feasibility of various assertions about how to manage time, stating agreement or disagreement, drawing on his backlog of personal experience to see how his time management technique compares with those written about in the text. This kind of evaluation, for many of our subjects, served as a means of making decisions about what material to use from the text; once they deemed something irrelevant or unworkable, they chose either to drop it or use their evaluative comments as the basis for their text. For Darnell, this is not the case. His evaluation of the source text gives him no clue as to how to manage it.

This is apparent as he begins his second reading of the text, claiming "I'm going to have to do a lot of rereading because I don't think I remember half of this stuff. . . . Let's see. . . . Every little thing had a different thing about time management. . . ." In this second reading, he sets about extracting gists for each paragraph, using none of his evaluative material. When he is done, he has a bare-bones list of gists, one for each paragraph. At this point, he ponders the task: "And I wonder what else I'm supposed to do for this assignment . . . Ok I have to make my interpretation . . . my statement about time management . . . ok what is my statement going to be?" He looks over his notes and finally writes a single sentence— **"Time management such as daily schedules are necessary for quality work that is meaningful to a person."** This sentence is a distillation of most of the gists he has extracted. Since he has not used his critical powers to help him construct a more fully elaborated, connected image of what is being said in this text, he has nowhere to go after that. This is apparent in his comments after he finishes writing his sentence: "Really, it's hard to make one basic statement, because there's like eight or nine different things that these people have said and that they mean, that they're trying to get across. . . . I don't know. . . ." He tries listening to his own protocol and decides that he sounds like "some illiterate jerk but God I can't come up with any statement whatsoever. . . ." He returns to his list of gists, notes that he has four ideas but can't figure out where to go with them. He rereads the task instructions and then decides "there's nothing I'm going to be able to do in this . . . I really don't know . . . I guess we're going to leave it at that."

What contributed to Darnell's failure to generate more than a single sentence? Among other things, he was apparently unable to build a substantive representation of the material he had to work with. What strategies might have helped him to do this? A closer look at his protocol suggests a few:

As Darnell read the material for the first time, he made quite a few elaborations and in doing so he generated a wealth of material whose value he clearly did not understand. For many other students, elaborative material was a gold mine. Elaborations that determined relevance enabled them to drop out material altogether, letting them skirt the issue of having to make connections between seemingly unconnected items. Also, such evaluative comments helped them make decisions about what kind of paper to write—that is, realizing that they disagreed with some of the advice given in the source text, they decided to use points of agreement, embellished by personal experience, as the structure for their own texts. Inferential embellishments, in which causal connections and scenario-building allowed students to see the implications of some of source-text advice, gave students a critical perspective on the topic and source text. Similarly, instantiations allowed students to flesh out bare-bones assertions enough to make them discussable. Darnell did all of these things as he read the source text the first time. But apparently he underestimated the utility of this kind of thinking.

Another kind of activity that might have proved useful to Darnell, but that he did not use at all, was structuring. Although he was able to pull out basic gists, he hardly even tried to discover what the connections between these gists might be. The source text had a number of contradictions embedded within it at the global and local levels. Working with these contradictions enabled some students to begin to see how things were and were not connected in the text. Darnell hardly noticed the local contradictions, and missed the global contradictions altogether. Nor was he able to find top-level organizers that might have helped him categorize the different assertions in the source text. Because he failed to do any of this, the source text remained an unmanageable morass of floating ideas, leaving him nothing to build his own text on.

In this context, the relationship between text and task is an important one. Students who come to an early understanding of what kind of paper it is they would like to write seem to have less trouble building a representation of the source text because demands of certain paper types dictate the way in which they will deal with source materials. For example, knowing early that you want to do a summary or synthesis carries with it the knowledge that you will have to find ways to account for all the material, which in turn seems to trigger strategies that will allow you to do so, such as structuring, categorizing, and gisting. Similarly, deciding that making a statement means some kind of personal response seems to trigger strategies for applying personal knowledge.

Yet, deciding on a certain task early is not always a guarantee of success in building text representations. Students may also have to understand that it is sometimes necessary to change tasks to get the job done. Claudia's protocol gives us an example of this phenomenon.

Claudia

After a first pass much like Darnell's, Claudia quickly began writing, with the intention, apparently, of writing a summary with comments based on her elaborations thrown in: **"Time management. There are many different opinions on time management. They vary from James who tells us to work past fatigue and reach a new level of energy. If we waited and worked toward this new level of energy we would probably all have died from waiting. On the other hand Guitton says we should rest at the first sign of fatigue. If we did this we'd never get any-**

where." But this approach doesn't seem to leave her anywhere to go ("Well, this is not enough, I have to write some more . . .") so she begins again: " **'Time management is important'** OK. So what?" She rereads parts of the source text and then expresses dissatisfaction with her approach: "I wish I could get an angle on this. How am I going to do this? Why do I want to do this?" The source of her dissatisfaction appears to be her inability to build an adequate text representation: "This data is garbage. Nothing fits together. This one's about students, this one's backwards, this one's forwards." Soon she realizes that a different approach is in order, one necessitating a change in task from summary to response, and she writes: **"Time management is relative to each individual. That is to say, everyone has a different interpretation. My opinion of time management differs from most of the experts quoted in the passage."** As she continues, she uses most of the material she generated before, but this time has no trouble fitting it into the structure of a response. Changing tasks helped her find a way to manage the material in the text.

These protocol excerpts show us a lot about the power of representation of both task and text. Both of these students were unable to write texts of their own because they were unable to make the source text work for them in an organized way. Claudia found a way around the problem by working instead on her representation of task. In these instances, however, switching tasks meant falling back on review plus commentary as a means of avoiding the problematic source text. But what of the student who seems adept at synthesizing, who has a more highly articulated awareness of the power of task representation, yet still cannot work it out? Such a student is Darlene.

Darlene

Darlene's teacher had identified her as one of the best students in the class, conscientious, motivated, and bright. Yet she seems to have had difficulty with this task. Her protocol, which runs to over thirty pages (more than twice the mean), shows she worked very hard at this task. For all that work, however, she was able to muster only a single paragraph on how she was unable to do the task. What happened to Darlene?

"How in the heck can you write a two-page statement about time management when they didn't tell you anything about time management?" she asked after her first reading. Upon hitting the interpret prompt, she wondered, "How can you interpret it? None of it's the same." She reread the task instructions several times after the first pass. She looked up the word "synthesis" to be sure she understood what it means, and focused on the word "comprehensive." Yet, after her third rereading of the task instructions, she decides that she will "just treat this like a journal . . . and write a statement," dropping entirely the notion of comprehensiveness.

Then she goes back to reread the source text, elaborating plentifully as she goes along, noting key points and points of agreement. But when she is done rereading, she again feels stymied by the source text: "I don't know what I have to write, I have to write something about time management. . . . I'm just doing it as a journal, I don't care what I'm supposed to do. Let's just start off with something about what I read." However, what she writes is not about what she read. It's about the trouble she's having fulfilling the assignment as she understands it: **"While doing the protocol on time management I had a hard time writing a comprehensive statement about time management because the notes I read didn't help."**

She starts a list of key points. However, "these notes just don't do anything" for her. "I don't even know what I'm supposed to be doing. I feel like such a wuss." So she makes a synthesizing move, trying to find "factors that influence performance." But working with the individual statements in the source text proves to be too frustrating and she finally says, "All right, forget it, I'm gonna give it another shot. . . . I'm just doing a journal."

Her very next move, however, is to read the task instructions again, focusing on the directive to "interpret and synthesize all of the relevant findings in the text." Ultimately she says "so I'm just gonna—I don't care, I'm going to interpret them the only way I can. . . ." but rather than begin her journal entry, she resorts to yet another synthesizing move, deciding to write about what the authors (not she) agreed and disagreed about. Unfortunately, this foray into synthesis proves unsuccessful, too. Finally, she looks at the one sentence she has written and changes it: **"I had a difficult time writing a comprehensive statement about time management because the notes I read did not seem to make a clear statement to me,"** saying "it's not that they didn't help, because I guess they helped. They didn't write the essay for me is the problem."

And so it goes. As she writes, she purposely determines to "go for vague words," as if underscoring her inability to deal specifically with the source text. After writing about instances of agreement between authors, however, she stops again and her frustration is evident: "Oh, I don't know! All I have is a half page of notes. How can I possibly make this into anything? I'm not doing well, but I don't know why."

She then tried to go "from the authors to [her]self. I have to write something that I feel." She writes **"To me it is obvious that organizing your time is an intrinsic part of time management. After all isn't that what management means?"** But when she returns to synthesis, looking for "opposites," the old frustration pops up again: "Can I leave it at that . . . oh give me a break, I don't know what I'm doing, I'm only a freshman, I have no idea what to do. . . ." She ends by writing:

> **I have tried to incorporate these ideas into my statement but I have been wandering in circles long enough. To continue to struggle for words would not be an efficient use of time and wasting excessive amounts of time does not seem appropriate, especially on a paper about time management.**

Certainly, Darlene's confusion about what task to do is apparent in her paper, which, read in its entirety, is a curious amalgam of synthesis and response. But what is perhaps more interesting is the fact that Darlene's paper is really not on the topic at all. It is instead a comment on the cohesiveness of the source text and her frustration with it. Darlene tried her best to find ways to make it all fit together, to do the synthesis task she thought she was supposed to do. Although she had an acceptable alternative, the response mode (called a journal entry by her teacher), she seemed unwilling or unable to commit herself to one task or the other.

Darlene marshaled considerable cognitive resources toward performing the task, yet she still came up short. What was missing from Darlene's repertoire? One move she did not make, that expert writers in similar situations may make, is to move at this point to active problem solving, focused on one's goals, alternatives, or the task itself.

Darlene's protocol points up an important aspect of strategic knowledge: simply knowing a few strategies is often not enough. You must also know when to apply them and recognize when they are failing you.

APPLYING PRIOR KNOWLEDGE

Prior knowledge has a number of uses in reading-to-write tasks. Use of formal topic knowledge or general world knowledge can foster development of critical thinking, aid in generation of new ideas and development of old ideas, and support the processes of monitoring, structuring, and planning. (For a fuller discussion of the application of prior knowledge in reading-to-write, see Chapter 5.) As such, therefore, application of prior knowledge can be a powerful strategy that shapes both reading and writing processes. However, as with any complex cognitive move, context enhances or constrains the effectiveness with which prior knowledge can be applied, and that means that students must develop some awareness of when and how it is appropriate to apply it.

As the following case histories show, some students use this valuable strategy with rigor and energy. At the same time, however, Connie and Elvin were unable to monitor their use of strategic knowledge, in this case, elaboration. Their inability to recognize that application of particular prior knowledge was inappropriate to the context of the topic and the source text almost subverted their attempts to do the task.

Both these students were candidates for the degree of Master of Arts in Professional Writing whose training in empirical research methods has provided them with specialized knowledge including precise definitions for certain terms and knowledge of the criteria for validity in such research. As they read the source materials, they immediately focused on the words "data" and "research." These terms apparently called up knowledge about research, including evaluative criteria, that they then tried to apply to the source text. The problem was that those criteria, and the reading strategy they suggested, were inappropriate for this task and that text.

Connie

This disparity caused a big problem for Connie. In her first comments after reading the source text she asks, "Why do they call it research notes?" Like the previous students, she is having trouble seeing how the text "hangs together," apparently because it violates her expectations about what research notes should be. After rereading the first paragraph, she says, "Now, what I'd like to know is, how did [the author] come to these conclusions? Did he observe a lot of people, did he do questionnaires?" She reads the second paragraph and wonders "Where did James get this stuff? Is it just his personal experience? What is the basis for his data? Too much acid in college? Did he do a scientific experiment, a repeatable experiment? Control group?" She continues to read the next couple of paragraphs, doing some elaboration, but seems to be having difficulty with the text. The source of her frustration appears to be her sense that the text does not live up to the expectations engendered by the words "data" and "research." This is apparent after she rereads the fifth paragraph, when she wishes the author had provided more specific instances (i.e., proof) of his ideas, and she writes "What was the nature of his research?" She says, "I mean, they never tell us how they did it. What method did he use? I could put that down for all these guys. I mean was this scientific research? Or was it mostly just opinions?"

She makes comments such as these after every paragraph that she reads, and her comments more often than not become notes. However, Connie never generated any text beyond those notes, and never reconciled the reality of the text with her expectations of what she thought it would be. Unable to let go of those expectations, she never focused on the substance of the text itself.

Elvin

Similarly, Elvin initially found his expectations tripping him up. After reading the source text, his first comment is "I was expecting more statistical data when I read the title." He begins to reread the text but soon wonders "exactly which data I'm supposed to be interpreting." Shortly thereafter, in the middle of rereading a paragraph, he says, "What I'm supposed to do is a statement about time management based on this data. And I still don't know which data I'm supposed to be interpreting, and I'm going to have to go back to the beginning again." But unlike Connie, he is able to get off dead center. After rereading the first sentence, he says, "Maybe I'll relate the data collected . . . data collected is always, data, data. Data. I don't think that's the right word for all the instances cited." He is able to let go of his strict definition of the word to be able to apply it to what is actually in front of him. He writes, **"data collected from authorities, professional settings and data collected from academic environments,"** and says, "So I think I'll set up a contrast between professional settings and academic environments . . ." and thereafter is able to come up with a plan, that allows him to focus on the content of the source text.

The protocols of Connie and Elvin highlight an important facet of strategic knowledge. Students may have developed strategies and evaluative criteria from their experience as writers and from their studies of a specialized field. But the development of such cognitive resources may be only the first step toward mastery of strategic knowledge. Students must also become sensitive to the context in which they apply these strategies. They must develop the kind of metacognitive awareness that will allow them to test for the appropriateness of application of a strategy; they must also make adjustments when the context of the text or task does not allow for successful application of a particular strategy.

AUTOMATED PROCESSES AND PRACTICED STRATEGIES

Some students seemed to have no trouble with this reading-to-write task. They moved from reading to writing with consummate ease, and appeared to have a well-established set of questions, criteria, and moves. Yet, as many teachers can attest, the fact that a student can do a task easily does not mean that she can do it well. In fact, as the following case histories illustrate, practice does not always make perfect; it can just as easily reinforce bad habits.

The terms "automated processes" and "practiced strategies," as they are used here, refer to well-rehearsed procedures that students have to some extent internalized. As mentioned before, most students have had years of experience with reading-to-write tasks, assigned by many different teachers with many different goals and in many different contexts. Often students do such tasks in one shot, perhaps because of time constraints, perhaps because they are not motivated to spend more time on them. Whatever the case, we hypothesized that students have had ample opportunity to figure out strategies for doing such assignments and rehearse them so often that using those strategies no longer demands much conscious attention—they have become tacit, procedural knowledge (see Anderson, 1983). In such cases, familiar task representations, and procedures for pulling together and packaging information would be used out of habit, almost as default processes. Use of such automated processes and practiced strategies would considerably streamline the reading-to-write process.

All of the students described here appeared to rely to some extent on sets of well-rehearsed procedures. They also all wrote the same kind of paper—one our raters called Summary with a Frame, in which the student provides a general topic statement in the first paragraph, provides examples in subsequent paragraphs, and closes with an iteration of the topic statement. Their protocols, therefore, give us some insight into how such processes yield this kind of paper, which closely resembles the five-paragraph theme; they give us some perspective on how the use of such processes affects paper quality, since our subjects' texts received quality ratings of between 1.5 to 3 on a scale of 3; and, perhaps most important, they show us the downside of using such procedures, especially for planning and monitoring activities.

Patrice

Patrice moved from reading to writing with hardly a pause for breath. During her reading of the text, she makes minimal comments, most of them in service to comprehension monitoring. She reads the task only once, and then, after a glance at the first sentence of the text, which seems to situate her in the topic, starts generating text:

> Ok, so well, let me see. . . . Time management of course is, well, it is of importance . . . it's of great interest to . . . people today because . . . I want to say that in today's society things move so quickly and there's so much to be done that every minute counts . . . so people are always trying to get the maximum done with minimum effort . . . like with computers, you can do so much more with them . . . so um okay **'time management is of great interest in today's society, a society which seeks maximum production and efficiency with the least amount of effort'** . . . they make it sound so easy to plan your time, it's not. . . . **'These studies make it sound easy to plan your time, to divide it between external and internal prime time. . . .**

This excerpt from Patrice's protocol is highly representative of how she went about writing this paper. She never stopped to make an overall text plan; rather, using elaboration to give her angles, she recaps portions of the source text, making comments about them as she goes along. For example, here is how she handled the third paragraph of the source text, which she moves to after she rereads what she's already written about the first:

> **"Walter Pauk's study is . . ."** really just common sense . . . is, it's not like it's some big discovery . . . I mean everybody knows about . . . everyone knows that you have to concentrate when you're in school, and that you can't concentrate if you've got like, loud music blaring in the background or anything. . . . And if you don't have enough time . . . um . . . . **"Walter Pauk's study doesn't really say anything that most college students don't already know"** . . . they may not practice what . . . they may not . . . I want to say . . . I mean, they know they should schedule time and that they should have a nice quiet environment, but it doesn't mean they practice it. They may not follow. . . . **'They may not follow his advice, but they know it's true."**

The rest of Patrice's protocol and essay are very much the same. She seems to have learned some conventions of form well: She writes a nice topic sentence that prefigures her attention to what people say and do about maximum efficiency with minimum time expenditure. She has a nice, if obvious, conclusion that ties it all together. (**"Obviously student strategies are inefficient, but will they ever change?"**) She accounts for most of the authors in the source text (for some reason, she seems to have skipped over James). By using her comments as a means of evaluation, she has found something beyond the source text to talk about. This knowledge of these conventions allows her to breeze along.

But there are other things that she did not do, that others did do, that might have improved her paper, which received a quality rating of 1.5. She never really monitored the task, asking herself "Is this enough?" or "Is this the best way to do this?" which might have led her to a more formal kind of task representation (such as Synthesis). Such a representation might have allowed her to use her critical evaluation more effectively. Nor did she posit an audience, a move that would have allowed her to develop a rhetorical purpose for what she was writing. And she never did any planning, except at a local level. Global planning may have given her a way to build more connections, dig deeper into the material, thus permitting an even closer, fine-grained analysis. Patrice was clearly able to elaborate effectively on a sentence by sentence basis. Pulling back and looking at the material from a greater distance might have let her use her elaborative skills even better.

Gracie

Gracie's paper received a quality ranking of 2, and an examination of her protocol reveals some interesting similarities and differences between her approach to this task and Patrice's. Like Patrice, she begins writing immediately, and like Patrice she is a prodigious elaborator who reaches quick closure. And again, as with Patrice, the move to quick closure prevents her from doing a better job of integrating the source material. In Gracie's case, the rapid application of practiced strategies in service to quick closure proves even more problematic as it leads to miscomprehension in some instances. But unlike Patrice, she does invest in some global planning, which gives her paper a somewhat clearer focus than Patrice's.

Gracie's notes, as she begins to read the source text, read more like text than fragmented notes. They include not only items from the source text, but also her elaborations. For example, here is Gracie's reading of the first paragraph:

> *"Time management . . . the key to success according to efficiency expert Alan Lakein in his recent book* How to Get Control of Your Time and Your Life *lies in pacing and planning."* . . . **"Time management. . . . How one goes about planning their use of time in the most efficient manner."** . . .*"He notes that planning is decision making, and that it is imperative that decisions on using time to best advantage be made"* . . . so **'If you don't use time wisely you'll never succeed at anything."** . . . *"There are two kinds of prime time to plan: external and internal"* . . . two kinds of prime time . . . so . . . **"time can be divided in two ways, internal and external . . . both help to organize the workday . . . every individual has a different time management because every individual spends time differently."**

There are several items of interest here. First, Gracie, preoccupied with using elaboration to build context for localized source text propositions, is generating text as she reads, not notes, but real, substantive text that gives her quick (perhaps premature) closure on the topic. For example, the idea that "every individual has different time management because every individual spends time differently" is a conclusion that most other subjects reached after spending a lot of time trying to get the pieces of text to fit together, and it became the focus of their writing, their topic sentence in effect. Gracie gets the picture early, but this valuable perspective is buried, obscured, because it is not used in a more global planning episode. Second, note how far she leaps in her elaborations. "It is imperative that decisions on using time to best advantage be made" becomes "if you don't use time wisely you'll never succeed at anything." These leaps indicate a lack of critical control, an inability to monitor the appropriateness of the material she generates.

Soon Gracie's drive for quick closure reaches almost comic proportions, as her efforts result in the kind of convoluted logic that make teachers wonder whether to laugh or cry. For example, she treats the student strategies at the end of the text, which many students recognized as being in complete contradiction to the advice of the experts, as if they were just as reasonable as the others:

> **Each of these deals with the allocation of time . . . one . . . first of all you do what's due and postpone big projects. This way you don't do what's not due and do what's due. That way you get it out of the way and the pressure is relieved. Or you create a crisis which pressures you to get the assignment done, or you get all the easy stuff out of the way. . . . By doing this you've spent the time wisely and have more time for the harder assignments. Next you allow the minimal estimate of time it will take to get a project completed. I guess they're saying not to allocate more than enough time to one project because you have less time to complete the others. . . . If you allow the minimal estimate of time then you'll know how to budget the time better and have time to do more than if you spend all your time on one project. Finally, students find that you shouldn't read material more than once and you shouldn't try to remember it until it's needed. . . . I guess by constantly rereading material you tend to confuse yourself and you may forget it . . . and spend too much time trying to memorize it before you get it down on paper.**

When Gracie has finished writing this series of text/notes, however, she takes a next step, one that Patrice, in her rush to closure, fails to make. Gracie makes a conscious investment in planning and structuring. First, she attempts to get a handle on the topic overall:

> Time management . . . the way in which some budget their time is founded on many factors. . . . Management of time is based on many factors . . . oh brother . . . Ummmm. . . . Time management is . . . Time management is needed so that every student expends all of their mental energy to complete every assignment. . . . If the student does not know how to budget their time correctly, then there's no way they can complete the assignment or produce quality work. . . .

Like Patrice, Gracie is searching for the topic sentence that will set up the rest of the paper. But unlike Patrice, Gracie does not settle on the first one. She keeps generating them until she gets to one she likes. She begins with a very general one, a paraphrase of the source text, and moves slowly toward one that gives her a specific focus, namely, students. It also sets her up with a problem statement of sorts, albeit a veiled one: Why do students need time management? Because they will not do good work without it.

Gracie's repertoire of automated processes and practiced strategies appears to include a greater awareness of the value of planning and structuring, but it still lacks the vital element of critical control. It is as if the emphasis is on the local management of propositions, and not on the development of a better understanding of the content of the source text at a more global level. The importance of a more global approach to comprehension and planning is exemplified in Leslie's protocol.

Leslie

Unlike Gracie, Leslie shows active critical control, and makes use of the value of monitoring and planning. She is able to use this knowledge purposefully and effectively.

Leslie resists the impulse to quick closure. She reads the text and instructions once without comment. Before she reads it the second time, she wonders about the purpose of the text: "Now, I'm supposed to write a statement about time management based on interpretation of this data. . . . Ok this passage is supposed to help students—give tips on how to improve study skills by arranging their time more efficiently." Her first reading has helped her get a handle on task and text: she understands the task to be interpretation and has a feel for the rhetorical intent of the source text. In her second reading, since she has a sense of what she wants out of this text already, she is also able to make valuable relevance judgments. For example, reading about Lakein's notion of internal and external prime time, she says:

> Now this is what is unclear. . . . How does that relate to the whole? This concept of internal and external prime time? I'm supposing that when he says "scheduling large blocks of time" he's referring to internal prime time, which is the "period in which one works best." [she makes a note of this] . . . well now that I think about it, perhaps "scheduling of large blocks" doesn't refer to internal prime time but to both and that . . . what you are supposed to do is set specific periods of time for dealing with

other people and specific periods of time for working. But I still don't, after reading this before, I don't think that this concept of external prime time and internal prime time is relevant at this time.

After she has finished rereading the text, she stops to make "some observations that I've made reading this":

[W]e've got two different environments that we're talking about: professional and academic settings. In looking at my notes, two paragraphs speak specifically about academic performance. So I'm going to write down academic performance and under-line it, and I'm going to write down the studies. Pauk, and I'm going to write factors that affect next to his name. Then the other one was student survey. I'm writing down strategies for overcoming poor study skills. The next thing I'm going to write is general performance and in parentheses academic or professions. I'm going to underline it and write down all the studies that fall into this category. . . .

Having noted specific differences and similarities in the ideas put forward by the source text authors, Leslie now engages in some more global planning:

Ok, so I've classified the studies according to what they're talking about. . . . Now I'm going to break these up under different criteria here. We have factors that af-fect . . . some studies have factors that affect performance versus strategies for man-aging time . . . ok now some of these studies can fall in both catagories . . . factors that affect performance—Pauk. Well, they're factors but they're also strategies: ability to concentrate, knowing how to study. I mean implicit in those are strategies. Actually you could list all of these in terms of strategies, instead of just saying factors. What we can separate by is not factors versus strategies but strategies for improving time management versus strategies for coping with poor time management skills.

But Leslie's planning does not stop with the arrangement of content into workable categories. Her next move is to find her rhetorical purpose:

Why is [time management] important? Who cares? Why is it an issue? Ok, I'm going to use the last paragraph as the problem statement: I want to answer the question, why research on time management? And the answer I'm going to give to this question is people tend to use ineffective strategies. . . .

Leslie had walked a very controlled path here. She takes the time to read the text carefully, to decide on the task, to find a good focus, to set up the problem statement, and to make sure to apply her criteria for success at every step of the way. In doing so she combines a wide range of strategies that include important moves for planning and monitoring.

BALANCING CREATIVITY AND CONTEXT

The students discussed so far have been intent on staying on task. Some have been more successful at producing papers than others, but they have all made persistent attempts to deal with the material they were given on its own terms. All of us, however, have at one time or another, received papers from students that seem so far off the mark that we wonder if they even bothered to read the assignment. How do students get off topic and off task?

This is the story of Travis, a Master's student whose paper was so far off the topic of time management as discussed in the source text that he might have been working on a different task altogether. This paper, which presented an extended metaphor on the thinking process, was rated as a "free response" by the raters. Given the indeterminate nature of this task, such a response was not necessarily inappropriate. Writing about a completely different topic was. Yet, a look at Travis' protocol shows that his journey from time management to thinking did, indeed, start with his consideration of the source text. A multitude of larger contexts, however, greatly influenced his odyssey through the process of reading-to-write. These contexts, unlike those explored earlier, are not defined by the task or those assigning it; they are defined by the person doing the task, who he is, where he has been. In Travis' case, the demands of those contexts proved to be more powerful than the demands of the task.

Travis

Prior to graduate school, Travis had gone to a small liberal arts college. According to him, most of his previous writing experience had been largely within the expressive writing tradition, with its emphasis on personal reporting, journals, and self-discovery. The graduate program he chose to enter, however, offered three semesters of intense training in professional and technical writing, with emphasis on identification of design and audience needs for technical documents such as computer manuals. Students are expected to write papers analyzing information in order to find the best way to present it, and they are also expected to analyze their own writing processes, in order to adapt them to various writing situations.

Travis had a hard time adjusting to the writing demands of the program overall, and to the specific requirements of the professional writing class in which he was given the time management assignment. He told his teacher that he found it very difficult to write analytic papers—indeed, even to think analytically. His protocol provides ample evidence of this. It presents a compelling portrait of a student unable to put his mind to the task.

Travis is a compulsive talker with a quick mind, given to fanciful leaps of imagination, facile turns of phrase, and off-the-wall free association in the manner of stand-up comics. Some of this is evident as he begins his task. For one thing, he seems extremely aware of the odd circumstances under which he's doing the task, virtually playing to the tape-recorder microphone ("We're going to open up the envelope here, folks . . . babble insanely for a while. . .") As he reads the source text for the first time, he makes notes of some gists and the like, but most of his effort goes into putting the assertions in the text into his own context by instantiating and free associating. Like Gracie, Travis is a prodigious and free-ranging elaborator. For example, when he comes across the sentence *"Time can be gained by combining activities which by themselves do not fully occupy all of a worker's capabilities"* (from the one additional paragraph in the Masters students' task materials described earlier), his response is, "I guess that means multiple . . . energy . . . if something is mindless you can put it together with other mindless tasks. This is sort of like cooking." This cooking analogy proves to be very seductive, with power enough to shape what will happen later.

Travis reads the source text through a second time, with the intention of doing a closer reading. The more he tries to concentrate on the task, however, the more difficulty he seems to have attending to it. For example, as he reads the task instructions, he muses:

> What's my statement. Is my statement . . . uh . . . criticism about how they're doing it? Or is my statement about how I would go about doing it if I had my act together. Which I do not . . . getting your act together is a very important thing, ladies and gentlemen . . . having it together . . . and of course, none of us ever has their act together . . . until we die, as Flannery O'Connor . . . Flannery O'Connor would say . . . what a Christian hero she was. . . .

Although he rereads the task instructions once later on, he never again attempts to define for himself what the task ought to be. In fact, he seems more intent on subverting the task. After he made the preceding comments, he read a few more source text sentences, and then decided:

> I know, I'll say everything that I'm writing in a French accent, then I'll know when I'm playing this tape back, where I'm writing down. . . . Hey coolness. . . . Ok well I gotta make sure I'm not speaking in a French accent when I'm not writing something down. . . . I'm such a funny guy (reads another sentence) . . . Ok when I'm reading, I'll do it in a German accent. . . .

Shortly thereafter, finally back on task, he decides it would be "a good idea to just go down this list and write my impressions of each point." This switch in emphasis from source text to his own impressions seems to trigger even more extreme elaborative behavior. For example, on reading that college students often "create a crisis" he wonders:

> Why would you want to create a crisis? To artificially induce labor, no, to artificially create a pressure situation because that is the way you believe to focus your energy . . . because you're too scared to be apathetic and easily distracted . . . OK, I'm distracted right now, my bum hurts . . . and I'm going to have to read this out loud or someone's going to be looking at this . . . they'll realize what a dangerous person I really am. PLEASE DON'T LET ME KILL AGAIN . . . (rereads note about apathy and distraction). . . . But to me when I'm in that situation I become more distracted than ever. I'm beginning to sound like Steve Martin. I become more distracted than ever, thinking "Oh my goodness, I have so much pressure on me. . . ."

The cooking analogy reasserts itself sentences later. When he gets to *"Read material once: don't try to remember it until it's needed"* he says:

> Yeah, that's like the crock pot situation. We're making a stew . . . ok . . . that's a good way of putting it . . . making a stew . . . we take information as vegetables . . . and meat . . . for all you vegetable rights activists, we take information . . . can see information as vegetables . . . and . . . let it stew . . . let it cook . . . we let it cook, we let it simmer, and the best way to do that is to gather your information, take notes on info so that you're concentrating on the information at first hand . . . and in the process of writing stuff down and jotting notes, your brain is actually recording it, I assume. Maybe I'm making the brain more wonderful that it is, but that's what I think is going on . . . and then . . . go on to planning and the daydreaming, letting the veggies of your mind, the information, that is, stew slowly and create new flavor combinations with each other. . . .

It is important to recognize that Travis is not merely fooling around in an attempt to avoid the task. To be sure, there are clearly moments when his attention seems to be wandering. But there are also moments, as the preceding excerpt shows, when Travis is working very hard, engaging not so much in critical thinking, as the term applies to analytical academic tasks, as in creative thinking. That activity provides him with a metaphor powerful enough to control his thinking, reading, and writing processes, which in turn affects the focus of his final paper. However, while the work and the effort he puts into expanding this metaphor are admirable, the work seems to be missing one important component: awareness that his metaphor will soon lead him off topic altogether, away from time management and onto creativity.

Shortly thereafter, while rereading the source text, he notes that "I did think of a good cooking metaphor pretty early." Later, rereading his notes, the power of the metaphor is again reinforced: **"You create a crisis in order to artificially create a pressure situation. Because you believe that is the most time-efficient way in which to concentrate and focus, because you're too scared to be apathetic and distracted** . . . like a pressure cooker."

Then he deems himself ready to write. He goes first to look again at the student strategies focusing on the sentence *"Students report the following for getting through assignments"* and wonders, "Are these written assignments or regular projects. We'll treat this as writing assignments . . . writing assignments . . . can be thought of . . . as making a stew." And so he is off and running. He is hereafter consumed with the desire to work out the cooking metaphor as best he can:

> We are making stew when we write. We take information (information as vegetables) and let it cook. Take notes on info, so that you are concentrating on info at first. And then go onto planning and daydreaming, letting the veggies of your mind stew slowly and create new flavor combinations. That is, let your mind make the combinations somewhat unconsciously.

It is perhaps not surprising that Travis was unable to stick to the topic, given the amount of effort he put into running away from the source text. In essence, Travis seems to have reinvented the task so that it looks less like a standard academic writing assignment and more like the kind of writing he feels more comfortable doing. In the context of that kind of writing, which is often used as a tool for self-discovery, it is quite acceptable to use the source text as a leaping off point to get to something more meaningful to the writer himself. This task, in contrast, required students to write about other people's ideas. Travis' previous writing experience, as well as his personal style, overrode demands of the task per se. The result is a final product that would puzzle any teacher expecting to read a paper on time management.

Looking for Patterns: The Quantitative Analysis

These case studies give us a sense of the delicate interplay of the independent cognitive systems of reading, writing, and task representation in reading-to-write tasks. We see that the comprehension work during reading affects the ability to write later on. We see that the way in which a student chooses to represent a task influences both his reading and writing behavior. We see that writing goals, such as being comprehensive, or including one's own opinions, similarly affect reading and task representation.

Further, we see that the families of strategies encompassed by our four coding scheme categories—monitoring, elaborating, structuring, and planning—serve crucial, and often very different purposes at different points in the reading-to-write process. For example, a student might apply a host of monitoring strategies while reading: She may have to make sure that she understands what is being read; that whatever prior knowledge she applies through elaboration is appropriate for the task at hand; and that the information she gleans from her reading and elaboration will help her reach her writing goals. This is to say, various contexts, such as the kind of subtask, nature of previous experience, and different types of writing goals, affect strategy use.

The first and foremost goal of this study was to map in some detail certain points of interaction between task, process, and context. As the exploratory study progressed, however, two rival hypotheses developed. One, the so-called frequency hypothesis, stated that the number of times a student uses a specific process can be correlated with such dependent measures as type or quality of paper, and that definitive relationships between amount of process use and specific outcomes can be described. The second hypothesis, called the "strategic knowledge" hypothesis, stated that these processes are best seen as strategies and that strategy use is not directly related to outcomes such as paper type or quality, but rather to goals, plans, and task representation.

The qualitative analysis just presented allowed us to explore this second hypothesis; hence its preoccupation with the interaction of strategic knowledge and context. However, such an analysis has some important limitations. It could only give us single instances that could not be used to generalize about relations within the group as a whole.

To test the frequency hypothesis—that is, to see the relationship between students' use of these cognitive processes and the papers they generated—a quantitative analysis was also performed. Independent raters were asked to assess the papers our students produced from two perspectives. They were first asked to make a determination about the structure of the papers, using the rating system described by Kantz in Chapter 2. After the papers were assigned to categories, different raters assigned quality ratings to the papers. The scale for these ratings was 1 to 3, with 1 indicating poor quality, 2 average quality, and 3 high quality. The raters were instructed to assign quality rankings within groupings; that is to say, the quality of a paper was judged relative to those of other papers with the same organizing plan.

Pierson Product Moment correlations comparing the numerical counts of process use to quality, paper-type ranking, and expert/novice status were performed, as were several regression studies. None of these analyses yielded significant results. That is to say, this analysis established no clear relationship between the number of times a student used a particular process and the kind of paper he eventually wrote or the quality of that paper. For the results, see Appendix XI.

Such results may lead one to reject the frequency hypothesis, however, such disconfirmation has to be taken with caution, for it may well be more accurate than this analysis reveals. That the quantitative analysis did not reveal any definitive patterns between process use and specific outcomes may be attributable to the scope of this study. In our analysis we had a relatively small number of subjects (36) and a relatively large number of paper type categories (7). Since the majority of our subjects (28) wrote some papers that fell into two of the Summary + Comment categories, there were not enough students writing the other kinds of papers to establish clear patterns of interaction between the number of times a student used processes and the type of paper she produced.

However, we do not believe that the frequency hypothesis, at least a simple version of it, will prove correct. One reason is that our subjects often combined strategies to reach a goal. For example, a student might elaborate in order to find the kind of connections between propositions necessary for structuring. Such combinations of strategies prove to be quite powerful for many students. But the value of the process depends on the current goal.

We also found that a large number of our subjects were what Wayne Peck (see Chapter 6) calls "intenders." These are students who believe they are writing one kind of paper (e.g., a Synthesis), yet produce a paper rated to be something else (e.g., a Summary). In this context it is important to note that twenty-eight of our thirty-six papers were rated as some form of summary, yet it is clear from the protocols that many students thought they were doing something else. That these students produced papers that went contrary to their intentions may be attributable to a number of factors: They may not have had sufficient command of particular strategies whose use, in different ways, may have been important to both kinds of papers. They may not have had sufficient knowledge of strategies to produce a certain kind of paper. Or, as discussed before, they may have had trouble and switched tasks without necessarily realizing that they were doing so. The frequency hypothesis, which assumes that we can predict process based on the final product, fails to account for the shifting goals and strategies we saw in these intenders.

It also became apparent that the frequency with which a student used a particular strategy was related to the ease with which students were able to do the task. If a student had relatively little trouble deciding what kind of paper to write, managing the reading, and doing the writing, he probably used these problem-solving strategies less often than his peer who had a lot of trouble with this task and had to marshall more cognitive resources to help her solve problems. Quite often a student having difficulty with the task, as shown earlier, may change task representations or reading strategies. But such changes would not necessarily be reflected in a statistical analysis.

Taken together, the quantitative and qualitative analyses provide converging evidence that the number of times a student applies a strategy may be less important than the context in which she applies it. Students must use strategies for monitoring, elaborating, structuring, and planning throughout the reading-to-write process; but how, when, and where they apply those strategies depends on the way in which they define the task and how reading and writing goals impinge on each other. While neither the qualitative nor quantitative analysis alone should be read as definitive, together they allow us to build a better data-based hypothesis about the way these students used these kinds of strategies to work through four important junctures in this task.

This perspective underscores the need for development of metacognitive awareness in the performance of reading-to-write tasks. Students need not only strategies for reaching goals, but also knowledge of the relationship between goals and strategies. Such knowledge enables them to look more critically at their armories of strategies, to engage in the kind of problem solving that will enable them to use the right strategy at the right time. This in turn may greatly facilitate the process of reading-to-write.

Appendix X: Summary Statistics*

	PT	G	Q	TOTEPIS	ELAB	WP	STR	MC
Number of cases	36	36	36	36	36	36	36	36
Minimum	0.000	0.000	1.000	16.000	2.000	0.000	0.000	0.000
Maximum	7.000	1.000	3.000	130.000	43.000	36.000	19.000	13.000
Mean	2.472	0.556	1.875	54.167	18.611	8.417	4.611	2.833
Standard deviation	1.682	0.504	0.637	25.295	9.601	8.069	4.871	3.203

Note: Total observations = 36

*Summary statistics show means and standard deviations. The three dependent variables are as follows:
   Paper type (PT)
   Group (G)
   Quality (Q)
The five independent variables are as follows:
   Total number of episodes in the protocol (TOTEPSIS)
   Number of episodes in which student elaborated (ELAB)
   Number of episodes in which student made writing plans (WP)
   Number of episodes in which student structured ideas (STR)
   Number of episodes in which students both elaborated and monitored comprehension (MC). Episodes in which students only monitored comprehension were not included in the analysis.

Appendix XI: Pearson Correlation Matrix*

	PT	G	Q	TOTEPIS	ELAB	WP	STR	MC
PT	1.000							
G	−0.015	1.000						
Q	0.244	−0.178	1.000					
TOTEPIS	0.033	0.080	0.126	1.000				
ELAB	0.141	−0.131	0.071	0.616	1.000			
WP	−0.089	0.230	0.033	0.497	0.068	1.000		
STR	−0.096	0.3000	0.071	0.595	0.059	0.638	1.000	
MC	0.169	−0.419	0.396	0.166	0.042	−0.026	−0.153	1.000

*Pearson correlation matrix shows no significant correlations. (See Appendix X for complete variable names.)

Appendix XII: Multiple Regression Results*

| | Analysis of Variance | | | | |
Source	Sum of Squares	DF	Mean Square	F-Ratio	P
Regression	5.534	4	1.384	0.459	0.765
Residual	93.438	31	3.014		

Dep var: PT; *N*: 36; Multiple R: .236; Squared multiple R: .056; Adjusted squared multiple R: .000; Standard error of estimate: 1.736.

*Multiple regression results using paper type as the dependent variable, elaboration, writing plans, structuring, and monitoring comprehension/elaboration episode counts as independent variables.

Appendix XIII: Multiple Regression Results*

| | Analysis of Variance | | | | |
Source	Sum of Squares	DF	Mean Square	F-Ratio	P
Regression	2.552	4	0.638	1.700	0.175
Residual	11.635	31	0.375		

Dep var: Q; *N*: 36; Multiple R: .424; Squared multiple R: .180; Adjusted squared multiple R: .074; Standard error of estimate: 0.613

*Multiple regression results using quality as the dependent variable, elaboration, writing plans, structuring, and monitoring comprehension/elaboration episode counts as independent variables.

5

Elaboration:
Using What You Know

VICTORIA STEIN

In the previous chapter, we explored the broad landscape of the cognition of reading-to-write, focusing on four cognitive processes: monitoring, elaboration, structuring, and planning. This chapter provides a more in-depth look at one of these processes—elaboration, the process by which students bring their own knowledge into the task. Students and teachers alike place a high value on "using what you know." Students see it as an expert move (see Chapter 3). Traditionally, teachers have often taught students to write what they know about. As is evident from Figure 15 in the previous chapter, it is the process the students in our study used most often, regardless of the kind of paper they wrote. In this chapter, we look at the many and varied uses of prior knowledge in reading to write, and the effect that importation of this kind of knowledge has on performance of the task.

In discussing invention and discovery, Booth and Gregory (1987) wrote of the primacy of memory in the writing process: "Our memory is . . . stocked with ideas, feelings and experiences. . . . On any given writing occasion only a few of these memories will be useful, but every piece of writing can be filled out or deepened to some extent by memories. . . . Most often, perhaps, we use memory simply to provide vivid details or images in support of points found in other topics. But often enough memory can provide just what we need—if only we can learn how to tap it."

This quotation highlights an important assumption that underlies both current reading and writing theory: that people, whether engaged in reading or writing activity, use what they already know of the world to help make meaning. Reading theorists of diverse perspectives, such as Just and Carpenter (1986), Bransford (1979), Kintsch and van Dijk (1978), and Schank and Abelson (1977), have noted that comprehension beyond the decoding level cannot occur unless the reader has some form of prior knowledge he can map the new information onto. Similarly, writing theorists representing different schools of thought, such as Langer (1984), Flower and Hayes (1980), Bartholomae (1985), and Elbow (1981), have advocated tapping memory as a fundamental means of invention and of critical thinking. Whether you call it world knowledge, general knowledge (Schank & Abelson, 1977), episodic knowledge (Tulving, 1972), personal experience, or simply "using what you know," one thing is clear: our understanding of the world affects the way we take in information about it and the way we communicate what we know.

One of the most commonly acknowledged ways that people tap memory is through elaboration, generally defined as the importation of prior knowledge during information processing. For example, a reader may draw an analogy between the actions of a character in a book to someone she knows in real life, thus validating the character's behavior. Similarly, a writer may search memory for relevant examples to include in an argument as a means of gaining agreement from his intended audience. Elaboration's usefulness as an aid to comprehension and retention is well established (see Reder, 1980). More recent theory on elaboration suggests that it enables deeper levels of processing and encourages critical thinking.

But Booth's remark also throws into high relief a dilemma that has long held researchers and teachers in sway: it is not enough to recognize that readers and writers have information stored in memory that can be of use. Reading and writing are, after all, goal-directed processes whose direction and shape change with task demands. We must also therefore understand how a reader or writer gets to appropriate and useful information, and once there, how he can make use of it most advantageously. Moreover, some tasks, including that most common of academic tasks, the reading-to-write task, necessitate the interweaving of reading and writing goals. This leads to more questions. How do people use prior knowledge in such tasks? Do the elaborations students make while reading have an impact on what they will write later on? And do writing goals change the way students read source texts, thus affecting how they elaborate while reading?

The purpose of the study described in this chapter was to explore the role of elaboration in reading-to-write tasks. It seeks to answer three questions:

- How do students use elaboration in this process?
- How much value does elaborative material add to source text material?
- How does material generated through elaboration during reading affect the essays students write?

To answer these questions, we looked more closely at the protocols made by the seventeen freshmen described in Chapter 4. One of the most interesting, and readily apparent, features of all of the protocols we analyzed was that all of our subjects elaborated abundantly as they read. Their elaborations contained a wealth of material that was not found in the source text: examples and counterexamples, instantiations, evaluations, criticisms, embellishments of old ideas, and wholly new ideas. Moreover, these elaborations did more than support basic comprehension. They allowed students to select or discard source text ideas, forge connections between previously disparate concepts, and create hierarchies of importance. Surprisingly, however, while elaborative material in the form of ideas and examples rarely transferred directly into the students' own texts, elaboration had important indirect influence, shaping the content and structure of the essays in a number of ways.

The Role of Elaboration in Reading-to-Write

To understand elaboration's role in the process of reading-to-write, it is necessary to explore the ways in which the reading and writing processes themselves can intersect. Current research sees both processes as constructive, in which readers and writers build "mental representations" of text. This involves selecting, connecting, and organizing ideas in such a way as to create a coherent, structured body of knowledge. This view is the basis for the constructive model of reading (see Spivey, 1987), which defines comprehension as an interactive process in which readers use both cues from a source text and prior knowledge to create meaning. That is to say, as readers compare information they are reading to what they already know about the topic as part of the comprehension process, they are selecting, connecting, and organizing information from both sources to create a new representation of meaning. This new representation may differ in content and structure from the source text because it contains additional information from memory that may have been organized differently.

Elaboration is the principle means by which information from memory is combined with source text material in the reading process. Reder (1980) defines elaboration as "extra processing that results in additional, related or redundant propositions," that is, the importation of information not found in the source text to the reading process. Such information serves several purposes: it aids in comprehension by creating context (see Reder, 1980; Whitney 1987); it provides redundancy for recall (Reder, 1980); and it provides salient exemplars of ideas found in the source text. However, elaborations have been seen as idiosyncratic, with the ability to lead the reader away from the "correct" meaning of the text (Reder, 1980). In this view, elaboration is seen as a secondary, supportive addition to the reading process (Reder, 1980).

More recent research, however, such as that of Hamilton (1987), Whitney (1987), and Weinstein, Underwood, Wicker, and Cubberly (1979), finds that purposeful instruction in the process of elaboration not only aids in comprehension and recall, but also facilitates depth of processing and encourages critical thinking. Whitney notes that when readers have a lot of topic-related prior knowledge, the comprehension process involves simply adding new information to already established schemata. However, when readers have no such knowledge to call on, comprehension becomes the process of *constructing* schemata. Elaboration, with its ability to provide context that includes information about objects and concepts and their relations, can greatly facilitate this process. Weinstein et al. note that as expert readers apply schematic knowledge, it is likely not only to contain information about structure and relations, but also provide expectations that, when violated, prompt the reader to process more. Thus elaboration does more than simply provide a basis for comprehension or strengthen recall. It enables readers to forge new connections, and encourages them to examine texts more critically when expectations are not met and to find new paths to understanding.

Much of the research done on elaboration and the writing process has focused on the role of elaborations in written products. For example, the amount of elaboration included in a text is often seen as an indication of writing ability (Benton, Glover, & Plake, 1984). Reder, Charney, and Morgan (1986) have found that writer-generated elaborations, in the form of examples placed in instructional texts, in some instances are not as helpful as reader-generated elaborations, such as analogies to personal experience that is more relevant. Thus, writers need to be careful about what kinds of elaborations they include.

It is important, however, to consider the impact of elaboration (as the importation of prior knowledge) on the writing process as well as on its products. Like reading, writing involves the generation of representations of meaning. Flower and Hayes (1984), in their multiple representation hypothesis, claim that writers generate a number of representations that may grow in purpose, fullness, and coherenc *:* as ideas develop. Again, the creation of such representations involves the selection, organization, and connection of ideas. But the writing process requires a student to translate that private meaning into public utterance. That is to say, the text she produces must not only reflect her understanding of the topic and the world, it must also be shaped so that the reader can draw on shared knowledge to get the author's point as she intends it. These two goals—to say what is meant and to make that meaning accessible—and the processes that support them—invention and audience adaptation—shape the representation of meaning as surely as schemas affect the creation of meaning during reading. As the writer invents meaning, he draws on his experience of the world to indicate what he believes to be most important to write about. As he adapts his prose for an audience, he draws on stores of shared knowledge and experience (e.g., knowledge of text structure conventions, of specific people in his audience, of experience with the world, of rhetorical commonplaces, and so on) to build a representation of meaning that guides the reader toward his intention. In this way, knowledge and goals interact to create meaning.

In the context of reading-to-write tasks, the role of elaboration in these processes merits attention because of the way elaborations made during reading shape text. As the student elaborates during the reading process, she is creating a pool of ideas from which to draw during the writing process. This pool is, to a large degree, custom built by the student, who selects ideas from the source text and from memory and arranges them on the basis of what makes sense to her. To some extent, then, the selection, organization, and connection of ideas that occurs during the reading phase may become the blueprint for what the student will write. The elaborative strategies a student uses while reading, as we shall see, may even become the basis of plans during writing. Similarly, comparison of source text ideas to prior knowledge during reading becomes the basis for invention during writing.

Thus, elaboration can provide many opportunities for inventive or critical thinking through the reading-to-write process. As this study shows, students take advantage of a good number of these opportunities during the reading and planning stages of the task.

The Protocol Study

The protocols analyzed in this study were those generated by the seventeen freshman subjects who thought aloud as they performed the Time Management task, as described in Chapter 1. One reason the topic of time management was chosen was because most students have had some personal experience with it. It is a topic freshmen often elect to write about in college composition courses, as they adapt to bigger course loads, more homework, and the temptations of life away from home. Also, many freshman orientation materials and programs center on the need for adequate time management skills in college.

The text these students were given was designed to mimic the kind of research notes they themselves might have generated had we assigned them the task of doing research on time management. Nelson and Hayes (1988) have found that, in doing research papers, many students simply more or less randomly pull appropriate books off the shelves, copy out the minimum amount of relevant material onto note cards, and then later copy their notes into their papers. The text on time management emulates such note cards. The six experts on time management whose opinions were cited represented diverse approaches to the topic: one was a psychologist; another was writing a "guide to the intellectual life"; one looked at time management from an adult business perspective; another looked at time management in academic settings. A survey of students citing their own time management methods was also included. The text included a separate paragraph for each author, which contained several main ideas without embellishment. Paragraphs were separated from each other by rows of asterisks. No effort was made to form coherent or cohesive ties from one paragraph to another.

The students were told to read the text and then write about it. As explained in Chapter 1, the exact specifications for their essay were left ambiguous because we were interested in seeing how students represent such tasks to themselves. Instructions included prompts to "synthesize and interpret all relevant findings," "make a statement," and "be comprehensive," concluding with an open-ended statement that "we are interested in your ideas."

Our students made an average of sixteen elaborations per protocol. Analysis of the elaborations indicated that they served three distinct purposes:

- To generate new ideas
- To develop critical perspectives
- To further develop ideas already found in the source text

A look at some of the elaborations our subjects made affords some perspective on these functions:

GENERATION OF NEW IDEAS

One of the most obvious functions of elaboration is the generation of various kinds of additional material, that is, information not found in the source text. Much of that material is at the level of detail, for example, an adjective. The goal of this analysis, however, was to capture those elaborations that represent a significant departure from those ideas in the source text and bring new top-level concepts into considera- Therefore, our coding for this category included only those episodes in which new ideas provided an organizational frame or superordinate concept that linked together ideas found in the source text.

Alice used elaborations in this way. She reads a passage that claims "will power alone can't induce concentration" and "motivation alone will [not] help students who don't know how to study and don't create a quiet distraction-free environment and don't schedule their time carefully." The author goes on to suggest that students who "schedule as much study time as possible into their days are likely to be better students." Alice responds as follows:

> Well I also think you need to do other things besides just work or you'll get kind of stale, but we'll get some of his ideas down . . . [writes] **Will power is not responsible for concentration . . . distractions disturb your concentration** . . . and you want to inundate **yourself with study time** and that will give you quality work. . . . But I think that sometimes you work better when you're under pressure and have very little time . . . but to each his own. . . .

The casual remark "to each his own" eventually becomes the organizing frame for Alice's essay, which begins "Time management takes a different course for various people" and goes on to discuss the importance of finding the mode of time management that is "right for you."

CRITICAL PERSPECTIVE

In our study, students used elaboration as a means of developing critical perspective more often than any other function. The term "critical perspective" is used here to indicate modes of evaluation. For example, development of critical perspective may come in the form of agreement or disagreement or qualification of an idea, or it may involve an effort to assess the validity or practical application of an idea in the real world. It may also include relevance judgments or an attempt to characterize an idea as conditional. Generally, efforts to apply prior knowledge in this way were signaled by certain kinds of language, such as "if, when, maybe/maybe not, I agree, that's garbage" and so on.

James's protocol provides some good instances of this. For example, while reading one author's advice to "find a place that is at once calm and stimulating" and "tolerate nothing that is not useful or beautiful," he muses:

> I think the problem is finding that type of place. It's very difficult. There's . . . if you study in your room it can be calm and stimulating, but you often find other things to

do. The library can be calm and stimulating, but it can be too boring and you don't feel right because there's too many other people studying around you. . . . Why do you have to have beautiful things to work with? I mean, just because I have a picture from a newspaper that happens to be a Picasso, does that mean that it helps me work? I don't stare at it. I stare at my grades, which are very bad. That's not beautiful. . . .

Here James, by generating instantiations based on what he knows about work environments, is able to test the assertions of the author. This testing procedure will, in the long run, influence not only the way he perceives this author's ideas, which he finds debatable, but also the way he treats these ideas in his own essay, in which he deals generally with the notion of developing a comfortable working environment, but does not mention this author's ideas at all.

DEVELOPMENT

Our students also frequently used elaboration as a means for developing ideas already found in the source text. In other words, they used prior knowledge as a source of examples, counterexamples, metaphors, analogies, and low-level connectives that provided context or support for things our experts said about time management. For example, almost all of our subjects, reading the passage that "advocated continued concentration in the face of apparent mental fatigue," which may "get worse up to a certain critical point" but then passes away when "we have tapped a new level of energy" said that this idea reminded them of the concept of "second wind" in sports, an analogy that in some cases made its way into final essays.

More often than not, however, students used elaborations to provide critical perspective and development of ideas in tandem. That is to say, a student might indicate agreement with a source text idea and then provide an example from memory as a means of validating the statement. Or, alternatively, she might provide a counterexample to think through why she disagreed with an idea. For example, Eddie, reading that some students "read material once [and] don't try to remember it until it's needed" says:

That depends a lot on what class or what material you're talking about. . . . It depends on which class you're talking about because something like physics, I can read the material once and then be refreshed constantly in recitation or lecture . . . however, if I'm reading for a quiz, or you know, something where I obviously need to know it and I'm not going to be able to check on it later, I'm going to have to memorize it right away . . . or, as in Economics, where the teacher is so bad that I had to do it on my own. . . .

Here Eddie creates critical perspective by conditionalizing an idea and develops his own perspective by providing different examples of when this idea may or may not work in a real-world situation. Later, both the notion that the usefulness of this idea "depends" on the circumstance and the actual instances generated by Eddie as he read find their way into his final essay.

Three raters looked at the elaborations generated by these students to see if, indeed, they allowed students to create new ideas, critical perspective, and idea development. They found that 83 percent of these elaborations functioned as a means of developing critical perspective, 29 percent functioned as a means of idea development, and 5 percent provided new ideas.*

Clearly the elaborations were affording students the opportunity for deeper processing, but how good were the opportunities? In other words, how good were the new ideas, how useful was the critical perspective for analytical thinking, and how much support did the additional development of ideas provide? To assess this, raters were asked to perform a quality rating for each elaboration to see how much value the new ideas, critical perspectives, and idea development actually contributed to the ideas in the source text. This was called a "value-added" rating, defined as "the extent to which the content of an elaboration enhanced the content of a source text proposition by adding valuable new material." Raters were given a four-point scale (0 = no value; 1 = some value; 2 = more value; 3 = great value).

The raters felt that the vast majority of these elaborations added value to the propositions in the source text. Fifty percent were rated as adding "some value." As an example of "some value," consider Michelle. She reads that "students may be breaking concentration whenever they remind themselves that they must use will power" and says:

> That makes sense. . . . If you think about it, then you're not gonna be able to do it. . . . It's just like thinking that you shouldn't . . . if you try not to think about anything, you're always thinking about something. . . .

This example was rated as having "some value" as further development of a point in the source text.

Twenty-seven percent were rated as adding "more value" to the source text. For example, Fred reads William James's assertion that pushing on in the face of fatigue leads one to a new level of energy and says:

> I don't know about this. I can relate to using your mental energy and when you're very fatigued and getting worse and worse, then after a point it does seem to get better. But I don't believe it's that you've suddenly found this new energy. I believe you've gotten to a point where you no longer can be concerned with your fatigue. It just doesn't bother you anymore. . . .

The raters deemed this as adding "more value" as critical perspective on the original source text idea. The elaboration conditionalizes the idea in such a way as to lead Fred to reject the author's notion out of hand and to generate his own account of the phenomenon.

Finally, 3 percent of the elaborations were rated as adding "great value." Eddie's previous consideration of the advice about "reading material only once" is an example of an elaboration rated as having "great value" as critical perspective.

Only 17 percent of the elaborations were rated as adding no value at all to source

---

*Because raters were permitted to code an elaboration as serving more than one function (e.g., critical perspective *and* development), totals equal more than 100 percent. Reliability for these figures was as follows: for new ideas, .76; for critical perspective, .78; for development, .81. All reliability scores computed using the Cronbach's alpha test for reliability among three raters.

text ideas. Thus, more than 80 percent of all elaborations were thought to enhance the meaning of source text ideas by providing valuable new ideas, critical perspective, or idea development.*

Having established the function and quality of these elaborations, it remained to determine how much of this valuable and useful information found its way into the students' final texts. The same raters were asked to evaluate how much of the elaborative material generated while reading made it into the final texts written by our participants. Another four-point scale was used. This time, 0 = no transfer, 1 = some transfer, 2 = rich transfer, and 3 = very rich transfer. This scale had two uses. One was to determine whether or not this material was transferred at all. The other was to determine how high in the structure of these texts the ideas were placed if they were transferred. Consequently, "some transfer" was defined as meaning that the information in an elaboration had only the merest mention in the final text. "Very rich transfer" meant that an idea from an elaboration assumed a major position in a student's final text. "Rich transfer" fell somewhere in between.

Results of this rating show that 78 percent of all elaborative propositions were not transferred to final texts. Of the material that was rated as having transferred, 12 percent was deemed as having only "some transfer," 7 percent as having "rich transfer," and 2 percent as having "very rich transfer."† In other words, while 80 percent of all elaborations made by our participants were rated as having at least "some value" as a new idea, a means of evaluation, or support for ideas already in the source text, only 21 percent showed up in recognizable form in the students' own texts, and most of that was at a low level in the structure of those texts. In interpreting this observation, we might ask if any transfer was needed, and the evidence of the papers suggests it certainly was (see Chapter 2). The essays were simple, underdeveloped in the way freshman essays often are, and they violated our strong expectations as academic readers and our request for more analytic thinking in the task instructions. While it may be reasonable to expect that not all elaborative material is worthy of direct transfer, the results of the ratings indicate that more direct transfer could have enhanced these essays.

The fact that so little of this information directly transferred does not, however, mean that the elaborations had no effect on the students' essays.‡ On the contrary,

---

*Reliability for this aspect of the rating was .59 using Cronbach's alpha. It should be noted, however, that 67 percent of the disagreements found two raters in agreement and one in disagreement, and in these cases, 72 percent of the time the disagreement was over the difference between "some value" and "more value." That is to say, raters were not disagreeing about whether an elaboration had value or not; they were simply disagreeing about how much value it had.

†Reliability for this rating (again using Cronbach's alpha) was .81.

‡The fact that so little material transferred made further quantitative analysis difficult. I wanted to see, for example, if the function of an elaboration (e.g., critical perspective) or the amount of value it added contributed to the overall quality of an essay or its length (since the amount of elaboration in an essay is often considered to be an indication of writing ability). However, the small amount of transfer made it difficult to establish with any degree of certainty whether or not such relations exist. Therefore, neither a correlational study, designed to connect functions and value of elaborations to quality of text, or a regression study, designed to see if function or value of elaboration could predict quality or length of essay, yielded significant results. This is not to say that such relations may not exist. Training students to use elaborations more effectively may be necessary to create a level of transfer sufficient to support this kind of analysis.

evidence suggests that the elaborations had a clear, albeit tacit, effect on these papers, which we called "indirect transfer." That is to say, elaborations made during reading shaped the way students dealt with source text ideas in their papers.

For example, as we have seen before, elaborations often serve as a means of selecting ideas, which means eliminating some along the way. Also, strong statements of preference for one source text idea over another affected how students created hierarchies of importance in their papers. Finally, we saw that in some instances, elaborative reading strategies eventually became the basis of writing plans along the way.

Suzie's protocol provides an example of the way elaborative reading strategies can metamorphose into writing plans. As she read the source text for the first time, Suzie's main strategy seemed to involve deciding whether she agreed or disagreed with source text ideas. As she rereads the source text, she decides to "put a star next to" all the ideas she agrees with and also decides to write down "the things I agree with—that I can comment on because I agree with. . . ." She decides that she will "put in two different parts in my paper—the things that I agree with and the things I don't agree with. . . ." Her elaborative strategy reinforced as a plan, she starts applying her own knowledge freely, moving from simple statements of agreement to generation of ideas and examples. When she rereads the passage urging "continued concentration in the face of fatigue," with its "second wind" idea, she notes:

> OK, I studied that last year in my movement class, where you would work so hard you would be doing tumbles and rolls and handstands and you'd get tired and you'd keep working through your tiredness even though you felt like you were about to die. And you kept working and working and working and all of a sudden you would find a new level of energy. That's true, so I'm going to make that comparison in my paper to my movement class to that exercise. . . .

Throughout the rest of her reading, she elaborates like this, providing extended examples and counterexamples, always noting what she will use and what she won't use. When she has finished her second reading she says:

> I think I have pretty much all I need to start writing the paper. I have all my notes. I have everything in order. I know what I want to say. I want to compare what I know to what they know, and tell my own opinions on what they said. So I think I'm ready to write the paper now. . . .

In Suzie's case, a simple elaborative strategy for providing critical perspective (i.e., noting whether or not she agreed with a source text idea) developed into a writing plan—to write about those sources of agreement—which in turn triggered more complex elaborative strategies that she could use in a goal-directed way. In other words, an elaborative strategy became a writing plan, providing a goal structure that influenced the way she read thereafter.

Conclusion

This study is basically the story of opportunity gained and opportunity lost. We see that students, without prompting and training, freely and routinely apply what they already know to what they are reading and writing about and, in doing so, generate a wealth of material that in and of itself may have considerable value. Further, we see that the process of elaboration itself has enormous potential to transform, potential that may too often be overlooked by students.

For example, we see that elaboration can lead to invention. The prior knowledge students import contains not only topic knowledge, but experiences, preferences, and beliefs. This knowledge not only gives them new ideas that help explain source text propositions, it also helps them discover what it is they think is most important about these propositions, which in turn leads to discovery of what they have to say on the topic as a whole.

Similarly, elaboration may promote critical thinking. Students use prior knowledge as a basis for comparison, a means of testing the validity of source text ideas. Such activity leads students to do more than simply accept what they read at face value. It provides them with a means to explore the implications of ideas, to find their strengths and weaknesses, to evaluate their usefulness in real-world situations. It enables them to draw inferences and analogies, to see ideas from a variety of perspectives, which may well influence the perspective they choose when they write.

Finally, we see elaboration's crucial influence on the process of representation building. The representation students build of the source text while reading contains propositions not only from that text, but also from memory. Some of this information may be "shared" in the sense that it is derived from a common base of gists from the source text and common experiences in the world at large (e.g., the "second wind" metaphor). Even so, the representation itself is highly individualized, containing each student's unique ideas, perspectives, beliefs, values, personality traits, interests, and style. Eventually, this representation becomes, to one extent or another, the basis for the student's own text. As students plan their own texts, making decisions about what it is they want to say, they will be selecting material from a personalized pool of ideas, one that does not contain all ideas from the source text and does contain specialized, already developed approaches to evaluating ideas.

Thus, we see evidence of elaboration's potential to shape the thinking processes that support the process of reading-to-write. Unfortunately, in the protocols we saw, relatively little of that potential was exploited. Most of our participants wrote papers that were essentially summaries with response; they did little more than restate a source text idea and give their own response to it. As the transfer rating shows, such responses, when they did transfer, were likely to be low-level, localized responses. Yet these papers do not reveal the depth of processing that elaboration led these students to engage in. As the protocols show, a good deal more thinking went on than is evidenced in these final products. But these students seemed unaware not only of the value of the material they generated through elaboration, but also of the value of the process of elaboration itself. Often we saw students taking tentative steps down the road to critical thinking or invention only to hesitate, turn back, or move on to the next paragraph. In some cases, it appeared that students simply devalued their own ideas. More often than not, however, it seemed that elaborative processing occurred without students' understanding or awareness of its effect on processing. As stated earlier, our students elaborated freely and spontaneously, but often automatically, without conscious control of the process. This should not be surprising, because they have probably never been taught to be aware of this process.

The results of this study suggest that teaching students to be aware of the outcomes of elaborative processing might be of value. We think there is real promise in sharing the results of studies like this directly with our students, to help them develop some metacognitive awareness of the functions of elaboration, the value of elaborative material they generate, and the impact of elaboration, directly and indirectly on the papers they write. This kind of awareness may teach students, first of all, to value their own ideas and experiences more and to bring themselves and their own beliefs into the domain of academic tasks. It may also help them to think more critically and inventively, to explore ideas and their ramifications, and to move beyond summarizing to more analytic kinds of writing. Finally, metacognitive control of the process of elaboration will help students manage the process of reading-to-write better, since elaboration plays such an important role in this kind of task. Students must be encouraged to use what they already know purposefully and wisely in reading-to-write tasks if they are to succeed in them. Perhaps Suzie said it best when she got her first glimmer of metacognitive awareness:

> You know what I just thought of . . . it seems that I'm making comparisons from my own knowledge to the knowledge that I'm reading—the knowledge of these people— the knowledge of Alan Lakein, William James, Walter Pauk. . . . I'm using my own knowledge in comparison to theirs and using things that happened to me to try to understand what they're saying and it's working. . . . I just realized this and that's kind of cool. . . .

6

The Effects of Prompts on Revision: A Glimpse of the Gap Between Planning and Performance

WAYNE C. PECK

One way of viewing the findings of this study is to picture yourself as a teacher confronted with seventy-two revisions of a previous writing assignment. How does one begin? What assumptions do we, as teachers, bring to a revision assignment? Do our assumptions match those of our students? This study addresses these questions and makes two observations regarding how students in college revised a written assignment. First, the writers we observed demonstrated different levels of "metacognitive" awareness and control (Brown, 1985) over the revision process. At one end of the spectrum, we observed writers spending considerable time in their think-aloud protocols actively building elaborate networks of plans and goals and tests, which they monitored as they produced their final drafts. At the other end of the spectrum, we saw writers who showed little, if any, awareness of multiple goals and options for the assignment. Instead, they immediately set to work applying a far more limited set of revising strategies, focusing almost exclusively on sentence-level changes. Second, after comparing the think-aloud protocols and the finished texts, we observed, in some of our writers, a gap between their planning process and their writing performance. Some of the writers explicitly "intended" in their protocols to transform their knowledge in significant ways, but for a number of reasons were unable in their final drafts to carry out their plans or have them acknowledged by the judges.

Procedure

The study to this point has shown meaningful differences in how students represented a common task to themselves. The various ways students represented the

156

task raised an important set of questions. Could students make significant changes in their writing, if they were prompted (1) to examine their task representation and (2) to attempt the demanding task of transforming their prose into an interpretive essay with a clear purpose? Moreover, how do students respond to alternative representations and to prompts to change their writing plans? Given the assignment, did the students perceive the prompt to be a real alternative? The revision assignment offered the opportunity to see how students used the different prompts to revise and helped assure us that simply revising, regardless of the prompt, was not responsible for the changes the student writers made.

The sixty-nine students were randomly divided within classes into Experimental and Control groups with thirty-six students in the Experimental condition and thirty-three students in the Control condition. The students in the Experimental group were presented with a forty-minute lecture on task representation, asked to complete the S-AC procedure, and then given the assignment "to revise their original essay, turning it into an interpretive essay that fulfilled a specific purpose." The students in the Control group did not attend the lecture and were simply asked to revise their essays making them "better." When the revisions were collected, fifty-seven students of the original sixty-nine students completed the revision assignment (thirty-one students from the Experimental group and twenty-six students from the Control group).

As discussed in Chapter 1, the prompt embedded in the original time management task was intended to be an open-ended invitation for students to think and to write an interpretive essay about time management. In the second phase of the writing assignment, we wanted the students to revise their papers to make sure they were "interpretive" essays. The experimental prompt was broad ranging in that its purpose was to make students aware of their options for transforming their knowledge. In the lecture the students in the Experimental group were presented with the various ways their fellow students had represented and completed the original assignment. By means of the S-AC procedure, students assessed the strategies they had used as they wrote about time management. Our aim in presenting such a broad-ranging and open-ended prompt as the "interpret" prompt was exploratory. Our main goal was not to design a prompt that was unambiguous and thus ideal for purposes of assessment (Ruth & Murphy, 1984). Our purpose instead was to spark students' thinking processes so we could observe the various ways students represented the writing assignment. We were interested in investigating the students' ability and willingness to change their prior representation of the task by restructuring their knowledge. We wanted to know if a prompt to revise a draft into an interpretive essay would lead more writers to transform their knowledge by changing their organizational plan than merely asking them to make it better.

Key Observations

OBSERVATION 1: NEGOTIATION VERSUS STANDARD STRATEGIES

As we began to examine the protocols of the students revising their time management essays, we discovered that writers were revising their papers in different ways depending on how they represented the task of revision to themselves. One group of writers, whom we ultimately called the Negotiators (Table 4), demonstrated by their comments a conscious awareness of alternative ways of accomplishing the assignment. This group of writers pursued a variety of tasks, such as reading and rereading both the instructions for the task and their original essays, considering what the assignment asked them to do, and creating plans, goals, and tests for their revisions. As we shall see, these writers demonstrated an awareness of a range of options for completing the assignment and indicated by the strategies and goals they selected varying degrees of metacognitive control over their thought processes.

A second group of writers, whom we called the Rereaders, approached the same task in a distinctly different way. Like the writers Bridwell (1980) observed, who failed to pause before they revised, the Rereaders in our study did not spend their time planning or considering their options. Instead, they read the instructions for their task and immediately set to work applying a rather uniform set of sentence-level revision strategies. These students reread their essays, working on sentence-level problems, primarily spending their time correcting their syntax and concentrating on making their essays "sound better." As we shall see, the comments of this group of writers revealed few, if any, signs of a metacognitive awareness and, likewise, paid little attention to the instructions of the particular assignment. For these students, revision is a familiar task. One student remarked in his protocol, "all revisions are alike . . . you clean up what you messed up."

Unlike the Negotiators, who consciously constructed a task representation for their revision assignment, the Rereaders came to the assignment with a set of local revision strategies, which they simply applied to the task at hand. The differences between these groups of writers led us to further examine the various ways in which students carried out their revisions.

OBSERVATION 2: A GAP BETWEEN PLANNING AND PERFORMANCE

Our second observation is best expressed in the form of a question: Do the revised essays we receive, as teachers, ever fully reflect the wealth of critical thinking that went into creating them? We found writers in our study who could not translate their sophisticated planning into equally sophisticated written texts. A gap existed between these writers' planning process and their writing performance. We identified as Intenders a group of thirty-five students in the original Negotiators group. These writers appeared to be asking the same kinds of questions and making similar strategic moves in their planning as students who were successful in transforming their knowledge for a specific purpose; but unlike their counterparts, they were unable to translate their plans and intentions into finished products valued by the

Table 4. Distribution of Revisers: Negotiators versus Rereaders ($n = 57$)

	Negotiators	Rereaders
Experimental	26	4
Control	16	11

judges. The Intenders were clearly trying to implement a rhetorical plan as they revised but, on the whole, were ineffective in communicating their intentions to their readers.

This gap between planning and performance led us to speculate that some writers are knowledgeable and in some sense skillful in planning a revision but, for a number of reasons, do not translate their complex planning processes into equally sophisticated revisions. We wanted to take a closer look at some of the reasons why the Intenders' plans either got lost in the writer's production of the text or failed to draw the reader into the writer's purpose for the discourse. To explore this gap between planning and performance, we first examine the texts produced by the students, noting the changes the students made in their organizing plans from the original draft to the revision, and then proceed to examine the protocol data, focusing on the students' writing processes.

The Effect of Prompts on Organizing Plans

The time management essays were read and evaluated by the judges and assigned to one of seven categories based on how the writers planned, organized, and wrote about the material (see Chapter 2).

0. Summarize
1. Review and Comment
2. Isolated Main Point and/or Conclusion
3. Frame
4. Free Response to the Topic
5. Synthesis
6. Interpretation for a Purpose

As stated earlier, we wanted to know if even a brief introduction to task representation and the prompt to revise a draft into an interpretation with a purpose would lead more students to change their organizing plan than merely asking them to revise their text and make it "better." The prompts themselves were presented in the lecture as a set or package of directions, options, and information that would be helpful to a writer in transforming information to accomplish a purpose. In the case of the students in the Experimental section, the students were instructed to reread their original essay and transform it into an "interpretive" essay that fulfilled a specific purpose. The students in the control group were simply asked "to revise their essay, making it better."

How did the prompts affect the revision processes of the students in our study? Did the "Interpret" and the "Better" prompts lead students to do different tasks? Did either prompt encourage students to restructure their initial paper?

Comparing the effects of the two prompts, we found the Interpret prompt only marginally more powerful than the Better prompt in encouraging writers to change their organizing plan to another plan. Roughly two-thirds (65 percent) of the writers in the Interpret condition (Table 5) changed their organizing plan, while a little more than one-half (53 percent) of the writers in the Better condition changed their

Table 5. Distribution of Revisions: Changes ($n = 57$)

Participants who changed their text plan	34
Experimental	20
Control	14
Participants who made substantial changes	23
Experimental	16
Control	6

organizing plan. Statistically, the difference between the power of the prompts was not significant. But, we asked, does this tell the whole story of the differences between the prompts? Measuring text change is a gross measure focusing on only visible changes in the text; as such, it did not fully account for a number of sensible reasons why people did not change their organizing plans. As we will see when we analyze the protocol data, a number of factors influenced both how the students carried out the task of revising their original essays and how the judges evaluated the students' final text products (see Chapter 3). While the different effect of the two prompts is not pronounced when only the text products are analyzed, powerful differences between the prompts emerge when the protocol data are taken into account.

SUBSTANTIAL CHANGES

While measuring the percentage of writers who changed their text plan is helpful in getting an overall sense of how willing or able the writers in our study were to restructure their ideas, such a measure is limited, if we want to know the various ways students responded to the prompts to revise. What does it take to encourage a student to consider a substantial reframing of the ideas of an original essay? A more precise way of examining the changes writers made in their organizing plans is to focus on the instances in which a writer decided to significantly restructure the original representation of information in the text. To distinguish substantial changes in text plans from less rigorous reworkings of the texts, we developed a set of distinctions that helped discriminate between significant and nonsignificant changes in organizing plans. We treated categories 0 through 3 as a single category. Our rationale for this decision was the observation that changes within these categories of text plans could be seen simply as variations on the theme of summarizing. Since changes within a summarizing scheme did not involve significant restructuring of the information of the essay, for instance, changing a text plan from a free response to an essay with a controlling concept involves the writer in transforming prior knowledge, we defined as "substantial" only those changes that involved significant changes in the text plan. For example, a change from a summary to a frame (0–3) was evaluated as "nonsubstantial" when compared with a change from a summary to a controlling concept (0–4).

Using this distinction between substantial and nonsubstantial changes in organizing plans to compare the writers who were assigned the Interpret prompt to those writers assigned the Better prompt, we found sixteen writers prompted with Interpret made substantial changes in their organizing plan while only six of those prompted with Better changed their plans in significant ways. The difference was found to be significant at a .02 level. Table 5 shows the number of students who, in the view of the judges, changed their essays and the number of students who were judged to have made substantial changes in their original draft.

Protocol Analysis

TASK REPRESENTATION

Text analysis provides a good "bottom line" for evaluating writing performance, but it sheds little light on how an individual writer approached the assignment and went about the process of deciding how to revise a draft. To gain access to this information, protocols were taken of the entire population of writers as they revised their original essay. As shown in Table 6, the ways writers approached and completed the revision task can be categorized in the following manner: intenders, transformers, low effort strategies, and rereaders. A kappa coefficient (Cohen, 1960) was used to assess interrater reliability of three judges evaluating twenty-five protocols. The kappa coefficient for this coding scheme was .93.

TRANSFORMERS

Dan's protocol is representative of a group of writers whom we called the Transformers. In the estimation of the judges, the Transformers were able to transform their original papers into essays with original purposes directed to specific audiences.

Dan (Experimental 5–6)

> interpret . . . let me check my notes . . . that means I'm going to have to change this stuff around. Originally, I read and looked for the main topic . . . my plan was a topical theme paper with a central idea, a topic sentence and an introductory paragraph. I didn't have an audience in mind because this was general information for everybody. In the revision I'm going to select information which supports my theory . . . also put in more opinions. I'll gear it to a certain kind of person. My purpose will be to argue with a bunch of freshmen.

Transformers were students who made plans to change their essays in significant ways above the sentence level. They read and reread the instructions for the task and

Table 6. Approaches to Task Representation

		$n = 57$	Percentage
Negotiators	Intenders	28	49.1
	Transformers	7	12.3
	Low effort	7	12.3
	Rereaders	15	26.3

thought about issues such as the intentions of their first draft, the audience they were addressing, what was going "right" and what was going "wrong" with their first attempt. Transformers acted on their plans by changing their essays and having them recognized by the judges as "interpretive" essays.

INTENDERS

Another group of writers whom we called the Intenders made plans similar to those made by the Transformers, but for a number of reasons their final products were not evaluated by the judges as "interpretive." For the Intenders, the prompts or written instructions that accompanied the task had a significant impact on the way these writers envisioned the task of revising their papers. The Intenders read, reread, and reflected on the instructions of their assignment. Certainly, not all the Intenders' plans were as lucid as the excerpt from Dan's protocol, but they did share these characteristics: they alluded to the intentions of their original draft, they mentioned and frequently changed the audience they were addressing, they evaluated to varying degrees what was going "right" and what was going "wrong" with their essay, and they made plans to change their essays. These writers demonstrated an awareness of options regarding possible organizing plans and created explicit plans for revision, which they monitored to differing extents throughout their protocol. But, in the eyes of the judges, they did not substantially revise their final text. Ed is an example of a writer who intended to change his essay but whose effort was not recognized as an interpretive essay by the judges.

Ed (Experimental 1–1)

> according to them I guess this (refers to his original paper) is a summary. I guess . . . I guess they want something different . . . something with my opinion in it (refers to assignment). They want me to have a purpose. I'll make it into an argument with my roommate . . . that will be my purpose. . . . I'll use the same material and make it into an argument I'm having.

Clearly, Ed intended to change his organizing plan from a summary to an argument with a purpose, but for reasons we will discuss later he was unable to communicate his intentions to his readers.

Since the Intenders group comprised 49 percent of those writers who completed the revision assignment, an obvious question is whether the Interpret and Better prompts had different effects on them. Assessing the impact of these two prompts on the Intenders group showed that eighteen of the writers who intended to change their essays were from this group.

REREADERS

While the prompts Better and Interpret had a significant impact on the revision process of the Intenders, the same prompts had only a marginal effect on the Rereaders. A group of fifteen writers in the study began their revision simply by reading the instructions for the task in a single pass, and then proceeded to work through the original essay on a local, sentence-by-sentence, problem-by-problem basis. Unlike the Intenders, the Rereaders tended to show little awareness of possible options for altering their text plan and did not pause to make any explicit plans or goals for their revision. An overriding concern for many of the Rereaders was the need to manage their time well. A good example of this group's perception of the revising task is summed up in the protocols of Bob (Control 2–2) and Jill (Control 4–4).

> this is just a revision . . . gotta get it done fast so I can study for the chemistry test
>
> revisions are just not that important . . . teachers make up their minds on the basis of the first draft anyways.

The majority of the Rereaders' revisions were finished when the last sentence was checked and edited by the writer. Only three writers paused long enough to reread their finished product. When the effect of the two prompts is examined, it was noted that eight of the fifteen Rereaders had been given the Better assignment.

THE LOW-EFFECT GROUP

A group of seven students read and frequently reread the instructions for the task, demonstrating an explicit awareness of possible options for restructuring their essays, yet chose instead low-effort strategies to revise their essays, concentrating on local revision. Indicative of this approach were the remarks of Rick (Experimental 2–2):

> the instructions are telling me to change my essay into an interpretive essay that fulfills a purpose . . . that's hard . . . that will be very hard to do. I'll need to shift the material. I need my lecture notes. . . . [rereads his lecture notes verbatim] I still don't know. I think I'll stick with what I got.

Writers in the low-effort group were cognizant of different alternatives to the original way they had dealt with the material but under the pressure of time or in the face of difficulty opted instead to carry out a simpler task.

DISCUSSION

Applebee (1984a) has noted, "Writing activities take their shape from the context in which they are embedded—we need studies which begin to explore the interactions between writing activities and the goals and classroom constraints." This study has attempted to examine the process of revision within the context of a reading-to-write college assignment. The findings of this study can help us describe some of the more problematic facets of the revision process, namely, some of the ways a reviser's cognition is shaped by the situation in which it occurs. We wanted to observe "cognition in context" in order to examine how writers represented the task of revision to themselves when given different prompts to revise. What we found challenged some of our assumptions about the revision process and how cognitive processes are mediated in the actual context of instruction in school.

Writers revise differently, in accordance with their goals, their knowledge, their detection strategies, and their overall writing competence. One tempting way to explain differences in revising behaviors is to assume that individual differences in the use of particular revision procedures is a function of an individual writer's skill in revising. For instance, mature writers are assumed to be more liable to revise globally, while developing writers are assumed to prefer simpler, more local strategies. We found something quite different. Just as Faigley and Witte (1981) identified the importance of "situational variables," such as, how good the text is to begin with, how much this writer knows about this topic or genre, or how high the standards for success, we also observed the importance of the writer's representation of the situation in which the particular revision was taking place. The assignment we gave our writers was certainly not the only one they were attempting to complete. From their comments, math tests, chemistry quizzes, and history papers were competing for our writers' time; this influenced the way they represented not only the importance of the task, but also how the task would be completed. Our findings encouraged us to find ways to explore and to begin to account for "situational" variables and their effect on the process of revision. In light of the situational variables and the variety of ways students approached the task of revising their essays, we began to view the revision process as a transaction between a writer's process and the situation in which the writing is being done. In fact, the protocols suggested that many students were negotiating their task, their text, and their situation as they planned and revised.

Negotiation Within an Instructional Setting

Revision begins, in an instructional setting, with the assumption that a student's writing needs to be changed, transformed, in some way, made "better." Revising a text is a collaborative act in that the writer and the instructor share a common goal of working to improve the student's writing. We found that the majority of our students (the Intenders and the low-effort writers) approached the task of revision as Negotiators, aware of the evaluative context of writing for instructors in school, and thus conscious of mediating their representation of the task and text with their perceptions of what the instructors wanted. Phrases in the protocols, such as "they want this" or "if they want a purpose . . . I'll change my first paragraph but I want to keep my second paragraph" were common among students negotiating in their minds what features of their essays they wanted to retain and what features they were willing to change. Moreover, many students frequently pointed out in their protocols the time constraints of writing within an academic environment and the need to manage their time effectively. More often than not, these writers solved their time problems by applying context-sensitive strategies for revisions. Al reported in his protocol,

> let's see I've got a history paper to write and this paper doesn't count as much so I am only going to go through and fix only the rough parts.

Other students, like Trent, showed an awareness of more complicated procedures for revision, and even contemplated doing global revisions; but, in light of their representation of the assignment, they chose to do an easier task:

> I could redo this whole thing . . . and show the reader the places where the sources don't agree and make more sense of what I am saying. I could make my audience a confused reader who just wants to know more about how to manage time but . . . but I'm pretty happy with what I have written . . . I don't think I will change my process for this assignment, it is probably not worth the effort.

Since many of the writers were aware that they could attempt more challenging revisions but chose not to, we became interested in the various ways the particular context affected the reviser's perception of the task. Taking such factors into consideration, we began to appreciate how complex and situational an assignment to revise really is and the myriad ways in which a situation shapes cognition and the revised product.

NEGOTIATING THE TASK AND TEXT

The analysis presented thus far has shown that the Interpret prompt was generally more powerful than the Better prompt; it produced more text change between drafts and encouraged a greater percentage of students to make significant changes in their revised essays. Moreover, the protocol data supported the greater power of the Interpret prompt in that it led a larger group of writers to make plans to change their drafts.

A critical distinction regarding the power of any prompt to effect change in students' process and performance is the extent to which a particular prompt either cues a student to perform tasks the student already knows how to do (Applebee, 1981) or evokes in the student's conscious problem-solving modes of thought (Newell & Simon, 1973). Given the fact that the majority of writers who retained their original organizing plans were assigned the Better prompt, we wanted to know what it was about this prompt that led students to consistently apply local revision strategies to their texts rather than global ones.

The protocol data revealed that the answer was, in part, the student's interpretation of what the prompt implied about their original draft. Don's and Sandy's remarks after reading the task instructions to make their essay Better are illustrative of how a number of students represented the task.

Don (Control 3–3)

> . . . make it better means I must be doing it right. . . .

Sandy (Control 4–4)

After reading the instructions and her original essay:

> . . . this is O.K. . . . sounds like I wrote it under the pressure of time which I did . . . my sentences are too long and involved. . . . I think I will do some dusting and cleaning and tighten the structure a little . . . that's all I need to make it better.

For both Don and Sandy, "make it Better" did not prompt them to further problem solving or coming up with new ideas. Instead, the Better prompt acted to confirm their original purpose, and the act of revising became the application of a series of corrective, sentence-level changes. In Sandy's case, the Better prompt cued a set of strategies over which she had considerable control. Her revision was completed within six minutes.

While the Better prompt was general and unspecified, the Interpret prompt, which included the S-AC procedure and the lecture, was more focused and specific; it suggested to students that certain features or aspects of their essays needed to be changed. The Interpret prompt tended to elicit more instances of problem-solving behavior than the Better prompt. The protocols showed that more than half of the students in the Interpret condition paused to reread the instructions and either elaborated on what they thought Interpret meant or searched their lecture notes to find a clue about what they should do and formed a plan of action. Only 24 percent of the writers prompted with the Better prompt made similar plans. Plans were defined as a writer's attempt to change a global feature of the text or address a different audience or change the specific way the information on time management was represented. Taking both the final texts and the process data into consideration, the Interpret prompt was consistently more powerful in engaging students in problem-solving activities and in encouraging students to change the ways they organized and represented their knowledge.

THE GAP BETWEEN PLANNING AND PERFORMANCE

Britton, Burgess, Martin, McLeod, and Rosen (1975) noted that writing is a "purposeful" activity through which writers carry out plans and accomplish goals. Focusing on the ways writers or, in our case, revisers negotiated their task, text, and situation, provided us with a unique window through which to examine how writers' purposes differed. Given our analysis of the protocol data, we wondered whether a writer's final text is really an adequate guide to the presence or absence of rhetorical purpose in a writer's own thinking. We hypothesized that students learn to manage different facets of the composing process in different stages, and one reason for the gap between planning and performance may be the students' struggle to let their purpose control the text. Throughout the protocols, we found evidence of students struggling with varying degrees of success to create rhetorical purposes and integrate them into their compositions. The following segments of protocols are good examples of the struggles of some of the Intenders who made plans to turn their essays into interpretive essays that fulfilled a specific purpose, but whose efforts fell short in the eyes of the judges.

THOSE WHOSE PLANS GOT LOST

Joel is representative of a group of writers who read and reread both the instructions of the assignment and the original essay and then proceeded to make explicit plans for revision.

Joel (Experimental 3–3)

> the problem is none of these people agree about time management and we are supposed to be interpreting what they think in a comprehensive way . . . it just doesn't fit together. . . . I could organize it by picking the ones I agree with but that wouldn't be

comprehensive. I'll try to find some points of agreement to start off and then I'm going to go through and praise what I like and criticize guys like Lakein . . . that way I'll be interpreting them to my audience.

In his protocol, Joel correctly diagnosed the tension between the fact that the sources do not agree and the need, stated in the instructions, "to be comprehensive." He remarked, "it just doesn't fit together." He proceeded to consider his options and devised a plan to find an organizing concept based on "points of agreement." Finally, he planned to add his personal evaluations. But, as Joel moved to translate his planning into his revised text, he reread his former organizing concept in his original essay and decided that he liked the sense of what he had written earlier over his new plan. His plan was abandoned as he chose to conserve the structure of the text he had already written (see Chapter 7). This preference among many of our writers to conserve the structure of a former text rather than transform its organization frequently resulted in revision plans being set aside. These writers consciously or unconsciously opted to carry out the simpler task of conserving their original text plan rather than pursue the more rigorous option of transforming their representation of their knowledge.

THOSE WHOSE PLANS DID NOT ACCOMPLISH THE DESIRED EFFECT

Another group of students also planned to change their organizing plans for their essays.

Liz (Experimental 1–3)

at first all I wanted to do was summarize and touch all the bases because all I could see they had in common was that planning was important to time management. (Rereads notes from lecture.) What I need to do is show I have a purpose and explain it to them. This time I am going to make planning my main topic and show other freshmen how they should plan their time to be a success. . . . I can still use a lot of my old material.

Liz's plan shows that she is aware that her original organizing plan needs to be changed from a summary to a more purposeful audience-based account. She designates "planning" as her main topic and "freshmen" as her audience. But, as Liz begins to translate her plans into action she makes the judgment "its not working . . . this stinks . . ." and abandons her plan. These writers were unable to carry out their plans to their satisfaction and decided, instead, to retain what they had originally written. For many writers, global revision is a high-risk enterprise for which there is diminishing commitment as the difficulty increases.

THOSE WHOSE PLANS WERE NOT RECOGNIZED

Another group of writers made plans to revise their essays, but their essays were not recognized as "interpretive" essays by the judges. Ed is a good example in that he made an explicit plan.

Ed (Experimental 1–1)

> according to them I guess this (refers to his original paper) is a summary. I guess . . . I
> guess they want something different . . . something with my opinion in it (refers to
> assignment). They want me to have a purpose. I'll make it into an argument with my
> roommate. . . that will be my purpose. . . . I'll use the same material and make it into
> an argument I'm having.

Ed's plan is sound in the sense that he recognizes his summary needs to be
changed. He makes a plan to argue with his roommate, but, as he turns to put his
plan into writing, he neglects to inform the reader of his new purpose. Missing from
Ed's revised text are the explicit references to his audience or the signals that he is
arguing rather than presenting information. On the whole, the organization of his
text remains the same with only a short phrase, "but in my opinion," inserted to
signal the reader that he is arguing. Writers in Ed's group frequently showed in their
protocols signs that their process was changing but failed to translate those changes
into explicit prose.

Another group of writers whose plans showed indications of rhetorical purpose,
but whose finished products were not recognized by the judges as being "interpretive essays," were the ones whose texts originally fell within the 0 to 3 range
of essays. These writers' plans are similar to those of Joan.

> I want to show them that time management matters and can make a difference if a
> student manages his time well. My topic is OK but it really doesn't have that much to
> do with the rest. . . . I need to find a way to tie Lakein and James in.

As Joan revises, she returns occasionally to her plan. Like Ed, though, she fails to
signal the reader that she has a specific audience in mind or that she is attempting to
make changes in the way she originally organized the material. While she was
successful in finding a way to relate Lakein and James to her original organizing
concept, the final result is a variation on the "review and comment" strategy rather
than a major transformation in her representation of the information.

Neither Ed's nor Joan's plan called for specific local changes to be made in their
text, and they gave no clue how the writers actually intended to put their plans into
operation. Instead of elaborating with specific strategies for making changes, Ed's
and Joan's plans were general, directional statements about the way they would like
their essays to turn out.

Writers Revise Differently

This study demonstrates that writers revise differently depending on how they
represent or negotiate their task, their text, and their situation. In examining the
protocols of writers planning to revise, one cannot fail to be impressed by the extent
to which a writer's representation of the task, text, and situation influences the
goals, strategies, and criteria that writers bring into play. Writers' representations
varied from relatively simple generic representations of "school" tasks to complex

multifaceted representations fashioned from writers' inferences about the cognitive, social, and rhetorical aspects of the task.

Given the fact that the process of revision within an instructional setting is complex and situational, we observed that revision is not merely a cognitive but also a complex social and political act. Writers, in an educational context, are always being asked to juggle priorities and serve different masters. Not surprisingly, students consciously choose strategies that are efficient and sensible, yet not always as rigorous as teachers would prefer.

Finally, learning to revise within an academic context is a tricky business for a freshman writer. What is a student to make of the prompts and goals teachers give them—"interpret," "make it better"? We found a sizable proportion of writers still developing a picture of what teachers mean when they make such requests. Often we found a mismatch between what our readers expected and what our writers delivered as final texts. In many of these cases, we were pleased yet disturbed to note that our writers' processes (as revealed in their protocols) were consistently more elaborate and sophisticated than their written products.

III

READING-TO-WRITE:
Social Perspectives

7

Translating Context into Action

JOHN ACKERMAN

Writing is a social activity, and as teachers and researchers we knew that our students' responses to a reading-to-write assignment were as much a function of larger social, economic, and cultural influences as of the immediate social context of a writing task in a university classroom. We knew that the reading and writing behavior we saw was strongly influenced (if *determined* is too strong a word) by these students' twelve years of public schooling and eighteen years (or so) of living in a literate culture. They did not walk into our classes or into our assignment as blank slates (Berkenkotter, Huckin, & Ackerman, 1988; Heath, 1983). They brought their lives with them, and our efforts to teach "strategies" for writing or "whole-text revision" or aims in academic discourse—as well as our writing task with explicit instructions to "interpret and synthesize" assigned readings—were scenes of negotiation. In a writing assignment, students and teachers negotiate what is expected and what can be done: the requirements in a writing task are tempered by what students know how and prefer to do as writers.

Recent work in rhetorical theory can help us understand the complex forces at work in this negotiation. When we say that writing behavior is "socially structured," we mean that the topics, rhetorical means, and linguistic conventions all have antecedents within a larger literate culture. Any given act of writing echoes previous literate practice and, more specifically, the literate practices of discourse communities (Porter, 1986). This means that the romantic image of the solitary writer, lost in a private war with words, is a myth (Brodkey, 1987a). The ideas a writer pursues through an act of composing are ideas that gain relevance because

173

they have been shaped through community action (Geertz, 1983; LeFevre, 1987). The extension, refinement, and transmission of those ideas are made possible because writers share rhetorical and linguistic conventions. Of late, researchers such as Bazerman (1981, 1985), Myers (1985a, 1985b), Swales (1984), and Huckin (1987) have demonstrated that the specialized knowledge displayed in social science writing is not only shaped through community action, it is shaped by the rhetorical and linguistic conventions in vogue in professional journals. The image of a writer belonging to and writing for a community with specialized conventions, in turn, is helping to clarify the difficulty some students have when they must write for university audiences. As Bartholomae (1985) has argued, freshman writers stand outside conversations between authorities in the university setting, and to answer our assignments they appropriate the language of an authority, "a reader for whom the general commonplaces and the readily available utterances about a subject are inadequate" (pp. 135, 140).

An act of writing is a social construct, but it is also situationally determined. A "rhetorical situation," as defined by Bitzer (1968), is the more immediate location and circumstance for writing, the "natural context of persons, events, objects, relations, and an exigence," which together invite an "utterance" (p. 5). Bitzer's theory is helpful because it reminds writing teachers that a classroom assignment, and certainly the class's response to that assignment, is a unique, local manifestation of larger cultural, literate currents (Bartholomae, 1986). Just as this theory refines our awareness of the immediate situation surrounding and provoking an act of composing, it appears to ignore the role of the individual and has been criticized for being deterministic (Vatz, 1973). Scott Consigney (1974) defused some of this criticism by arguing that a coherent view of rhetoric, or in this case a coherent view of student writing, includes both a "rhetorical situation" and the acknowledgment that writers are agents within a rhetorical situation. Thus, the writer determines the rhetorical situation as much as the situation gives meaning to the utterance. Through an act of publication (making ideas available to a reader) within a rhetorical situation, a writer establishes or reestablishes her individuality within that culture and community.

This view of the interplay between a literate heritage, the immediate social or rhetorical situation, and a writer's ability to affect change within a discourse community balances the sometimes deterministic flavor of some theories of writing as a social activity:

> Even if the writer is locked into a cultural matrix and is constrained by the intertext of the discourse community, the writer has freedom within the immediate rhetorical context . . . successful writing helps to redefine the matrix—and in that way becomes creative. . . . Every new text has the potential to alter the Text in some way; in fact every text admitted into a discourse community changes the constitution of the community—and discourse communities can revise their discursive practices. . . . (Porter, 1986, p. 41)

Sociolinguists also recognize that language users are agents within communities and cultures. Hudson (1980), paraphrasing LePage, points out that a writer can belong to and write for more than one discourse community. An act of writing can be thought of as an act of *positioning* oneself at a point within a "multidimensional" space, so that writing within a rhetorical situation means *choosing* the means to address one community without denying wholesale the topical, rhetorical, and linguistic conventions of other discourse communities. In any one act of composing, then, a writer's behavior is a composite of years of literate practice, and a negotiation between the more immediate rhetorical situation, which echoes those years of practice, and the individual stamp a writer can bring to the circumstance for writing. We believe that writing instruction and guidance should help our students "choose the means" to address a language community. And we believe one way to being is to search out the antecedents for an act of composing in rhetorical and cultural contexts.

Most theories of writing and rhetoric, however, are built from images of accomplished writers who have made the transition to full membership in a discourse community and a literate culture. When we think about the relative success our students have had in high school English class, as evidenced by "A" papers and acceptable proficiency test scores and college entrance exams, our students (in a sense) successfully publish for an academic audience. But the gap between the reading and writing skills that provide access to the university community and those necessary to thrive there is known to many and is commonly articulated as a university's commitment to undergraduate- and graduate-level writing instruction. We would not say that our students are "redefining" the university community every time they publish a paper for a teacher in freshman writing; for lack of practice and exposure, they do not yet know how to act in the role of an accomplished member of a specialized discourse community. They are students who have succeeded in one environment and now must transfer their know-how to a different setting, with sometimes very different requirements for performance. As we watched our students write, we noticed what we thought were traces of our students' history as readers and writers in school as they first represented the reading-to-write assignment to themselves. For many students, "schooling" created a bind between the habits and assumptions they brought to the immediate rhetorical situation and their efforts to *re-represent* the assignment, to take their writing a step beyond the "commonplaces and readily available utterances" they first thought were expected or acceptable.

This bind partly explains why freshman writers and the teaching of reading and writing fascinate us. Freshman writers are both experts and novices: they bring years of practice with academic discourse, bound up in the habits and assumptions exhibited in our classrooms. They are novices in that they have had less practice with the assignments and expectations common to the university setting: an act of publishing a paper for a teacher in freshman composition (or history or psychology) is as much a reliance on these habits and assumptions as is the acquisition of new rhetorical or linguistic skill. As Bartholomae points out, freshman writers falsely assume, often with the very best intentions, that commonplaces such as the five-paragraph theme will be read and accepted by a knowledgeable audience composed of readers who have long-since distanced themselves from such conventions.

What students need to be helped to see, then, is that fluency with certain rhetorical and linguistic commonplaces—the specialized conventions of an academic or professional discipline—comes with practice, and in the time being the more comfortable, routine commonplaces—the reading and writing habits that won them success elsewhere—must be examined, refined, and extended. Students also need to be encouraged to understand that the choice to rely on or depart from a commonplace is theirs to make. As linguists and scholars suggest, since specialized rhetorical and linguistic conventions exist, we ought to teach them directly to make students aware of the expectations of new language community (Bizzell, 1982; Swales, 1984). But that awareness and practice ought to build on the knowledge of when to rely on or depart from more general reading and writing skills. Commonplaces, such as stuffy academic terms and phrases, deductive informational patterns, or a conclusion that mirrors the introduction, by themselves are not the problem; they echo literate practice. It is when a writer (young or not-so-young) uses them without knowledge of their commonality and, thus, without care for their limitations that readers see them and turn the other way.

For our purposes, original writing, the writing we expected to see in response to our reading-to-write assignment, is generated by writers who bring a healthy skepticism. They actively question a writing situation and their invested responses to that situation. Decisions on how to begin, how to make sense of assigned passages, or how to construct a plan for writing ought to invoke questions by students about the origins of their literate practices and their appropriateness to the rhetorical situation at hand as well as their own sense of who they are or want to be as writers. It is, in fact, the interrelationships among cultural and immediate rhetorical contexts and how a writer translates those contexts into action that interests us here.

Locating Context: In Writers, In a Culture

How is it that the "cultural matrix" of literate behavior influences the reading and writing practices of a student in freshman composition? Or, from the perspective of the writer inside a linguistic community, how do these students translate context into an intellectual act? If for a moment we adopt a theory of memory from cognitive psychology, we might say that context is stored in the form of schemata (Bartlett, 1932; Rumelhart & Ortony, 1977), and that schemata provide procedures for acting in accordance with cultural and contextual expectations. Schema theory posits that shared experience becomes ingrained in the individual and, when the situation invites, is replayed through common procedures for living our lives. We can see socially derived schemata at work when students demonstrate test-taking know-how, or when a reader assumes that a story should include characters, plot, climax, and resolution, or when we enter a restaurant and pause at the door to be seated. In all three cases someone supplies or infers missing information; these actions and expectations are guided by schemata that are habits of mind formed through years of practice. Cultural influence, then, is not a static phenomenon. The fact that freshman writers have resided in a literate culture and have accumulated hours upon hours of experience reading and writing—all of which is brought to bear on a writing situation—means that context reveals itself in the form of procedures. Conversely, the literate procedures students used to represent and act on our assignment can be traced back to their contextual antecedents. It is the procedural form of stored schematic knowledge that takes the longest to develop, is the most deeply rooted in specific learning situations, and finally is the most useful in helping a problem solver succeed at a complex task. (For an extended discussion of procedural versus declarative knowledge, knowing *how* versus knowing *that,* see Anderson, 1983.)

The analysis of student writing in this chapter begins with two observations: first, a writer's history in school acts as a *legacy of literate behavior* in that the habits and assumptions from schooling appear as procedures for reading and writing and are evident in the opening moves by students to represent and translate a writing task into a draft. When a freshman writer receives an assignment, there is a good chance that the task at hand is ill-defined because requirements and materials are newly encountered. Thus, when students face an unfamiliar writing task, we can expect them to begin with what they know how to do as stable, productive first moves to make the unfamiliar more familiar. A second observation is that our students' opening moves, which translate the assignment into something familiar and doable, often became a *legacy within the composition of a draft.* The first impression of the assignment, and especially the initial moves to comprehend the readings, became a lasting impression. Students' opening moves to understand and initiate the assignment narrowed the choices in the composing behavior that followed. In other words, for many students the first impression and accompanying procedures—born from their reading of the task directions, materials, and the rhetorical situation implied by the assignment—were indelible.

Our first task in this chapter is to describe these opening moves and to study them as a legacy of literate behavior and as strong influences on the immediate rhetorical situation. Our second task is to explore how the imprint of those procedures, the legacy within the composition, directs the composing that follows in completing the first draft of an assignment. To help us think about the legacy of an opening move, we conceptualized each student's composing (represented in the protocol data) as two broad yet distinct episodes. Episodes of *early comprehension* temporally and procedurally are those opening moves in which students represent and initially act on an assignment. Early comprehension consists of several common behaviors: perusing the explicit requirements of an assignment, taking whatever practical steps are necessary to define and limit that assignment (questions, comparisons, models), and reading the assigned passages primarily to surmise topical and textual boundaries. Collectively these behaviors are the procedural counterparts to a represented task and predictably are partial evidence of a student's history with writing in school and out. Episodes of *translation* begin when students in some way move beyond initial representations and procedures, by planning a written response or rereading for a specific purpose or reviewing notes to consolidate and order ideas. These behaviors, like the outward behaviors associated with early comprehension, are not by themselves distinctive. What we found remarkable was the linearity and causality suggested by these clusters of behaviors and their eventual effect on a written product. We wondered what conscious decisions or habits of mind guide the translation of early comprehension into a course of action.

We split our students' reading and writing behavior into two episodes for several reasons. First, we needed a conceptual tool to guide our observations. The opening moves by students to understand the assignment and familiarize themselves with the readings (found in early comprehension) were distinct from the moves to actually begin writing out a response. And because these moves appeared to be familiar, habitual, and practiced ways to begin, we took them to be the best example of how the influence of schooling reveals itself in an immediate rhetorical situation. Students read first to learn what the authorities on "time management" were talking about as if to learn the lay of the land; the episode of early comprehension was thus often marked by questions such as "What are these people talking about and what do you (the teacher) want me to say?"—questions (and answers) these students had seen before. To gauge by their actions, students responded to these questions with the sure-footed expertise that comes from years of practice.

The episodes also enabled us to label differences in physical behavior associated with composing. When students shifted from early comprehension of the task and readings to efforts to translate this information into a plan to write, there was a proportional shift in the amount of energy devoted first to reading and taking notes and then to reading notes and writing sentences. The shift in activities seemed to correspond to the prominence of a new question: "Ok, I've got my notes, now how can I use them to begin writing?" How a writer answered that question was indicative of the degree to which a writer was re-representing a rhetorical situation. In the period of translation, a writer in some manner faced the legacy of schooling. Schooling, which provided the student with the procedures to begin the assignment, either continued as a legacy that shaped the composing of the draft to follow, *or,* if the act of translation became a scene for *continued negotiation,* students tried to re-represent and redefine the task before them.

If we want students to redefine a rhetorical situation, and perhaps alter the direction of an act of composing, we are not advocating that they deny their literate heritage—as if that were possible. They can, however, slow and complicate the act of translating context into action by consciously examining the know-how they bring to an assignment. This know-how, as it appears in an opening move, is typically beyond the purview of a teacher. After all, though assignments in a sense begin with course descriptions and handouts, they begin in earnest away from the classroom when the writer addresses not only explicit directions but also the blank page. When students return with a draft for sharing or clarifying the assignment or evaluation of work completed thus far, the opening moves to represent a doable assignment are already indelible. Research on revision has underscored what writing teachers and writers see time and time again. The first response to an assignment, by habit and practical necessity, is an investment writers do not easily cast aside, even when they benefit most by rethinking and starting anew (Flower et al., 1986; Sommers, 1980).

THE LEGACY OF SCHOOLING

The opening moves our students used to begin reading and writing can be inferred from their drafts and from the comments they made as they composed. If we wish to trace the origins of these moves, their antecedents in a literate culture, we must decide how to view the cultural and rhetorical contexts in which our students' writing is located. What, for instance, does a social or cultural context for writing consist of? Are there observable characteristics that could allow researchers, teachers, and students of writing to differentiate among various contextual influences? One thing is clear: larger cultural and more immediate rhetorical contexts are two sides of the same coin; our students compose in a number of contexts, all of which reflect larger cultural and political pressures as well as more immediate situational concerns. By first specifying and briefly examining these contexts, we can perhaps more accurately address the interplay between culture, rhetorical situations, and our students' unique roles as writers. We also found that the exercise of describing and differentiating these contexts helped us make explicit some of our underlying assumptions about where language comes from and how it is put to use. We do not presume to capture or fairly represent the complexity of a cultural matrix, nor to adequately represent how various sociocultural elements are interrelated. Here are seven perspectives on context, our way of defining the "cultural matrix," and our paths to a consideration of why our students' writing is a "social activity."

Reading and Writing in Society

Reading and writing are learned technologies that reflect the cultural needs of a society. Reading and writing taught in school are responsive to the aims and preferences of the dominant linguistic culture in which school is embedded. The students in this study are members of a literate society insofar as they have successfully completed their public education while at the same time acquiring the normalized forms of literate behavior favored in a variety of situations and mediums (Jameson, 1980; Ong, 1982).

Schooling

School mirrors society and disseminates, through academic language and practice, society's values for knowledge and communication. Learning to read and write is not the same thing as learning to read and write in school, even though these abilities are mostly bound up in the culture of schooling. School teaches students to read and write while it inculcates well-defined habits and assumptions that help to sustain the larger society (Baliber & Machery, 1981; Heath, 1983; Scribner & Cole, 1981).

Academic Discourse Communities

Specialized groups exist within school and elsewhere in society with relatively distinct forums for communication, case-building methods, rhetorical conventions, and a canon of topics. To be a member of a discourse community means participating in the relevant issues of a professional group, a demonstration that a writer's contributions have currency. Though the students in this study come from various backgrounds, they attempt, through their writing, to participate in a local expression of academic performance, the university, and more specialized groups such as majors and departments (Porter, 1986; Swales, 1987).

Linguistic and Rhetorical Practice in Communities

Discourse communities and even specific classrooms are marked by preferred forms and uses for reading and writing. These textual conventions are the boundary markers for a literate context in that reading and writing are visible and permanent indices of social interaction. In this way, textual features demark a context. Commonality across discourse practice is evidence of the social foundation behind a discipline, a discourse community, or a classroom (Gilbert & Mulkay, 1984; Myers, 1985a, 1985b).

Classrooms

Classrooms form ad hoc discourse communities within school, each with routines, codes, conventions, and ethos defined momentarily by the actions of the class. The classroom is also the locus for the expression of the literate practices of the class members as the teacher's assumptions and objectives for the course and the students' experience in school merge (Herrington, 1985; Richardson, Fiske, & Okun, 1983).

Assignments

A writing assignment is an immediate context in that it is a situation for composing, triggering the "exigence" for a writer, and outlining explicit directions and materials in a rhetorical situation. Task directions, parameters for performance, and situational constraints create a local context, an occasion to read and write. Assignments are acts of negotiation, revealing the habits, assumptions, and expectations of both teachers and students (Bartholomae, 1983; Ruth & Murphy, 1987).

A Student's Own Intellectual History

To acknowledge a personal "frame of reference" is to acknowledge that contextual influence is uniquely represented in each of us. A point of view is both idiosyncratic and evidence of socially constructed knowledge—a personal, intellectual history does not at all deny the effect of social interaction. As mentioned earlier, the vitality of linguistically defined social groups depends on the creative acts of publication by individual members. People do have their own perspectives, frames, or points of view, and do surprise us, in acceptable ways, with their idiosyncrasies. Those who teach are reminded of this claim when students return each semester to solve our assignments in varied and meaningful ways (Bereiter & Scardamalia, 1983; Hayes, 1985).

These contexts remind us that the lines separating the larger, cultural context and the immediate rhetorical context for composing easily blur. The effort to understand how contexts overlap offers both a vocabulary and a vantage point for talking about the origins of reading and writing procedures. For example, a convention such as a purpose statement in an opening paragraph can be argued to be more of a local convention of a writing class than an accepted convention in written public discourse or a specialized discourse community. The rhetorical situation in which our students composed was a convergence of a range of socially derived influences. As noted earlier, students not only wrote in response to an assignment or situation, they wrote in a multidimensional space where home, school, class, assignment, and their unique habits of mind converge. The student writers in this study provide glimmers of all of these contexts in their writing—with the predictable exception of full membership in a specialized "academic discourse community." From our perspective as college writing teachers, freshmen in college can be thought of as situated between communities. They are longstanding members of a rambling discourse community called public education, and we can expect to see traces of this membership when they read and write for us. The point of continuing their education is (for many) to embark on specialized careers, which will eventually include specialized language practice.

The convergence of contextual influence appears in all kinds of behavior in the classroom—from the way students granted a teacher authority to the manner in which our assignments were addressed. We saw the convergence especially in the procedures, the opening moves, students demonstrated as they first responded to our reading-to-write assignment. As we have stated earlier in this paper, students read first to gauge the lay of the land, to see what the assigned authorities and the teacher (through the assignment directions) were talking about. Independent raters reported little trouble isolating the outward signs of a shift in attention from reading to understand the boundaries of topic and assignment and to making and acting out decisions on how to create a draft (100 percent agreement for three raters). Our two-part classification scheme of periods of early comprehension and translation was general enough to allow for false starts, rereading for clarification, or puzzling over an appropriate "angle" for an essay. In other words, the two episodes encompass a range of composing styles while still helping to draw our attention to a common set of moves in the period of early comprehension.

Our three raters also looked for specific commonalities across the seventeen student essays and think-aloud transcripts. Once the boundaries between the major periods of early comprehension and translation were established for each writer, raters isolated a few widely shared moves. Early comprehension can be characterized as an exercise in summarization and recitation. Students tended to read quickly to summarize, reducing material to gists and grafting their experiences with time management on to key ideas in the readings without apparent concern for explicit task directions or the more implicit task to craft an original statement by "synthesizing" the available information with their own beliefs and experience. They read initially "to get a sense" of the main points of each authority, often restating main ideas and writing them in their notes as if they were mining the assigned texts for nuggets of truth. Because of habit and necessity students brought a remarkably well-formed set of reading strategies to this task. By restating the authorities' main ideas they efficiently reduced the assigned readings to manageable units of information, using their experience most often to screen the main ideas for their relative popularity. Without much interruption, an idea was located and then validated ("I agree . . . that's good . . .") as to whether the writer recognized or approved of the authority's position. When students did pause to explore an idea, they typically related a recent experience in school that matched or complimented a scene an authority had just described. The commonality across the opening moves of our students and the self-assured way these moves were invoked surprised us, although we predicted that students would rely on their expertise. Since our task was ill-defined for them (at its inception), we imagined that students would spend more intellectual time asking what a synthesis or original interpretation might consist of.

The students' early efforts to comprehend and manage the readings did appear to be quite practical. That a student would plunge into a writing task that requires a synthesis of diverse information, and rely on well-learned behaviors, is not surprising on several levels. First, these students surely recognized characteristics in this task that were common to past writing assignments. In school, students routinely find themselves—for example, in an entrance examination—needing to manage information quickly to construct a written statement. And our students all reported experience writing "research papers," which to varying degrees, called for canvassing diverse sources of information to support a thesis. In this way, their opening moves to summarize and reduce the assigned readings fit the task at hand in that students were asked to produce a draft by analyzing assigned materials and craft a response in one sitting. Also, as was mentioned earlier, the decisions a writer makes in this situation happen away from the influence of a teacher or peer, and we can expect a student to draw on familiar, well-learned routines. Hence, the absence of hesitation in acting out the assumption that this assignment involves, for example, summarization suggests that this sequence is practiced and, because of its familiarity, is a safe way to begin. Alone, these college students depended on familiar, successful, efficient comprehension strategies to gain control of a composing situation. Research on problem solving (Newell & Simon, 1972) has shown repeatedly that the first stages of searching for solutions are understood as the act of *finding* the problem and building a representation. Our students wanted to succeed, and success began by representing the reading-to-write task in a familiar form in which well-learned procedures were appropriate and practical. In this way they performed as experts by quickly recognizing the usable elements in the writing task (the main ideas, for example), which in turn invited ways to comprehend and begin to organize the required (as they saw it) information in their synthesis. (See Glaser, in press, for a summary of "expert" behavior across specializations.) In sum, these students were experts at recognizing the features of familiar school assignments and engaging, however superficially, appropriate procedures for comprehending the assigned readings. In doing so, they took the first practical steps to translate a representation of what they were supposed to accomplish into a plan for action. Their notes, chock full of salient main ideas, were poised for the construction of a summary essay.

The Students' Opening Moves: Origins in a Literate Culture

The opening moves, the procedures our students used to represent and act on the reading-to-write task, are similar to what a number of researchers and theorists have observed in the way reading and writing are taught in school. As mentioned earlier, certain features of the writing task were recognizable to students and invited familiar procedures to begin a response. In this case, the practical requirements in the rhetorical situation seemed to bring those literate behaviors closer to the surface, but the task alone did not create or invoke them. National studies of achievement and instruction point to a tradition of knowledge compilation and recitation—similar to the orientation to knowledge and composing seen here—rather than a tradition of exploration, criticism, and thoughtful interpretation (summarized in Applebee,

1984b). For example, for many students the lack of accord between the authorities on time management was not seen as an invitation to impose a personal order on the subject matter, or a chance to sort out the validity of distinct arguments on the topic. Ambiguity was more a hindrance than an invitation, something to be quickly circumvented if it was noticed at all. A student's success at avoiding ambiguity and reciting main ideas mirrored what national assessments predict: this success is partly due to the ability to record and recite facts and concepts, not to critical interpretation.

When students did turn to their relevant experience or opinions, they provided examples and counterexamples but rarely pondered for any duration the validity of what (we thought) were sometimes quite novel connections between their experience and the ideas before them in the readings. Instead, they relied on a "agree/disagree" framework to judge the issues in the readings. For example, one student chose a first sentence for his draft built on the idea that "many of the suggestions . . . seem very sensible." To find out "how sensible are these suggestions," he reread to "agree" with an author's contention. Right and wrong, good and bad, agree and disagree are all examples of what William Perry found as college students' avoidance of ambiguity and intellectual complexity (1968). Ten of seventeen freshmen in this study used this dichotomous frame in essence to clean up the ambiguity found in early comprehension. National studies and Perry's developmental scheme suggest that the opening moves demonstrated by these students reflect common practice within public education. The student behavior illustrated thus far echoes a *culture of recitation* (Applebee, 1984a, 1984b), in which the emphasis is on accuracy of learning and routine recitals and not reasoned exploration and debate. The opening moves appear to coincide with an "inert knowledge" epistemology (Bereiter & Scardamalia, 1985), behavior similar to what Nelson (in press) labeled low-effort strategies demonstrated in writing research papers and projects over several weeks.

This paper began by proposing that a coherent image of writers at work would include contextual and cultural influences as well as each writer's efforts to re-represent and redefine an immediate rhetorical context through an act of publication. Looking only at the common opening moves in the period of early comprehension, the writer's role as agent within a linguistic community is not particularly apparent. Even though the assignment, to our eyes, calls for repeated examination of the task and chosen response, and even though the researchers and theorists mentioned previously imply a united front in support of original, critical interpretation, students responded in a largely unoriginal (but practical) manner. As mentioned earlier, the literate behavior that students brought to this task constituted a form of linguistic expertise in the general community of *assumed* academic readers and writers. Students did not (initially) block when they faced an unfamiliar set of readings (Rose, 1984). Instead, the opening moves succeeded as a form of "relative fluency" (Rose, 1985), in which, in spite of the students' unfamiliarity with the excerpts or lack of involvement with the topic, they were able to recognize familiar features in the assignment and proceed. Their moves became a kind of "practical" cognition, a term Scribner (1984) has used to explain how, in specific, everyday circumstances, people work efficiently with little awareness of the economy of their effort. Later in interviews and during classroom discussion, students reported that the assignment reminded them of writing tasks they had seen before in school. When a student was asked whether she had ever written a "synthesis" and what the term meant prior to this course, she said that to synthesize meant to summarize, a task assigned to her many times in school.

The practical, knowledge-telling orientation ensures membership in one type of discourse community, a middle-ground that many "successful" college writers inhabit in advance of full participation in more specialized discourse communities. The discrepancy between writing to succeed in high school or to prepare for college and writing to be accepted by college readers can be glaring. The habits and assumptions that students depend on when they write to the *assumed* discourse community of "theme writers" (Coles, 1978; Heath, 1983) does help many of our college-bound students negotiate the entrance and essay examinations for acceptance into the university fold. A generic academic literacy, then, may be a precursor to more refined and specialized professional "conversations" (Bazerman, 1985), which develop later in a student's career. But students' relative fluency does not come without costs. The facility our students displayed in representing and inaugurating this task, we believe, complicates the rigorous struggle to acquire different habits of mind. If students begin a reading and writing assignment with the assumptions and habits we saw and characterized earlier, the legacy of a common literate behavior interferes with acquiring new literate behaviors, those more specialized rhetorical and linguistic conventions in various areas of the university. The compatibility between a common set of opening moves and the assumed requirements for successful academic writing is more troublesome than it is convenient.

TRANSLATING COMPREHENSION INTO A DRAFT: THE LEGACY OF OPENING MOVES

In the preceding section, we argued that the immediate social situation for composing cannot be understood fully without taking into account currents within a larger literate culture; that these currents reside in the individual and are displayed through observable procedures—here, the opening moves of a student to respond to a writing assignment in school; and that these opening moves to comprehend the assignment and authorities in question quickly suggest a practical but limited representation of what could be accomplished. Throughout the rest of this chapter, we argue that consequences associated with "early comprehension," a student's first pass at translating an assignment into action, create a second legacy. Students who rely primarily on the common set of opening moves (described previously), as often as not find themselves in an arhetorical situation. Their role as agents, with the opportunity to affect change within a community of knowledgeable readers, is diminished. To see how this occurs and to explore alternative habits of mind, we begin with a closer look at the opening moves and especially how they continued through the period of translation.

The time and effort students devoted to configuring and acting on a plan for writing suggests two versions of how a student negotiates a reading and writing task. Students may too readily accept the procedures accompanying the legacy of schooling in that they remain faithful to the assigned readings and the well-learned habits of summarization and recitation. Or they may tend more to question the familiar and the habitual, promoting their own values and ideas on the topic at hand and on acceptable prose. Finally, our goal is to help our students (when possible) consciously control the influence of their literate heritage as it interacts with the practical concerns of the immediate rhetorical situation for writing.

The opening moves seen in the period of early comprehension encumbered many students by issuing an orderly but rigid inventory of information on which they based their drafts. When students shifted attention toward the blank page, this inventory not only informed the next raft of writerly decisions, for some students, it also dominated their composing. In effect, early comprehension produced a template for the emerging text that they just could not deny. To look again at the opening moves students used to construct this template, here are the set of early comprehension strategies used to initially respond to the assignment. In all but a few cases, these strategies constituted all the moves we observed in the episode of early comprehension:

- Restating an authority's ideas
  by paraphrasing
  by finding key words in the passage
  by categorizing the readings by assigning a persona
- Comparing personal experience to an author's ideas
  by imposing an agree/disagree framework to evaluate or to elaborate
- Connecting excerpts, ideas, or authors
- Acknowledging the task

The students used three basic comprehension strategies: restating main ideas, comparing the readings and their experience, and connecting issues or authors in the readings. The variations (paraphrasing, finding key words, etc.) essentially gave students ways to label, classify, and arrange the assigned material. This inventory of main ideas, for the most part, became the tangible by-product of early comprehension, and the value of an inventory of ideas for this assignment is perhaps obvious. It is an efficient way to amass and connect disparate ideas quickly. This otherwise virtuous schema for ordering and efficiently arranging ideas, however, suggested a straightforward reading plan that, if allowed to go unchecked, sufficed for a writing plan. To a much lesser degree, the set of opening moves contained efforts to connect ideas in different passages and to briefly acknowledge task requirements. The students who did the latter only momentarily puzzled over terminology for example, and they continued reading or rereading with little deviation (Kennedy, 1985).

Translation began when students actively sought ways to translate into written form the products from a first reading and a first brush with the task. This translation can be characterized in several ways, depending on the degree to which writers accepted or questioned the progress of their drafts. First, some students appeared to accept (whether consciously or not) the usefulness of a ready-made template of ideas with its implied organization for a draft. When this happened, little or no hesitation was apparent. Other students hesitated, but only momentarily, to puzzle over what they might do with their recent investment in a summary of the readings or the absence of an angle to pursue to start writing. This hesitation *could* have developed into a fruitful examination of the rhetorical problem of translating early comprehension into a writing plan, except that these students seemed to have ready-made answers to their own questions. When they asked, "How do I make sense of the reading?" and "What is my angle for the paper?" they answered with two popular representations of ways into and out of the problem of finding a plan for writing:

- If I can find an idea that will account for the readings, I can use it to order my draft.
- I can organize the readings by whether they agree or not with my experience.

These representations imply procedures similar to what we saw in the set of common opening moves: reducing concepts to key ideas and using experience as a filter to qualify information. These representations assume that somewhere there exists an ideas that will simultaneously tame the inchoate nature of the assigned readings and provide a script for writing. And they assume that connections made between personal experience and an authority's assertion warrant the inclusion of ideas in a draft. As we have proposed before and will demonstrate in a later case study, these assumptions bear some truth insofar as these representations do lead to written products, however ordinary.

Other composing behavior in the period of translation suggests an alternative characterization, in which students more actively negotiate their roles in a reading-to-write assignment such as the one they completed. Some students seemed to *recognize* that they have a choice in how to construct and act on this assignment—as if not only to ask "How do I account for the readings?" and "How do I begin writing?" but to pose the answers to those questions as two reasonable alternatives among many others. If students appeared to hesitate, to ponder where their representations of the readings and the task are taking them as writers, they purposefully complicated the period of translation with different perspectives on their composing thus far, which were accompanied by statements such as

- I need to consider my audience, the task to "synthesize and interpret," and my own goals in order to write my statement.

With this comment, students were closer to recognizing that codifying the authorities into key concepts could actually interfere with translating text ideas into a working frame for writing, or that a summary essay with a thin rhetorical purpose ("Time management is important . . .") might produce uneventful prose for a reader. What was most exciting to us was that the question of how to translate comprehension into a written product was couched in terms of larger, more situational issues. Some students noticed that any solution to the dilemma must take into account the rhetorical situation they faced, a composite of task- and class-based expectations and their own expectations for performance. When they addressed this composite, they took steps toward strengthening their roles as agents within the immediate composing situations.

If students adopted this frame of mind in the period of translation, they began to turn a potentially arhetorical situation into a rhetorical one in which "finding something interesting to say" was at least as important as carefully representing the printed materials before them. In the think-aloud transcripts, and later in class, several students talked about how stock introductions and list of facts did not produce particularly readable, interesting essays. Other students never outwardly realized this. What follows is the story of how one student writer, Nancy, proceeded arhetorically, using a search for encompassing main ideas and her experience to qualify the information. She accounted for the authorities, and this account became her draft—a safe path out of the assignment but, on another level, a trap.

A Case Study: Nancy

Excerpts have been pulled from Nancy's think-aloud transcript to show generally how early comprehension leads to translation and how specifically a student represented the reading-to-write task as, first and last, an exercise in finding (to use her words) the "relevant" main ideas on time management. Nancy begins by scanning the task and reading, demonstrating many of the opening moves common to the period of early comprehension (her writing is in italics).

> [After reading a passage] . . . *so the most important thing to understand is that decisions on how to use the time is one of your best advantages* . . . [after another passage] . . . *so he's saying that even if you think you are too tired* . . . *you should keep concentrating* . . . *it's like having a second wind* . . . [another passage] . . . *so, fatigue passes with concentration* . . . *that makes sense* . . . *if you think about it. . . .* [She continues reading] . . . *so schedule is an important part* . . . *but there are other things that are important too* . . . *like, uhh, knowing how to study* . . . *to create a quiet environment* . . . [another passage] . . . *that's true but you do what's due first* . . . *it's easier if you do a first draft in one sitting* . . . *but you shouldn't write the whole paper at once because you might have a change of ideas. . . .*

From these comments we can see Nancy restating the author's main ideas and linking some of the ideas to her experience. After her first pass through the readings, she momentarily addresses the written directions in the assignment and invokes her representation of a key activity in the writing assignment. Although she does not state it directly, she implies in the following comments that to synthesize means to select the "relevant findings." Without hesitation, she begins rereading, taking notes, using similar opening moves:

> . . . *what do they want us to synthesize?* . . . *so first I'll say what the relevant findings are and interpret them and try and figure out what "synthesize" means* . . . *so both James and Pauk are saying that concentration is a big part of pacing and planning. . . . Lakein* . . . *he says that* . . . *it has to do with pacing and planning. . . .*

She does draw a comparison between two of the authorities, James and Pauk, but primarily begins to build her list of discrete, relevant findings. Several moments later, as she begins to translate her reading of the authorities into plans for a draft, she notices "categories," a nondescript concept that allows her to circumvent the ambiguous nature of the readings. She begins to build her draft by stopping reading (for the most part) and drawing on her notes for ideas. With her notes complete and in front of her, she discovers a plan for her first paragraph, an idea ("pacing and planning") taken directly from the reading. Using the ideas recorded in her notes, she fills in her supporting detail. All of this is done with little hesitation or any outward self-criticism.

> . . . I'm writing down notes and then I'll go back and revise the notes and put it into a better paper. . . . There are basically two distinct categories here . . . the first part is how to set . . . set the right mood and this part of the paper tells what people really do. . . . Ok, so now I have notes and now I have to write the response statement. . . . basically time management is broken into two parts . . . pacing and planning . . . *with good time management and optimal study conditions you can achieve . . . the best work possible* . . . so that's the first paragraph . . . and how each of these people, James, Pauk, and Guitton talk about it. . . .

To finish her "statement" she uses a rhetorical move similar to the agree/disagree move common in early comprehension. She distinguishes the authority of students from that of the time management experts in the readings and applies her "right and wrong" analysis.

> . . . And now I go to the second part of the paper, which is discussing these strategies that students use . . . and I guess instead of an interpretation it's an analysis . . . what's right with their strategies and what is wrong. . . .

Because we see no overt objection to her emerging draft, we can assume it is acceptable to her. She now calls upon her knowledge of essay conventions and is soon finished.

> . . . uhh, I need a conclusion . . . what's in my introduction. . . . Did I answer everything I said in my introduction? . . . Talked about management . . . talked about optimal conditions. . . .

Many of Nancy's responses to the assignment resemble those of her classmates, and her moves support our characterization of how a well-formed set of summarization strategies and comparisons between experience and the readings can build a template for a draft. For her, the shift from comprehension to translation came with little apparent effort. The goal to "revise the notes" led smoothly to a writing plan. She also used a version of the agree/disagree strategy to help her frame the remaining ideas in her final paragraph. And in her closing comments, like several of her peers, she gave some indication that she was familiar with the conventions of short essays in the English classroom. She demonstrated her know-how in moving from reading passages to reviewing notes to writing a draft with a coordinated introduction and conclusion, and her comments seemed to forecast this progression. Returning to our characterization of paths through the period of translation, she accepted her initial representations and saw no need to reexamine her early interpretations and strategies; she found a paper in her notes (Kennedy, 1985).

In this way, Nancy successfully completed the assignment; but in another sense she was trapped. She was trapped not by the absence of an approach or skills to respond to the assignment, but by the limitations her response placed on her thinking. Her reading and writing habits and her assumptions about academic writing created a legacy within the act of composing which functioned as a prescription for how she would complete the assignment. Independent raters labeled the organizing plan in her first draft a "frame," meaning she created (for a reader) a superstructure for her summarization and commentary but not an original interpretation. Even after revising, her draft remained, in her readers' eyes, a frame—a well-structured inventory. We believe Nancy misread an opportunity. If she had noticed and evaluated her early comprehension moves and the way she turned them into a design for writing, she might have asserted herself more in this assignment. It would be hasty to conclude that a heightened rhetorical sensitivity would lead directly to a more sophisticated draft, or one that would at least feature more of Nancy's own ideas on the topic. Yet, Nancy, because of the way she saw and responded to the reading and writing task, composed her essay with less rhetorical information at hand than others. For example, would it not be useful for Nancy to be aware of the similarity of her moves to those of other writers, the shape those moves gave her draft, and how they interfere with other rhetorical concerns? If readers consistently notice the generic nature of writing plans, then there could be a real gain in helping students to analyze the origins of those plans and, thus, the consequences of their initial representations of a reading-to-write assignment.

Asking Questions of a Legacy

The legacy of schooling provides our students with paths into and out of academic writing situations and assures them a form of fluency for minimum competency. Our students appear to know how to read for main ideas, to summarize those ideas, and with common conventions to arrange those ideas in an essay *about* the topic at hand. To conclude this chapter, we want to argue that students also have the instincts to question a legacy of schooling and especially the procedures this legacy gives them to address a writing assignment. Since students bring these instincts along with the rest of their habits and assumptions, the instincts are available but unfortunately less practiced. And they are not reinforced in academic environments where a faithful recitation of information is valued. We found instances of students laboring (in our eyes) to question, if not the antecedents to an act of composing, the more immediate consequences of their initial representation of the task and their opening moves to complete it.

We noticed students who more directly addressed the immediate rhetorical situation and their role as writers in that situation, especially in the period of translation. At this juncture, a key goal arose, one which largely determined the composing to follow: to "find a good idea." Students referred to "a place to begin," "the big picture," "an angle"; and in each case this happened students appeared to pull back from a reading plan and search for a topical focus that often included a rhetorical purpose. As noted earlier, for some students this angle was assumed to accompany the assigned readings or to magically rise out of a set of notes. After a first pass through the readings and the task directions, one student asked,

> How can you "interpret" it. None of it's the same (followed closely by). . . . I am doing an interpretation. . . . I guess I go to the next page and write my notes . . . and . . . look up "synthesize." I know what that means so we have to combine everything . . . one "comprehensive statement" that's supposed to make sense but nothing relates. . . .

The writer, like Nancy, assumes the task and the readings allow for a "combination" of information, and the diverse nature of the material confounds his efforts. Other students pursued a "good idea" differently. As a counterexample to the quick march from an inventory of ideas to a plan for writing, this student invested more time in the period of early comprehension and especially in her interpretations of the authorities and language she could use to present this interpretation. In doing so, she gained control over the readings and the writing task.

> [Reading] . . . ahh, well it seems that . . . umm . . . Guitton in talking about how one prepares for peak performance that is . . . by getting enough sleep . . . getting enough sleep and being . . . relaxed . . . [repeats last phrases] . . . umm . . . hmm . . . reinforces Pauk's comments about the environment . . . um . . . environment is crucial . . . the right environment is crucial to a peak performance . . . ahh . . . the right environment is one . . . is one without distractions, no noise . . . no noise . . . no distraction . . . no noise . . . so both Pauk and Guitton believe in the importance of environment. . . .

Although perhaps difficult to see in this short excerpt, one difference in how this student's reading practices differ from Nancy's is the pace at which the assigned readings are read and accepted as understood. In the moment shown here, the student is ratherly arduously making sense of the main ideas from two authorities, struggling to find the right words to capture her thoughts and arrive at a conclusion (however tenuous): the two authorities share some common ground. When the student finished a complete pass through the assigned readings, she too moved fairly quickly from reading and taking notes to text production, with the same outward ease as Nancy. The difference was in the amount of energy directed to understanding and reconciling the authorities in early comprehension. The creation of her inventory of ideas about the reading came far more slowly and was accompanied by a search for language that would best let her make a point. The reward for these "inefficient" moves in the period of early comprehension was evident in the way readers responded to her writing. She produced a more complex "synthesis" of the readings with a novel organizing idea and structure for her statement.

Other students reconsidered the consequences of their early comprehension as they continued to search for controlling ideas and relevant material. One student went through four cycles of trying out organizing concepts that fit her interpretation of the readings and the assignment. This search amounted to a considerable intellectual investment as she moved from ruminations on "an important key to quality work" to "important characteristics" to "things to remember in order to enhance time you set aside" and chose "good advice for any student" before she quit. The fact that this student took the time to find four concepts that would suffice as an organizing concept should not be downplayed. Through trial and revision she questioned the use of stock leads such as "Time management takes a different course for different people," "Time management is of great importance," "Time management is relative to each individual," and so forth.

When we see students question a stock approach, as in the search for a controlling idea or a plan for writing, we cannot say how *conscious* any of these students are of their actions. We can say that their literate procedures effectively pose the question:

"How will readers respond to these controlling ideas?" or "How will an investment in a summarization of the readings complement larger rhetorical considerations?" An action becomes a question, of course, only when students are truly aware of their habits and their consequences. Perhaps it is less that these students lack the ability to think and write critically than that they are not aware of their options. They are less practiced at risk taking, in this case delaying successful publication by questioning their own habits and assumptions and by complicating the act of translating a reading plan into a writing plan.

Our sense is that this awareness is limited by our assignments and the environments we create for self- and social-criticism more than an inadequacy in our students (Brown, 1986). At any rate, we know from talking with students and studying their writing and think-aloud transcripts that alternative representations and procedures do not need to be taught as completely new information, as we would teach a specialized academic convention. There are ways to celebrate and reinforce those occasions when students actively throw into question their immediate rhetorical situation and early comprehension and a reading plan are seen only as raw material with which to study the design of a paper, not declare it finished. If students can consciously slow the shift from early comprehension to translation, they practice a form of rhetorical sensitivity that can help establish them as writers within a rhetorical situation.

AWARENESS IN A RHETORICAL SITUATION

What we want our writing students to learn is how to examine their composing processes, especially their opening moves to comprehend a task and assigned readings, and to locate these moves within the immediate rhetorical situation. This examination can include a self-study of the origins of a writer's literate habits and assumptions, the history each writer brings to a rhetorical situation. The place to begin is with a writing assignment and the composing behavior at hand. If writers must negotiate assignments and responses and negotiate current reading and writing expectations and time-honored expertise, we suggest the juncture between early comprehension and translation as a place where this negotiation can be examined. It is here that a freshly constructed reading plan became (for our students) a blueprint for writing a first draft.

Through the semester, we found that teachers and students can make more explicit the routines and expectations they bring to a reading-to-writing assignment. It was illustrative to ask, for example, how the features of a given writing assignment matched assignments students had been given before in high school or other writing classes, and to explore how students responded to those features, how they defined success (how a reader responded or evaluated their work), and what they believed a teacher, school, or literate system wanted from them. Through open discussion and examples from drafts and think-aloud transcripts, students and teachers learned how they valued printed authorities, what a "controlling idea" is really supposed to control, and the relative value of a summarized idea. By doing so, students began to realize that a controlling idea controlled more than the order of ideas in a draft. It controls the character writers project with regard to topics, readers, and the larger community of readers and writers in which they compose. It was instructive, also, for students to watch as other writers wrestled with the lack of accord in the assigned readings and questioned commonplace rhetorical conventions. By sharing think-aloud transcripts and linking these oral texts to their written ones, we located commonalities and idiosyncrasies in the way students represented and acted out an assignment.

In some cases, a study of opening moves and how comprehension translates into action and a plan for writing helped students examine the local context and communities in which they reside. In this way, the relatively short-lived decision to question the practicality of a controlling idea or angle for writing, or the decision to search for an alternative representation of the printed authorities, could act as a vehicle for a student's self-critique of his or her role in a language community. This kind of awareness requires writers to step outside of the act of composing to strive for a critical distance from a specific decision and to locate that composing act in a larger setting. Recognizing the characteristics of literate practice could provide students with the raw material to begin a critique of self and society, looking at and deciding on a writer's role within politically and culturally defined communities (Chase, 1987).

If students and teachers study together the antecedents to literate behavior and study the consequences associated with habitual and less-habitual procedures for writing, they do so because of the need to create a meaningful piece of writing. The immediate goal for our students (we think a good one to pursue) is to produce interesting and useful writing. When this goal is extended to a larger critique of the writer's continuing role in a community of writers, in this case the role of writers in school, students are moving toward a positive form of "resistance," a term used by social and educational theorists to denote a political struggle against a dominant ideology (Giroux, 1983). We are happy if our students rethink a stock approach to a reading-to-write assignment and consider alternative behaviors. But we are aware that this rethinking can carry forward the self-critique as a revealing activity, one that offers a student the opportunity for self-reflection and self- and social-emancipation. Recalling our preference for writing and writers who bring a healthy skepticism to academic writing in order to continually and creatively push out against the discursive practices around them, a theory of social and educational resistance can benefit from a cognitive equivalent. The mental tools for examining, redefining, and following through on a act of translation can spark a larger critique, if student and teachers are willing.

Besides this kind of political and social awareness, other researchers and scholars emphasize reading and writing instruction that builds an awareness of and control over students' habits and deep-rooted assumptions about language. Peter Elbow (1985) believes we need to "develop more control over ourselves as we write so that we can *manage* [his italics] our writing process more judiciously and flexibly" (p. 300). Poststructuralist theories of how readers construct meaning rather than passively encode information suggest instruction to help students consciously explicate the repertoire of strategies and assumptions they bring to an act of composing (McCormick, 1985). Research on the rhetorical and linguistic case-building techniques in specialized discourse suggests exercises in which students recognize conventions in a specialization and in their own composing. Analyzing various conventions can suggest why a commonplace fails to engage a reader who may expect a certain rhetorical move in a particular genre (Huckin, 1987; Swales, 1984). And an arm of educational research is now exploring the value in and methods for "teaching thinking" (for a comprehensive review, see Nickerson, Perkins, & Smith, 1985), exploring both domain-general and domain-specific strategies (Voss & Post, 1988).

After all our illustrations and discussion, we would be remiss if we characterized rhetorical awareness as an act of devaluating or rejecting the ability to summarize and recite information. Even though we necessarily pointed to summarization and recitation procedures as a limiting "legacy," these skills serve as a superstructure on which to base rhetorical awareness and the procedures that complement it. In fact, current research and classroom practice suggest that students can be taught to increase their expertise in summarization and comprehension (Afflerbach, 1985; Brown & Day, 1983; Brown & Palincsar, 1989). Training and practice in summarization in this way contributes to a writer's growing awareness and control over reading comprehension and can augment otherwise typical composing routines (Tierney & Pearson, 1985). Direct attention to early comprehension and summarization, in turn, might facilitate the recognition of alternative perspectives for truly original interpretations (Applebee, 1984b) and the recognition of the features and conventions of college-level academic discourse.

In this chapter, we have tried to build detail into the image of how a freshman writer confronts the unique problem of representing and acting on a college-level writing assignment. We can expect our students to rely on their literate heritage, and in so doing to use that expertise as a basis for "appropriating" rhetorical and linguistic conventions and topical authority that is not yet theirs. Young college writers facing the demand of new contexts for reading and writing, with new linguistic and critical expectations, need not rely exclusively on the habits and assumptions accrued through years of schooling. By looking closely at the juncture between early comprehension and translation, we find evidence that awareness and alternative routines are there. With help from teachers, students can return to this juncture, drawing on these habits as well as others, and can begin to translate their immediate rhetorical situation into a more self-directed event. Instead of casting false starts, hesitations, and second thoughts about a writing move as wasted energy, informed reconsiderations can heighten a young writer's rhetorical awareness and help keep that writer's ideas and knowledge of logical and linguistic conventions at center stage in the act of composing academic discourse.

8

The Cultural Imperatives Underlying Cognitive Acts

KATHLEEN McCORMICK

The Need to Place Student Writing in Broader Cultural Contexts

In Chapter 7, we began to place reading and writing in a social context involving academic and nonacademic influences. We focused on how students' first responses to the Time Management text were rooted in practices they had learned—and learned well—in school. This chapter explores some ways in which both those very educational practices that students say influenced them and their varied responses to the time management talk are symptomatic of broader ideological practices. By largely focusing on the "interstices" of students' reading and writing—their class comments, interviews, and protocols, as well as some less easily studied aspects of their time management essays—this chapter investigates some of the cultural imperatives that may underlie the particular cognitive acts our students performed. As Mike Rose (1985) has argued, we need to create a "rich model of written language development and production" that will honor not only "the cognitive" but also the "emotional and situational dimensions of language . . . and aid us in understanding what we can observe as well as what we can only infer." In short, our earlier observations on the cognitive dimensions of writing and on the contextual nature of task definition must be integrated with larger cultural dimensions in which students learn to read and write.

It is primarily in Rose's realm of inference that this chapter necessarily works, attempting to tease out of students' comments more broadly based cultural and institutional factors that are silently but powerfully influencing their reading and writing behaviors. As such, most of these inferences are subject to interpretation by rival hypotheses. Nonetheless, by looking at our students' work on their time-management tasks within larger institutional contexts, we suspect their reading and writing acts can be seen as much more culturally motivated, directed, and constrained than we might have initially thought. Enabling students to develop the strategic awareness necessary for college-level success requires that they become aware of the cultural, as well as cognitive, forces that are directing them to read and write as they do.

In the first part of this chapter, we examine the methodologies involved in reading students' papers and listening to their remarks. We explore some students' and educators' positions on the nature of reading and writing to discover some of the ideological assumptions that compel certain reading and writing acts. We explain some of the ways in which ideology functions in a society and in educational systems in general by drawing on the work of some recent cultural criticism.

In the second part, we explore three interrelated culturally based assumptions that seem to have guided many of our students' determinations of their task definition for the exercise: the desire for *closure;* a belief in *objectivity;* and a refusal to write about perceived *contradictions.*

Learning to Recognize Assumptions Underlying Students' Writing

None of our students' assumptions about closure, objectivity, or contradiction is explicitly mentioned "in" their essays on time management; but their interviews, protocols, and class comments suggest that these assumptions nonetheless motivate many of the cognitive acts they perform. Because reading and writing are learned in rich social contexts, they are always influenced by complex cultural assumptions and expectations, many of which are at best implicit in students' written work. One of the reasons students may have such difficulty developing strategic awareness of their reading and writing options could be that these patterns are influenced much more than we generally acknowledge by broadly based cultural assumptions concerning the nature of reading, writing, knowledge, and the educational system in general.

For example, quite apart from any specific task, many students believe they have to write a "perfect first paragraph" that will unify their whole paper. In addition to (sometimes) impeding their ability to write, this assumption also suggests that students possibly misconceive the nature of writing by confusing the thinking *process* with the written *product* and by viewing writing as a procedure whereby the writer puts closure on ideas rather than explores and develops new ones. It may make their writing a dull process in which they can develop only the ideas they set out in the first paragraph (see Chapter 7). As one student commented in class when discussing how he wrote the first draft of his time management essay:

> I'd go back and read the first paragraph. Because, like they always teach you in high school, you should always say what you're going to say, say it, and then tell them

again. So, I looked at what I said in the first paragraph and repeated it even better than I did in the first paragraph in the last paragraph.

The repeated rereading of this first paragraph and reliance on it as a gauge for how his paper should develop prevents him from developing new ideas about the subject during the act of writing.

Another student unconsciously presents some insight into what he thinks it is to acquire knowledge. For him, it is simply a matter of discovering what other people have to say and then passively paraphrasing their points rather than questioning them, bringing his own information to bear on the subject, or criticizing the authors' positions. In discussing how he wrote his paper, he commented in class:

> I had to go back and reread each point and I got an idea of where I should start. I then wrote a paragraph about each point. I looked it over really carefully in my mind, and I tried to figure out what it was saying. And then I wrote about it. And I think that worked really well for me.

For this student, like many others, writing a summary seems like an appropriate task because it is straightforward and it demonstrates that he read the material. Notice that he derives a certain degree of pleasure from his achievement, an achievement for which he was no doubt rewarded in high school and which is important for reading comprehension. But because of his training in high school, this student, like his classmate quoted earlier, did not imagine that his finished paper could be dull or tedious to read or that it might not be what this particular educational system wanted him to produce (see Chapter 7).

Comments such as these imply that students believe their writing will be most valued if it is something unified and without contradiction, if it appears closed and objective, even though their most interesting positions in their protocols were often where they took up distinctive positions (see Chapter 5). For a number of reasons, many of these positions did not make their way into students' final papers; clearly one reason for this is that students believe the educational system wants them to produce texts with closure, without contradictions, and apparently objective. Since such a large number of students suggest they feel this way about writing, knowledge, and the educational system, we might profitably study how, why, and in what circumstances they are developing such notions—notions that do not necessarily prepare them for developing critical interpretive abilities. We might then share our findings with our students.

Developing Complementarities Between Rhetorical and Literary Theories: Reading for Absences

Our desire to develop complementarities among cultural and cognitive theories of reading and writing is one that many teachers of literature and composition share (see Bartholomae, 1985; Bizzell, 1982; Faigley, 1986; Heath, 1983; Lunsford, 1980; McCormick, 1985; McCormick & Waller, with Flower, 1987; Waller, McCormick, & Fowler, 1986). One productive way to do this is to explore the methods of investigating cultural marking developed by poststructuralist literary and cultural critics over the last twenty years. It is, of course, as difficult to generalize about "poststructuralist" literary and cultural theorists as about composition researchers. But a variety of theorists such as Louis Althusser, Michel Foucault, Pierre Macherey, Fredric Jameson, and Terry Eagleton have taught us to look for what is "absent" as much as for what is "present" in any data—that is, look for unstated or unacknowledged cultural assumptions and institutional pressures motivating cognitive actions. Their methodologies and insights can help us develop analyses of our students' reading and writing processes in broader cultural and historical contexts. So, for example, when students are instructed not to say "I" in their papers, as many of our students report they were in elementary or high school, their teachers may have thought they were teaching them a stylistic rule, associated with academic writing in which the "I" is subordinated to "objective" evidence and ideas. Or the teacher may have seen the stylistic rule as a way of helping students develop a more public voice. There is, however, often a gap between what the teacher taught and what the students learned. From this supposedly "innocent" stylistic rule, students report learning that their opinions are not valued, that their essay must sound "objective" instead of "subjective," and that they can best succeed in school by ignoring rather than developing their own ideas. They believe that more accomplished writers are capable of using their own ideas, but they themselves seem unable or unwilling to do so (see Chapter 3).

This gap between what the teacher is supposedly teaching and what the student is supposedly learning should not be dismissed lightly as a simple misunderstanding. To be told that one cannot say "I" in a culture that continually emphasizes the significance of the individual subject can cause the student to become alienated and disoriented. In "innocently" moving the child into the public sphere by instructing him or her not to use "I," the teacher may be simultaneously (and contradictorily) cutting the child away from this sphere: on the one hand, to be "public" the child learns that he or she cannot say "I"; on the other hand, the public sphere, from its advertising to its disciplining practices, is continually interpellating, in the sense used by Louis Althusser, of "summoning" or "calling out to," and defining the child as an individual. The situation is confusing—others can speak to the child as an individual subject, but the child cannot speak of himself or herself as an individual—and on some level the child is aware of the situational and cultural contradictions in which he or she is situated.

One of the major tensions of our culture that is surely a "present absence" in this particular moment of learning is between individualism and conformity: the child must conform to the teacher's rules in order to get good grades, and perhaps to communicate and succeed in a world much larger than the classroom. Learning to succeed by effacing oneself as a subject is just one of the many social apparatuses that helps to fragment and decenter the subject. Although decentering students is generally not likely to be a goal of teaching syntax, it is one of the likely results because rules of syntax help to determine ways of thought that extend beyond the classroom and that will help constitute the boundaries of students' views of reality. Such rules are, we might say, one type of *signification* of reality.

The institutional pressure not to say "I," with all its attendant, mixed assumptions, cannot be articulated directly in the actual texts that students write for class;

rather, it must be teased out, often years after it was first learned, from the students' interviews, protocols, and in-class discussions. Even there, however, the institutional assumptions may be only implicit: the pressure of institutions is often felt to be so natural it does not require explicit acknowledgment. Looking further at these absences, we can begin to explore some of the powerful ideological antecedents for individual writers' goals. Attempting to express the silent, or at least the not fully articulated, pressures of the educational institution and locating this expression in the broadest possible cultural context will help us *suggest* (because we can never fully determine) some of the cultural imperatives that underlie acts of cognition.

Ideology and Students' Writing

To argue that reading and writing are inextricably embedded in rich cultural contexts is not new; what is new is the insistence that such a context can be illuminated by the intellectual categories developed in the past two decades by poststructuralist literary and cultural theory. Power, Foucault has remarked frequently, resides in the details of social life: in the way people dress; in how they sit in a classroom; in what newspapers they read, if any; in the books they value as "literature"; in their notions of what it is to be educated, elegant, or successful. It is in such details that we can see the pressures as well as the permissions of power. Students naturalize (both in the sense of adapting and seeing as natural) the demands of the particular educational structures in which they are trained. They choose certain strategies of reading and writing for their apparent effectiveness—but effectiveness is a cultural category, defined by institutions, social structures, the everyday practices of the culture. In short, effectiveness is defined by and within a particular *ideology*. Increasing our students' strategic awareness, that is, their rhetorical options and control of their own cognition, therefore, should involve their ideological awareness.

Since "ideology" is both a frequently misunderstood term and one central to my analysis, it is important to define it carefully. Ideology is frequently thought to be a system of false beliefs, often those of one's political enemies; for example, "The Russians were speaking ideology" (with the assumption that *we* speak the truth and *they* speak out of vested political beliefs). But ideology is not something that only other people have—it is inescapable. Ideology refers to the shared, though very diverse beliefs, assumptions, habits, and practices of a particular society. Most of the members of a given society are not conscious of the ideological nature of their beliefs. They simply take them for granted, seeing them as "normal." For example, most Americans assume that classrooms should be arranged so that students sit in neat rows facing the teacher whose chair and desk is larger than the students' and who is always positioned at the head of the class. Such actions in themselves are not ideological, but the assumptions behind them are—assumptions that students should see teachers as authority figures who are superior to them, who will "impart" knowledge, rather than "share" or "participate in" it. These ordinary assumptions are part of a way of life, a set of values about what constitutes the "good," "proper," or "civilized" view of life. But such assumptions are clearly not "natural"; they are learned, conventional, part of a historical and cultural context.

When we turn to our students' time-management task, we can see how their writing, like all writing, is full of ideological assumptions. Look, for example, at the following extract from a student's in-class explanation of her procedure for writing drafts of her time management essay:

> Through revisions, I found out the author's purpose. Once my conclusions explained the main points of the passage, I found the true purpose and could begin my actual paper.

Let us explore some ways in which an ideological reading could suggest possible origins for this student's quite clearly articulated goals. How could we discover some of the unstated assumptions underlying her position and articulate some of the absences in her discussion?

The phrases, "author's purpose," "true purpose," and "actual paper," are key terms for an ideological analysis. They are "absences," as discussed in the previous section, because the student seems unaware of their cultural significance, unaware that they are historically situated, value-laden terms, not natural truths. They are present as influences on her, but absent from her consciousness as anything that needs to be thought about critically. These phrases suggest the student believes that the text will have a unified meaning, that she is finding rather than creating that meaning by her "revisions," and that "actual" writing can only begin once she has developed a coherent, unified idea. We saw in Chapter 4 that most students, like this one, expected the material provided by the teacher to be coherent. Unlike this student, however, a number of other students (understandably) found it difficult, if not impossible, to create a coherent representation of the material and did not finally write an essay in response to it. It is important to see that despite the differences in their responses, these students are all privileging coherence as an attribute of texts, indeed a prerequisite for responding to them. So strong and unquestioned is this particular student's belief in the unity of the text on time management that she fails to note that each paragraph was written by a different author. She will not acknowledge fragmentation even when directly confronted with it both by a line on top of the essay explaining that the essay is a series of quotations from a variety of sources and in the obvious disjunction between paragraphs. This student's discussion of her writing process suggests even more deeply rooted ideological beliefs. Her faith in authority and her assumption that she must make her paper echo the "truths" of the authorities trap her. For it requires that she maintain an intellectual passivity and an unwillingness to read the text critically in order to be able to write about it (see Chapter 7).

If this analysis is even partly accurate, we clearly need to place more emphasis on teaching students to argue with authorities. By this we do not mean to imply that students should not read arguments carefully to discover what the authorities have said or that they should argue willy-nilly with them just for the sake of argument. Being critical does not mean being perverse. What we are suggesting is that it is impossible to separate fully the stages of reading to discover "the facts" from reading to develop a position. Since any summary is always perspective, it is crucial that students recognize the role of their perspectives in reading texts. The student just quoted looks for coherence in the time management text at least in part because she has learned that coherence is a mark of authoritative texts, and as a student, fairly low in the power structure, she may feel that her safest strategy is to accord to the text the authority of "truth" that school texts are generally given. Paradoxically, her desire to be "faithful" to the text, coupled with her apparent belief that all texts are unified, prevented her from seeing the contradictions inherent in the text. If she were more aware of her own assumptions and of their root in larger ideological structures, she might have been able to alter them when she came upon a text that did not conform to them, and she might have been able to see that this text is fragmented and contradictory, not unified.

The Invisibility of Ideology in the Educational System

Ideology is expressed in the educational systems of any society. Educational systems, like any cultural system, are always historically *situated,* that is, a product of particular cultural and historical forces. Thus, what students are taught about any subject necessarily values certain aspects of that subject over others. While this process of selection is inevitable, it is not uniform either across cultures or within a given culture at a particular time. Foucault argues in his essay "The Order of Discourse" (1971) that "any system of education is a political way of maintaining or modifying the appropriation of discourses, along with the power and knowledge they carry" (p. 64). Consequently, the educational system can be as much a means of repressing certain groups of people as it is a means of empowering others. While many students and educators may be intuitively aware of the repressive as well as the enabling function of education, it is only when we begin to investigate systematically the ideological reasons underlying the ways in which students are taught that we might possibly begin to change these educational inequities.

Such a task is very difficult, however, because ideology typically functions as invisibly as possible. For instance, we take for granted the practice of students putting their names on their papers. How else could the teacher grade them? This practice, however, emphasizes one belief: that an individual is distinct from a group and that he or she should be evaluated independently from that group. We can easily imagine a situation in which the members of a class worked together on a group project, but it is harder to imagine a situation in which the students who participated remained anonymous. The need to put one's name on a paper or project, the need to say "This is mine" is ideological. Similarly, the need to evaluate and be evaluated individually rather than collectively is also ideological.

In both instances the ideology seems invisible; but its effects, even in the earliest years of education, are obvious once we look for them. During a recent workshop, a high school administrator in English recounted a particularly insightful story that illustrated the subtle workings of ideology. One evening, she asked her third-grade daughter, who was writing a paper about a story she had read for English class, if she had talked about the story with her classmates. "Oh no," the girl replied reproachfully, "that would be cheating!" The notion that the individual exists outside a group and must be evaluated as such has been turned into a moral principle by this and many other young students: to share knowledge is wrong unless you have already gotten your grade (by which time the significance of the knowledge is frequently forgotten). One can see that such supposedly moral views carried to extremes can cause one to become authoritarian and elitist, and yet this girl in no way means to be either. She is only trying to be "honest." Moral values such as these seem "natural," "correct," and "unquestionable" to students and teachers alike because they are driven by ideologically invisible classroom and examination practices. The very topic of our study, "time management," is also influenced by the dominant ideological forces in America—it grows out of a distinctively (though, of course, not exclusively) American preoccupation with efficiency and progress. Ideology is also infused in the language system of a culture, a system that makes perception possible rather than, as was commonly thought, a tool by which people express what they have already perceived.

Ideology, therefore, preserves order in a society by delimiting its linguistic and social practices. That ideology restricts social practices, however, as it did with the young girl mentioned earlier, does not of course mean that it is pernicious. Most societies want to believe that they are unified, coherent, devoid of contradictions, and that their customs and beliefs are "true" and "objectively correct"; ideology is what enables them to maintain this illusion. For example, one of our students stated in class, "I don't think when I read. It just somehow sinks in in some strange way. And I comprehend it." This student's apparent lack of awareness to her reading strategies points to a larger lack of awareness that she brings complex sets of cultural, as well as cognitive, assumptions to bear in any perceptual situation. The ideological nature of her expectation of closure and coherence, and of her attendant assumptions that language is transparent and that texts and readers are unified, is invisible for this student. We can get further insight into why this is so when she goes on to explain what she does when she is reading to write: "What I usually do is read through it, and then I go back and I pick out main points and I usually write the assignment from there." This student not only does not question her reading process, she also does not question the strategies of the texts she read. She talks as though texts, like her reading process, are straightforward, objective, and naturally correct. She talks this way because she has been trained to think this way.

Our culture's belief in objectivity comes out in the most seemingly mundane social practices when, for example, students are told to write a "coherent" essay. Such instructions suggest to many students that incoherence, ambiguity, or contradictions are the mark of a poorly written essay, even though when almost any subject matter is investigated including time management, one discovers that many experts contradict each other. Having been instructed from an early age to be coherent themselves, students not only expect coherence in the texts they read, they will ignore the subtleties of an argument in the name of coherence. One might argue (as a reader of an early version of this report did) that this behavior is simply the result of laziness—students perceive the contradictions but choose not to write about them because they are afraid that if they mention them, they will have to resolve them. Such a remark, however, is still caught up in the ideology of objectivity and coherence: it assumes, first, that it is *intrinsically easier* to write about coherence than ambiguity, and, second, that all ambiguities must finally be resolved. Even if students do find it easier to create coherence than to acknowledge incoherence—a dubious assumption in this case, since it took much more work for students reading the time-management essay to create a consistent argument than simply to acknowledge the inconsistencies—we must still recognize that the ability to create coherence is an ideologically produced practice, not something that is natural or value-free. Further, if indiscriminately privileged, it is a practice that can impede the recognition that not all ambiguities or contradictions are resolvable.

We should keep in mind, however, that many of our students, particularly in their protocols, did disagree with one or more of the positions in the time management text. That a large number of those positions did not make their way into the students' final essays (see Chapters 5 and 6) suggests not laziness but rather that students may hold certain assumptions about moving from informal writing or thinking aloud to more formal essay writing: assumptions such as the need to move toward coherence, to summarize uncritically the source text's viewpoints rather than foreground one's own positions, to write what seems objectively correct. That students often wrote simplistic essays while they had developed much more complex elaborations further suggests the power of a dominant school ideology encouraging intellectual passivity. The strength and interest of many students' elaborations, however, imply that they have enormous potential to develop strategic and ideological awareness and thus a more active relationship to the texts about which they read and write. What follows is an analysis of three aspects of our students' responses to the time-management essays to show the invisible influence of our culture's ideology, particularly our educational system, on their reading and writing. It focuses on students' seeking closure, trying to be objective, and avoiding contradictions.

Three Ideological Assumptions Guiding Students' Writing
THE DESIRE FOR CLOSURE: THE FAILURE TO BE TENTATIVE

Closure in writing means coming to explicit conclusions about a particular issue that rules out alternative ways of conceiving the issue. Closure can be achieved either by arguing against these alternatives or by failing to take them into account. Experts more frequently achieve closure in the former way; novices, in the latter. A number of students expressed pleasure in the closure that writing a summary affords. One student, for example, remarked after writing her first essay:

> I read each paragraph, figured out the main idea . . . and when I had a few main ideas, I wrote the paper and concentrated on each one of them—just going from one idea to the other—and it just fell into place, and everything was pretty much all right.

Her strategy is to go straight to a summary that follows the order of the text; these remarks indicate that she has the metacognitive ability to explain in general what her primary writing strategy was, but not to explore why she employed it. This strategy seems simple enough—so simple, natural, or obvious that the student does not think to address, either in her essay or her comments on it, the cultural factors that have motivated her *choosing* this strategy over other possible strategies. Further, she does not acknowledge that she could have used other strategies—tentative, explorative, questioning strategies—to approach the text. Why does this student, and others like her, feel the need to place closure on the text in the form of a summary, especially when she later proved capable of developing a more complex interpretation in a second draft? Why does she feel the need to have everything "fall into place"? Some would argue that having everything fall into place is a universal human desire, though at this point in our analysis, we should begin to recognize the ideological impulses behind assertions of universality. Experts in any field—from literary study to physics—knows that things never fall into place, that they are always in a state of flux. The more one knows, the less one can be sure of. Nonetheless, television sitcoms, politicians, advertisements—all major ideological influences—tell us that we can attain closure, get it right, know (or have) it all. It is these ideological apparatuses, along with much of the educational system that values closure over exploration, that are influencing this student, and she is responding as sensitively and sensibly as can be expected under the circumstances.

As they are traditionally taught—despite the supposed widespread use of the process approach to writing in the classroom—interpretation and summary require students to focus on their final reading of a text rather than on their reading process, that is, to come to a conclusion, to achieve closure. Traditional interpretations and summaries generally demand that readers ignore or explain away any sense of ambiguity or confusion when they begin to write about a text they have just read, even if they found those to be characteristics of the text itself or had those reactions themselves when reading. Tentativeness, students are taught, just is not the way to go; it is often seen as a mark of an ignorant rather than an explorative mind.

A tentative reaction, unlike the seemingly objective summary, has costs and benefits for students, but most students seem to know only about the costs. Tentativeness can occur in expert writers' early drafts in many forms: they may write with a tentative prose style, asking myriad questions of themselves; they may write in a seemingly authoritative style, but include contradictory perspectives among which they know they will have to adjudicate in a later draft; they may ask questions of themselves parenthetically or in the margins of their drafts. Tentativeness suggests that problems or unresolved conflicts exist and that more reading and thinking needs to be done. Therefore, regardless of what form experts' writing takes in a first draft, it generally bespeaks an open-mindedness to revision, a willingness and an awareness of the need to rethink ideas. While most expert writers and teachers would probably agree that tentativeness almost always characterized their first drafts, they will frequently not accept it in their students' final drafts (which, alas, in many instances are also their first drafts). Thus, students like the one quoted earlier learn to shut off nagging internal voices that suggest new ways to piece material together or that the material does not fit at all. While many teachers want closure to occur in students' essays after they go through elaborate procedures of synthesizing the material for their own purposes, students get the message that they should reach closure immediately at any cost. And the cost is generally in terms of the subtlety and creativity of their own work (see Chapters 5 and 6).

What are the advantages of students' writing more tentative responses to texts? First of all, it opens the text up to multiple interpretations rather than closing it off, thereby potentially giving students a voice in their essays. It makes the text available to readers with diverse perspectives and demands that the reader consider his or her perspective. Tentativeness implies that meaning is not derived solely from the text, but rather is produced as a result of a complex interaction of cognitive and cultural, as well as textual variables—any or all of which could possibly become the subject of analysis in a later draft. A tentative, open approach that stresses issues and questions rather than mere statement of "facts" further allows students to develop, and possibly even change, their position on the subject about which they are writing *during the course of their writing*. A tentative, as opposed to a closed approach, leaves interpretive options open and regards writing as an occasion for discovery rather than a tool for recording what is already known.

Tentativeness is a necessary part of the process model of writing which advocates that students and teachers focus on the writing act rather than just on the writing product. But without encouraging students to be tentative and without teaching them why a tentative, open, questioning approach can be regarded as a clearer sign of thinking than a paper that all "fits together," most students will be loath to try it. This is not to say that tentativeness must necessarily oppose coherence in an early draft, but rather that the desire for coherence frequently causes students to create closure prematurely, and that premature, superficial coherence is not preferable to the tentativeness of a complex argument (see Chapter 2).

The summary seems to be one quick, easy method for students to attain the near instantaneous closure teachers seem to demand, because it is a process of both reading and writing that deemphasizes the dialogue in which the student engages when reading. Although a necessary and significant first step to understanding, the summary is an inadequate stopping point for more complex kinds of thinking. Many students, however, largely because of their desire for closure in both reading and writing, do not see it this way, and it seems that many are not being rewarded for developing an alternative task representation. As Richard Richardson notes in *Literacy in the Open Access-College* (1983), many students find themselves daily in "information-transfer courses" in which the teacher, using texts like ours on time management, "disseminates" information to the students and the students, by and large, play the role of the "attentive audience" or "active non-participants." In such situations, students attend class merely to take in information so that they can later give it back, unedited and pretty much unconsidered.

Institutional Encouragement to Write with Closure

In studying the French educational system, Etienne Balibar and Pierre Macherey (1981) observed that only "basic language" is taught in all French primary schools while "literary language" is taught in advanced levels. Such a division in the educational system allows one group of students to learn a language that is more highly valued in society than another. A similar stratification may exist in the American education system at even higher levels of education regarding the teaching of summarizing as opposed to critical thinking skills. Braxton and Nordvall (1985), for example, report that more selective (regarding admission standards) liberal arts colleges tend to demand "higher order levels of understanding" on course examinations than do less selective liberal arts colleges. By "higher order" Braxton and Nordvall, following Bloom's taxonomy, mean "application" and "critical thinking" questions. These are opposed to the simple "knowledge" questions asked more predominantly at less selective liberal arts colleges. These data, however, should not encourage universities who place themselves in the first category to pat themselves blithely on the back. Most students we interviewed at Carnegie Mellon, after they had completed all phases of the time management task and had been told that they were expected to develop a position of their own and integrate it with what they read, nonetheless reported that they would not immediately use sophisticated interpretive strategies when they wrote for another course. As one student commented, "It depends on what the teacher wants. . . . They want you to analyze sometimes. But in a lot of cases what they want is just 'list and gist.' " This student is suggesting, therefore, that, at least in his perception, a division exists within the university itself; many teachers ask questions requiring simple information transfer rather than more sophisticated interpretive strategies. Of course, this still leaves open the question of whether this student is correctly assessing the demands of these other instructors, whether he is missing their perhaps inexplicit cues that ask for more than a simple "list and gist."

Thus, we can see two major reasons why students would try to produce closure in the form of a summary in their papers. The first results from a kind of misunderstanding between teachers and students. Teachers want a polished, organized, coherent, and unified final draft; students often want to write only one draft, and hence to achieve closure, by refusing to engage with the text in a questioning, tentative, or argumentative way. The second results from more significant institutional problems: training students at particular educational levels in only basic modes of thinking and writing; rewarding students in classes for "actively nonparticipating," for listening and giving back unreformulated information that the teacher has presented to them; requiring students to be capable of answering only simple "knowledge" questions. Both situations—the first indirectly, the second directly—fail to encourage students to think critically about the material they read, their responses to it, or their own opinions.

Why would teachers or entire educational systems develop programs of training and testing that ultimately inhibit rather than stimulate students' thought? Foucault (1971) suggests subtle ideological reasons for this practice. In "The Order of Discourse," he analyzes various procedures and principles by which the ideology of a society controls and delimits discourse in order to ensure the successful reproduction of the current social system. Among these is the principle of *rarefaction*, a process whereby one is encouraged to analyze a text, not to discover multiple and often contradictory meanings but to demonstrate a limited, single, unified meaning. The discovery and reproduction of a unified meaning in texts is just one way in which a society asserts its consistency and stability. A major procedure by which discourse is "rarefied" is through *commentary*. According to Foucault, commentary "allows us to say something other than the text itself, but on condition that it is this text itself which is said, and in a sense completed." Although Foucault acknowledges that a commentary always says something that the text on which it is commenting did not say, because a text cannot be reproduced objectively, he recognizes that commentary so defined "exorcises the chance element of discourse" because "by a paradox which it always displaces but never escapes, the commentary must say for the first time what had, nonetheless, already been said, and must tirelessly repeat what had, however, never been said." In other words, summary will necessarily differ from the sources it is summarizing, but its rhetorical and ideological strength lies in its supposed faithful reproduction or reduction of those sources rather than in its deviation from them.

The effacement or downplaying of differences between summaries or commentaries and their origin contributes to the particular sense of order, objectivity, and truth that are so much a part of any ideological system. One of the goals of the educational system is to teach students to function in the existing society. In so doing, it must necessarily give priority to those practices that will ensure the survival of established modes of thinking and marginalize (and frequently exclude) what Foucault terms "the chance elements" of discourse that could disrupt the existing order. One effective way of stifling the development of potentially disruptive discourse is to teach students that there is a greater value in learning to reproduce "faithfully" the "truths" that allegedly exist in already accepted texts than in learning to read against the grain for absences, discontinuities, and the purposes of developing a counterargument. While oppositional reading may remain within the accepted limits of a particular discourse, it runs a much greater risk of introducing disruptive chance elements that might themselves be true but are not, as Foucault says, "in the true" (*dans le vrai*)—that is, not within the accepted discourse of one's time. If trained to avoid digressing from acceptable discourse, students writing an essay about something they have read will probably try to be as "true" to the text as they can, to try to keep out as many chance elements as possible. Such a goal can perhaps best be accomplished by writing a summary in which the new elements that students introduce are effaced and in which their own texts can be seen as subservient to the text they were assigned to read and write about.

THE GOAL OF OBJECTIVITY: THE NEED TO QUESTION
THE SUBJECTIVE/OBJECTIVE PARADIGM

Some students felt a strong tension between their desire to be "objective" and their desire to develop their own ideas. The wish to be objective seems to derive from three related assumptions: first, students believe in (or at least act upon) a subjective/objective paradigm—that opinions are either personal, emotional, and *subjective,* or factual, verifiable, and *objective.* Many appear to believe that an objectively true position on any subject can be attained. Second, students tend to attribute objectivity to the authority of an expert's printed opinion. Third, students seem to regard their own positions and ideas as subjective, personal, likely to be wrong, and lacking authority. One student, for example, who became so frustrated that he did not complete his time-management paper, commented in class:

> When I read, I tried to get just one idea out of the thing—just to condense each point . . . and try and get it together. . . . I did the same thing with writing, and it was really bad because I tried to just take it from a totally objective point of view. . . . Finally I stopped and said I have to take this totally from my own point of view, but first I have to get a point of view. And I wasted so much time, that I never got done with the thing. . . . And I'm really sorry I didn't keep going with it, because I did get some really good ideas.

Why is this student incapable of putting his own ideas on paper? What cultural and institutional pressures are simultaneously warring within him, one telling him to be "objective," the other to take a position of his own?

This student seems to be hampered by a belief in the subjective/objective paradigm. He wants, on the one hand, to overcome it, to get away from being "totally objective." He implies that his reasons for getting away from objectivity are that this stance is rather dull and also that he has been told in class to include his own opinions. On the other hand, however, he seems incapable of writing a paper using his own ideas, even if he thinks some of them were "really good." This student does not seem to know *how* to write a paper in which he uses his own ideas. Why should this be? Rather than lacking the cognitive capabilities necessary to integrate his own ideas into a paper, our work suggests that he lacks the practical strategies to do so. It is very likely, especially given other students' comments about the inabilities to use their own ideas, that this student's cognitive problem is culturally induced: he does not know how to use his own opinions in a paper because he has not been *taught* how to. In fact, in most circumstances, his perceived need to be "objective" has discouraged him from even trying.

Let us look at some comments of other students to further our understanding of the ways in which the subjective/objective paradigm constrains students' use of their own ideas. One student discussed in an interview why he did not use his own opinions: "I've always had difficulty on formal papers bringing my own ideas. I never thought that was right." This student's choice of words suggests that he believes it is almost immoral (or at least incorrect) to express his own opinion in an essay. He said that for him "interpreting [was] like summarizing." When asked whether he had ideas of his own to express, he said he most definitely did, but that it was wrong to bring them up and he demonstrated how the seemingly simple and innocent rule of not using "I" discussed earlier effaced him as a thinking person with valuable ideas:

> They were always discouraging me from using "I." I always felt awkward in saying "the writer's opinion is." So I was never comfortable expressing my own ideas in a formal paper.

This student's teachers probably did not want him to interpret their instructions as he did. They most likely had in mind the idea that "I" is not necessary because whatever the writer states in his or her own paper is obviously his or her own opinion. But, as this student inferred, one can state many things in a paper that are not one's own opinions, but are, rather, the opinions of others—since these opinions are in print, they often seem "correct." If always correct, the experts' opinions are, by extension, objective and true; the student's opinions, in contrast seem subjective, and likely to be at best, "inappropriate," at worst, wrong.

Another student made the following statement:

> I didn't believe that it was right for me to put a lot of my own things into papers. I thought that I had to take a lot of things just from the text. And even with organizing concepts, a lot of times I would just take them from the text. I never had the feeling I had the right to have my own. I guess it's because I always figured that this person was the author. And if I was to be writing a paper, it would be more of a summary than an interpretation.

Underlying these comments is the sense that "the author" is a term one can give only to an expert. The student, although a writer of papers, is not in his own mind an author but a transcriber, a conduit through which information is passed rather than an organizer of information or a developer of new ideas. These three students are intimidated by what they perceive as experts' objective knowledge, and seem to feel unauthorized to explore and analyze their own opinions. Again we should remember that many students did express their own opinions quite freely in their protocols, class discussions, notes, or interviews, and some did in their final papers; but the fact that students often offered less developed opinions in their papers than they recorded elsewhere suggests an ambivalence regarding the appropriateness of using their own ideas in a formal essay.

Many proponents of the process model of writing have attempted to counter the objective model by asserting that the individual student writer is unique, and, therefore, must be allowed to express himself or herself "freely." D. Gordon Rohman (1965) and Donald Stewart (1969) advocate the use of expressive theories of writing to help students like the one mentioned previously get over the fear of using their own opinions. Rohman argues that "'good writing' must be the discovery by a responsible person of his uniqueness within his subject." Although this subjective, expressive model of writing may be laudable in many respects, it can nonetheless put students in a bind that is as problematic as the traditional text-based, product-oriented, objective model. According to the expressive model, students must have integrity and be sincere, qualities that can supposedly be determined objectively by teachers but in fact are always inferred by certain value judgments. So, although students are told to "be themselves," teachers still have the right to say whether or not they have been. Further, while students must rely solely on experts' opinions in the objective information-transfer situation, under the subjective paradigm, they must rely completely on themselves. This can lead to two obvious problems: students' drafts and papers can be loosely impressionistic, uncritical, and "touchy-feely" or simply misinformed because students are not encouraged to go "outside their own heads" for information. Expressive theories, therefore, like objective theories ignore the fact that the subjective/objective paradigm is a false one.

What are the implications for students of such a critique of the subjective/objective paradigm? What are the implications of their recognizing that there is no one correct and objective answer to a given problem? Many teachers are afraid that such a recognition might lead to a pernicious kind of relativism, that students will then think that "anything goes," and that they will argue that their own opinions, however vacuous or uninformed, are as valid as those of the most knowledgeable experts. Such a fear is unfounded for at least two reasons. First, it is still based on a residual assumption that if positions are not objective, they will become subjective. Second, it assumes that we cannot tell students an important piece of information that all of us know: that rival hypotheses exist, and that texts and contexts are always subject to multiple, overlapping, and frequently contradictory interpretations.

Failing to inform students about the reductiveness of the subject/object dichotomy is similar to the failure discussed earlier to teach students the value of maintaining a tentative position in early drafts of a paper. Most of us are opposed to thinking in black and white categories, yet if we imply to our students that they must, we are depriving them of creative and critical cognitive options in which we as writers, thinkers, and researchers engage all the time. If students recognize and are required in their papers both to address the fact that experts disagree about almost every important issue today and to explore *why* those disagreements exist, they will not be plunged into relativism. They will discover that disagreements are not arbitrary, subjective, or a result of believing "anything goes": experts disagree because they develop arguments in diverse contexts and from divergent underlying assumptions. As a consequence of recognizing the situated—not arbitrary—nature of all positions, students may see that in order to take a certain position themselves or to agree with a particular expert, they must explore (while reading) and explain (while writing) the assumptions underlying their particular stances. In taking a particular stance, they will also have to acknowledge that they are always choosing among diverse assumptions and that these choices must be justified. This justification cannot occur on the basis of an absolute "right" and "wrong," but must result from situating the positions in larger cultural contexts and examining the *contexts* in which an argument would seem "right." Such writing requires students to maintain positions of their own, to recognize and explain how these positions are situated— in short, to become articulate critical thinkers, a goal writing teachers have always cherished. This goal, however, can be attained only in a rich cultural context that rids itself of the subjective/objective paradigm, that situates the positions of experts, and that grants credibility to the positions of students by giving them, indeed requiring them to develop, a voice that must be as closely scrutinized as those of the experts.

One of the first steps in effecting this end, the subject of the next section, must be to get students to see that contradictions exist among experts and to recognize that it is the very presence of these contradictory positions that leaves room for them to enter meaningfully into the conversation.

THE AVOIDANCE OF CONTRADICTION

Categorizing Students' Essays

One of the most striking aspects of our students' responses to the time management text was that so few of them discussed the contradictions in their essays despite the fact that many students discussed these contradictions in their protocols. Many student essays did not even acknowledge that the text was composed of extracts from various sources. Struck by this observation, we decided to categorize the essays into five types: in the first (0), students did not mention the contradictions; in the second (1), students mentioned the contradictions only in passing in the form of a summary; in the third (2), students attempted vaguely to reconcile the contradictions; in the fourth (3), students attempted to explain and analyze the contradictions in terms of larger cultural or cognitive considerations; and in the fifth (4), students noted the contradictions and attempted to resolve or explain them by presenting their own opinion. (See Table 7 for categorization of essays; this analysis is limited to the fifty-seven essays for which both drafts and revisions were available.) Recall that each student wrote a pair of essays. (Table 8 categorizes essay pairs.)

Sixty-seven percent of all the essays written did not mention that contradictions

Table 7. Students' Reactions to Contradictions

Coding[a]	Number of Essays	Percentages
0	76	67
1	24	22
2	3	2
3	4	3
4	7	6

Note: $N = 114$, total number of essays

[a]Key:

    0 = did not mention contradictions
    1 = mentioned contradictions but does not analyze
    2 = attempted vaguely to reconcile contradictions
    3 = attempted to explain contradictions in terms of larger cultural
        and/or cognitive considerations
    4 = acknowledged contradictions and developed own views on time
        management in the context of contradictions

existed in the text (0). Looking at the essays in pairs, 54 percent of the students did not mention the contradictions in either of their essays (pattern 0/0). This is the only significant pattern of pairing that occurred among the essay types.

Twenty-two percent of the essays were of the second type; students noted that the experts disagreed but mentioned this only in passing in summary form and, for most of their essay, ignored this fact. A student in this category typically opened his or her essay with a paragraph like the following:

> Time management has been the subject of numerous studies, but the issue is by no means resolved. Most experts agree, however, that an effective method of time man-agement increases an individual's efficiency; what they do not agree on is how one should go about implementing such a program.

Table 8. Students' Reactions to Contradictions in Essay Pairs

Coding	Number of Essay Pairs	Percentages
0/0	31	54
0/1	7	12
0/3	1	>2
0/4	1	>2
1/0	4	7
1/1	3	5
1/2	1	>2
1/4	3	5
2/1	2	3
3/1	1	>2
3/2	1	>2
4/1	1	>2
4/4	1	>2

$N = 57$, total number of pairs of essays

This particular student continues in five discrete paragraphs to summarize each of the five different sources but does not compare and contrast them in any way. By keeping each in an isolated paragraph she is able to avoid addressing the disagreements and contradictions among the sources. This pattern of mentioning the contradictions in the opening paragraphs and ignoring them for the rest of the essay was the most common one for essays of this type. Variations on this pattern included putting a paragraph such as the one just quoted at the end of the essay or at both the beginning and the end. Regardless of their format, however, none of the essays in this category attempted to explain either why the experts disagreed or how they themselves agreed with the experts and disagreed with others.

Students who mentioned the contradictions in passing in one of their pairs of essays, unlike students in the first category, did not generally write in this manner for their other essay. Only three students stayed in this category for both of their essays. Other patterns, however, seemed random: seven students moved from type 1 in their first essay to type 2 in their revised essay; four students moved from type 2 in their first essay to type 1 in their second essay; eight other students moved either forward or backward into this category from other higher categories, but again no discernible pattern could be noticed, nor did any significant differences occur between experimental and control students.

In the third category (2), students noted the contradictions among the writers cited in the text, and sought to reconcile them in a vague and general way, usually by suggesting that some general concept probably existed that might subsume all positions. Only three students (or 2 percent) did this, so we cannot discuss many "typical" characteristics of this kind of writing. We can nonetheless categorize students' attempts to reconcile divergent positions as "general" because they were neither developed nor expressed directly as students' own opinions. For example, one student wrote, after having distinguished between people who are "in a work situation" (according to him, the students) and people who are "detached from the actual places where time management is employed" (according to him, the researchers):

> Those involved in time management personally assume there is very little time and they must rush. Those observing and advising say there is lots of time and the slower you go the better. Perhaps if these two views could be integrated better, a full understanding of time management would result.

Note that this student does not say how the two could be integrated, but expresses a wish that this integration might occur. The three essays that discussed contradictions in this manner did not follow any discernible pattern of combination with other essay types, that is, they did not seem to be related to the students' treatment of contradictions in their other essay.

In the fourth category (3), students sought to explain either the cultural or the cognitive reasons why such disagreements occurred. The four essays of this type set the contradictions in a broader cultural context and tried to explain why they might have occurred. Their explanations ranged from looking at the large context of various researchers studying different populations to the more local context of why contradictions occurred in the particular text they were given to read. What follows is the opening paragraph of one of the essays in this category.

> The value of the given texts is not in their content relating to the idea of "time management," because when considered in relation to this subject they provide no useful insights whatsoever. They are useful in another respect, however, and it ties in interestingly to the topic at hand, that is, time management. The true value of these texts is found by viewing the assignment as a whole and using them as examples of inadequate resource material. The point of this essay, therefore, is not to make a comprehensive statement about time-management, but rather to provide a different perspective for the instructor by examining the problems that can result when an open ended question is combined with limited reference material.

This student's ability to distance himself from the immediate subject matter of the text, to set his remarks in the context of his institutional setting, and to analyze both the cognitive and cultural effects of being given assignments such as this is indeed impressive. But that only 3 percent of the essays approach this assignment in this way must give us pause. Later in the section I consider some of the implications of results such as this. Essays in this category were not paired with other particular essay types.

In the final category (4), students not only noted the contradictions and tried to explain why they might exist, but also gave their own opinions both in an attempt to resolve or explain these differences, and to let their own voice be heard in the debate. Only 7 (or 6 percent) of the 114 essays were of this type, so as with the previous two categories, we cannot easily talk about a "typical" response. But one aspect these seven essays have in common is that the students offered their opinion on the issue, not just as something they tacked on to their essay at the end but as a direct response to their recognition of the contradictions within the text. For example, one student wrote the following:

> The dissimilarity of advice given by all these selections makes the reader tend to question their validity. What should the reader do to avoid being totally confused? I presume it is best for the reader to choose all of the bits of information s/he feels is best for his or her needs. It would seem that the following best suits me: schedule as much time as possible for study in a quiet, non-distracting environment. . . . Do not read unnecessarily; work through mental fatigue whenever possible.

Again, little discernible pattern could be noticed in this category of essays except that apart from one student whose first and second essays acknowledged contradictions and developed a particular view on time management, four of the remaining five essays in this category occurred as second essays. No difference occurred between control or experimental students; that is, being told to write an "interpretation" as opposed to a "better" essay had no effect on students' ability to write about contradictions. This suggests that even when students are capable of seemingly more sophisticated writing tasks such as interpretation, they may still value closure and unity, even if it is superficial, over a more thoughtful analysis of ambiguity or contradiction (even if they discussed ambiguities or contradictions in their protocols).

Analyzing Students' Failure to Discuss Contradictions

One might argue that we are unfairly valuing the discussion of contradictions as a synthesizing concept when in fact a student could develop any number of equally valid or interesting synthesizing concepts that would not discuss the contradictions. (And it is clear that many of our students who did develop synthesizing concepts talked about something other than the contradictions.) Students' failure to discuss contradictions points not to an inability to organize an essay around *some* concept, but to a refusal to acknowledge in writing that a source text may not provide objective facts and that it should be read critically rather than simply for information. Discussing the text's contradictions, therefore, is not just one of many possible synthesizing concepts students could have adopted. It is privileged here because it requires an ability to develop a position of one's own in direct conflict with an authoritative text that the other synthesizing concepts did not. Why, after all, did so few students choose to address the contradictions?

That more than 65 percent of the student essays did not even mention the existence of contradictions in the assigned texts needs to be explained. Interviews and student in-class and protocol comments suggest that many more students observed the contradictions while reading than wrote about them in their papers. How can we account for this? It helps to examine both cognitive and cultural factors. A number of students may not have the strategies to write about contradictions just as they did not seem to have the strategies to write about their own opinions. Most students' task representations did not seem to regard mentioning contradictions as necessary or even relevant to the task, even if they were very conscious of them. Some students, however, reported that suppressing or avoiding contradictions was part of their task representation—something that we would not have discovered merely by examining their papers. Why should students who perceive contradictions in a source text decide either that they are not relevant or are not appropriate to write about? This is a particularly important question since, as discussed in the previous section, experts disagree on almost every subject in every field from foreign policy, to economics, to social history, to psychology, to time management, and it would seem that students should see the analysis of such disagreements as a viable paper topic.

Some students who did not write about the contradictions at all or in detail (i.e., wrote either type 0 or type 1 essays) explained in interviews why they were reticent to do so. One student, for example, who mentioned the contradictions in a summary form in both his essays (type 1), provided insight in his interview as to why he did this. He argued quite forcefully that he recognized many contradictory points of view in the text but felt that he definitely could not say anything about these contradictions because he regarded contradictions as flaws in an essay and did not want to have any in his. He felt that the only way he could resolve contradictions was to "use only the information that fit together." He seemed quite frustrated with his essays and the assignment, but his desire for a unified argument was so strong that he had to write a "resolution essay."

> There was so much information there that first of all I felt I should summarize everything I said. . . . As I was reading through it, a lot of what was said was contradict-

ing. . . . In high school, I probably would have thrown out the information that contradicted and just used whatever information was there that I could use for my thesis. But here I just tried to think through everything until I resolved it.

Why does this student have such an intolerance for ambiguity or contradiction? He suggested that in high school he always had to make unified arguments and that he often did this by ignoring contradictory information. By the time he was interviewed, he sensed that this strategy was insufficient for the tasks of his college writing class. But because he has never been trained to write in a manner that could accommodate diverse perspectives and because he still was unsure that such writing was "correct," he reported that he would still be unable to write about contradictions in his future essays.

Another student who did not mention the contradictions in either of her essays (0/0) clearly acknowledged in her interview that she noticed the contradictions when reading. Resolving them was one of the most difficult aspects of writing the essays for her because they kept preventing her from developing "one organizing concept over the whole thing:"

And then some parts of the original information didn't fit in. It just didn't make sense with my organizing concept. And so I had to revise my organizing concept—my purpose—or what I thought was the purpose of the articles, until all of the information fit together.

The way this student was able to get around the difficult and, perhaps for her, insurmountable problem of writing about contradictions was to write an exciting essay about the relationship of time management to success. She did not refer directly to the text on time management she had to read, but rather used the material indirectly for her own purpose of explaining how good time management leads to success. Although her essay has an obvious purpose, her interview suggests that it also has another purpose, one not obvious in the actual text, but a very present absence—to avoid responding to the contradictions in the source text.

Using Cultural Theory to Supplement the Teaching of Reading and Writing

The desire to avoid contradictions can be seen as a corollary to the need for closure and the belief in objectivity, and these two culturally learned beliefs may impede the development of the thinking strategies for invention and organization necessary to write effectively about contradictions. Some aspects of poststructuralist cultural theory can help students understand the situated nature of all information, which, in turn, could enable them to develop the strategic awareness needed to write about contradictions.

Students' reticence to discuss a text's contradictions is clearly both a cultural and cognitive problem. Some students may fear that in discussing a text critically they are implicitly criticizing the authority of the teacher who they imagine thinks the essay is coherent. In such instances, students often find it safer to assume that the contradictions might be the product of their own inability to comprehend the essay, and they try, therefore, to explain them away or ignore them. Whether or not students respond to the teacher's authority, however, they are certainly aware of the authority of the printed word—and that authority generally carries with it connotations of unity and consistency. Contemporary cultural criticism tries to dispel such textual authority by making readers aware that texts are always contradictory. As Roland Barthes (1981) says, "the text explodes and disperses"; it always opens itself up to multiple and opposing readings. Even texts that appear coherent, therefore, can often be regarded as sites of struggle, as semiotic battlefields in which diverse and often contradictory meanings compete for dominance. Because the dominant meanings of words change over time and because, in any given cultural period, contradictory views exist on just about any subject, the meaning of a given text can never assuredly be pinned down. To encourage students to look for the cultural contradictions in the texts they read—in essays, fiction, film, newspaper stories, the evening news, poetry, rock music, as well as in their own material practices—and to make them realize that contradiction is a part of all our lives, can free them to look for and acknowledge contradictions in texts without impunity. This is hardly to suggest that students must always write essays about contradictions, but rather that unless students are taught that contradictions are a vital part of all their experiences, they cannot develop the strategic knowledge necessary to analyze contradictions and use them constructively in their own essays.

Becoming aware of the cultural factors operating in the reading situation will not cause students to abandon rigorous reading and writing practices; far from it. It can demand a level of critical thinking about students' own texts and the texts of others that will encourage students who discover contradictions in texts to explain them rather than explain them away. As one of our students wrote on the time management assignment:

> In my studies here at CMU two points have been emphasized over and over. First that questions should be answered in a clear, concise manner, and secondly that you must first support your claims with firm evidence. I believe both of these to be valid points and helpful guidelines and as such it is always my first goal, when approaching any writing assignment, to answer the question as asked. I begin the process by fully examining the question before reading or writing anything, then with the question firmly in mind I begin the assignment. Thus the form of the question is just as important as the answer.
>
> If a question is vague, or the reference material constraining, it will only frustrate the writing process, particularly in an academic environment. Here is where the problem ties in well to the given topic of time management. In the face of the unpredictability of academic life, involving various courses and assignments which change on a daily basis, scheduling time runs head-on into the problem of uncertainty. An assignment based on a very broad question, when coupled with restricting reference material, puts a great strain on the writing process, particularly in the presence of additional pressures such as concern about the grading, or assignments due in other course. Our latest writing task is a perfect example of this problem.
>
> My initial problem with this particular assignment was the wording of the question itself. I was confused by the directions to write a "brief comprehensive" statement, which seemed to be a contradiction of terms. Next I read the texts and began to organize my thoughts as to their similarities and differences, in an effort to find a common theme. What I found by using these content strategies was that all of the authors believed that scheduling your time will help your production and organization.

With this earthshaking revelation in mind I changed the direction of my analysis and turned to using situation strategies.

As I considered the authors and topics some interesting questions came to mind: Who is Jean Guitton? Are the statements from the students representative of the entire group surveyed? What qualifies Alan Lakein as an efficiency expert? My point is that five points from five different sources, taken out of context, are a good basis for further investigation but are by no means a sound basis for a comprehensive statement about any subject matter. The only statement that I could legitimately make, based on the given reference material, is that there are different views on the subject of time management which revolve around a common theme of scheduling. This is definitely not the complete statement that the assignment calls for. As a result of this I found myself confused and my writing process completely frustrated.

Thus the writing of a question is just as important as the answer. Academic assignments should be given careful consideration and be presented with clear expectations. The question, in turn, should be formed in a way that will convey these expectations to the student with equal clarity.

This student's essay is unusual in its ability to argue persuasively for an opinion that not only differs from the text but from the opinion he assumes that his teacher may hold. He is an older student and it seems that the seven years he spent outside of school has given him the ability to assess his institutional setting and to argue effectively and self-consciously for the value of his own opinion. He recognizes that there is no one right answer and hence he is not afraid to point out contradictions in the time-management essay, the assignment, and the educational system, particularly when he feels these contradictions place unnecessary pressures on him.

But we cannot send our students away for seven years in hopes that they will discover "what they can't learn in school." Although it is important to recognize that some students who developed their own idea of what they were supposed to write about were able to write more comprehensive statements about time management than this student could, his comments and criticisms seem valid. We need to change some of what we teach our students so that they can learn what, paradoxically, we think we are already teaching them: to become critical thinkers, capable of reading carefully and writing persuasively; to recognize not just gross contradictions, but subtle nuances in texts; to explore the assumptions underlying those nuances; and, finally, to write interested and interesting essays.

Appendix XIV: Interview Questions for Students
OPENING STATEMENT TO STUDENTS

We found your series of assignments particularly interesting and would like to interview you to discover some more about your process of writing and your attitudes about writing. While any information we learn about your reading and writing process may eventually be shared with all the staff of the Reading-to-Write course, it will all remain confidential during this semester. In other words, there are no "right" answers to the questions you will be asked, and we are not grading you, but are, rather, only trying to gain more information on your particular reading and writing processes. The interview will be taped and at times I will be jotting down some notes just to ensure that I understand all the points you are making.

AREAS OF INFORMATION TO EXPLORE IN INTERVIEW

I. Preliminary Warm-Up Questions

1. The assignment for your self interview required that you stop periodically, pause, think, and talk into the recorder. Can you reconstruct how this worked for you?

2. **Follow Up:** In general, did you feel comfortable doing the self-interview? How did you react when you went back and listened to the tape?

3. Did the information you discussed about your *revision strategies* (we can fill in various terms here) seem useful to you in any way?

Students' Definition of Interpretation

1. You've been learning a lot about interpretation in this course, and we would like to know how you would *now,* after x weeks, go about working on an essay that interpreted a text. What might you say are the three of four most important things you would need to know?

Interviewers will take notes while student explains relevant features of an interpretive essay and then ask the following:

> Option A: **Follow Up:** (If student has been clear) I want to make sure I understand you correctly. Are you saying that to do an interpretation you must do x, y, z? (Wait for student to confirm.)
>
> Option B: (If student has not been clear) I want to make sure I understand you correctly. Are you saying that to do an interpretation you must do x, y, z? (Wait for confirmation.) I'm not really sure what you mean by x. Could you please elaborate on this?

2. Does your sense of what you do when you interpret differ from what it was before you took this class? If so, in what ways?

III. Students' Task Definition

Bring out students' essays and response statement
Statement

When given a writing assignment, students often ask teachers, "What do you want," because they need to figure out how they're supposed to do the assignment. We want to get a sense of both what you decided you ought to do on the two essays you wrote and how you decided it. We also want to see if your sense of what you should do changed from the first to the second essay. *Show student first writing assignment and response statement and give time, if student desires, for him/her to look back over assignment.*

1. Try to think back to when you wrote the first assignment. What did you think were the most important things your particular teacher in reading-to-write expected? Feel free to look over your first assignment and response statement before you reply. (Optional **follow-up**—see above.)

2. Try to think back to when you wrote the second assignment. What did you think were the most important things your teacher expected? Feel free to look over your second assignment and response statement before you reply. (Optional **follow-up**—see previous page.)

3. Did your sense of what was important in the second writing assignment differ from what you thought was important in the first? Why?

4. I'm really interested in how you figured out that you should do x. In deciding how to do an assignment, students often use various clues such as information written on the assignment itself, comments that they get from other students, points that are outlined in class discussion. **How** did you figure out that x was important for each of these assignments? (Optional **follow-up**—see previous page.)

IV. Some Explicit Questions on the Costs and Benefits of Students' Writing Strategies

I'm also interested in the writing strategies you used to write these two essays and in your rationale for doing so. In other words, I'd like to find out what you think the advantages and disadvantages or the benefits and costs are of using these strategies.

Bring out students' match for first and second essays.

1. Here's a copy of the match exercise you completed on your first and second assignments. Could you explain what you feel are the advantages and disadvantages of using these particular strategies?

2. Did you consider using other strategies on these assignments that for one reason or another you finally decided not to use?

Follow-up:

A. Are these strategies that you often use?

B. Why did you decide not to use them on these assignments?

3. Here's the strategies you thought expert writers would use on these assignments. Why do you think expert writers would use these strategies?

V. Closing Questions

1. What do you feel you have learned most from the course so far?

2. Do you plan/have you used some of the strategies for writing/reading learned in this course to other courses? Why/why not?

IV

**UNITING COGNITION
AND CONTEXT**

9

Negotiating Academic Discourse

LINDA FLOWER

A Conceptual Framework

In many ways this study is the story of students' success. It is a study of writers in the act of entering a university-level academic discourse, who come with an impressive range of abilities that are fundamental to academic writing: the ability to summarize, to get the gist, to see key points and connections, and not least, to execute moves that make an essay seem coherent and on topic. The interviews and protocols show students who are also working and struggling with this assignment, wanting to appear smart, trying to say something "interesting," wanting this paper to show what they can do. Yet, despite their effort, these typical freshmen papers still fall short of the critical and creative thought we expect in academic writing. These students, like most freshmen, are in an important transition; there is another river to cross. The problem is how to characterize this transition.

A deficit model, in which students are presumed still to lack basic "cognitive skills," to be unable to think "analytically" or "critically," or to be still in some "egocentric" state of intellectual development is emphatically denied by our data. Such a model has been criticized by other educators who see students sadly pigeonholed when we conclude that students "can't think" in certain ways because certain school tasks fail to elicit the evidence of such abilities (Rose, 1988). Our interviews and protocols of students in the act of planning, elaborating, and intending echo Labov's (1972) compelling picture of streetwise verbal intelligence, in the way they show ample evidence of savvy, reasoning, and sensitivity to conflict, as well as confusion over how to negotiate this new situation. When a large group of students is assumed to labor under a basic intellectual or basic cognitive deficit because of some limit in performance, we may need to ask how much of that deficit is residing instead in our own methods of measurement and observation (see the Introduction).

A traditional, staged developmental model may miss the mark as well. We do not see compelling evidence that this particular transition into academic discourse takes a linear developmental path marked by distinct stages of growth. These freshmen do not appear to be climbing up the ladder implied by a "taxonomy of intellectual skills," up the steps of "cultural literacy," up the "great chain of being," or up other stepwise value systems we academics love to create. Doing academic writing, for all its virtues, does not appear to be a necessary stage in the unfolding of the literate mind or to require the addition of missing cognitive capacities. In the next few pages I sketch half a dozen elements that, taken together, could yield a more con-textualized, more strategic picture of this transition.

ENTERING A DISCOURSE

A more accurate conceptual framework, we believe, is one which sees this freshman transition as at once a social and cognitive event, in which students are attempting to *enter a new discourse community posed by college* and, more particularly, by this freshman composition class. To enter such a community, students need to learn the textual conventions, the expectations, the habits of mind, and the methods of thought that allow one to operate in an academic conversation. And, in some cases, they will need to learn a body of topic knowledge as well. To this task, students bring a wealth of prior knowledge, past practices, and tacit assumptions about school writing—some of which support this transition and some of which compli-cate it. Conceptualizing this transition as a social/cognitive act of entering a dis-course emphasizes both the problem-solving effort of a student learning to negotiate a new situation and the role the situation will play in what is learned.

STRATEGIC KNOWLEDGE

Learning to negotiate a new discourse, we suggest, calls for a rapid growth in *strategic knowledge,* defined in terms of three key elements: *the goals writers set for themselves, the strategies they invoke, and the metacognitive awareness they bring to both these acts.* Although strategic knowledge is not the only kind of growth or the only form of knowing involved, it appears to play a special role. The three elements of goals, strategies, and awareness, make strategic knowledge a form of knowing geared for action within a specific context. The cognitive and rhetorical strategies within a writer's repertoire are linked to/cued by the goals the writer sets, which in turn are a response to the social and rhetorical context as the writer interprets it. Awareness of any of these elements increases the writer's power to negotiate that context. Strategic knowledge is contextual in another sense: like other schema-based understandings (Fiske & Linville, 1980), it develops over time in response to past experience—in this case as a response to twelve years of school-sponsored reading and writing.

Our interest in studying strategic knowledge is motivated by a desire to see the individual student as a goal-directed thinker and agent operating in a complex social and educational environment (Flower, 1988). John Gumperz (1982) has called for a similar shift in sociolinguistics, from correlational studies of group patterns to the study of "discourse strategies" that reflect the context-specific purposes of a speaker. "There is a need," he says, "for a sociolinguistic theory which accounts for the communicative functions of linguistic variability and for its relation to speakers' goals without reference to untestable functionalist assumptions about conformity or nonconformance to closed systems of norms" (p. 29). Applebee's study of *Contexts for Learning to Write* (1984a) concludes with a similar turn toward the importance of writers' goals: "The most rewarding approaches to the study of writing may be those which include writing processes as strategies that are orchestrated in the course of a particular communicative event, with its own network of purposes and outcomes."

The combination of protocols, interviews, and texts in the present study helps build a picture of strategic knowledge in action, revealing patterns in the ways these students engage with academic discourse and suggesting paths by which their powers could develop. As the first part of this study demonstrated, students in this setting need an enlarged image of the task of academic writing; they must be able to give themselves relevant and challenging *goals* and to invoke the criteria and standards the community employs. But goals alone are not enough. To carry out complex tasks such as interpretation or synthesis, or to engage in the knowledge transformation academic writing often calls for, writers need an enlarged repertoire of *strategies*—of rhetorical, textual, interpersonal, and writing process strategies for managing these tasks. The ability to enlarge this repertoire quickly may depend on the third element of strategy knowledge—*awareness*. In the process of negotiating a new discourse, students, we claim, need a strategic awareness of their own options; they must learn to adapt the thinking and writing skills they already possess to the new expectations of this discourse. When this metacognitive awareness is limited, tacit, or unexamined, academic writing is likely to seem an inscrutable task that requires some unknown set of skills. With increasing awareness, students can turn this freshman transition into a context-sensitive negotiation with a new situation, an act of adapting what they know in tandem with a more sensitive reading of the rhetorical situation.

ACADEMIC EXPECTATIONS

But what is *academic discourse?* Reading this new rhetorical situation and representing the task play a major role in this transition, as we see it, because the expectations of the academic discourse itself are often tacit. Academic discourse operates with its own peculiar, socially constructed conventions and norms which liberal education has valorized for their time-tested ability to support reflective thought and build new knowledge. But in acknowledging that potential, we must not assume that these specialized habits of mind and ways of talking that a person *must learn* are a "natural" form, much less a simple indication of ability or intelligence. In fact, we propose that freshmen whose "legacy of schooling" includes practiced strategies and strong assumptions about school writing (see Chapters 1, 7, and 8) may fail to appreciate the conflict between those prior assumptions and the unstated expectations of an academic discourse community. Even though many freshman are familiar with academic writing from high school, the demand actually to enter a community as a contributing member can require important changes in students' image of writing and sense of authority, as well as changes in their strategies for creating text.

The students' problem is further confounded by the fact that there is no Platonic entity called "academic discourse" one can define and master. The "academic community" is, if not strife-torn, certainly rife with disciplinary and theoretical disagreement about how arguments should be conducted, what constitutes good evidence, and how correctly to format one's bibliography. Scribner and Cole (1981) describe similar problems in the attempts to conceptualize "literacy" as a single entity. They argue for a focus on context-specific literate *practices,* which they define as "recurrent, goal-directed sequence(s) of activities," developed and patterned to use "technology and knowledge to accomplish tasks." Literacy as a whole is the sum of this "set of socially organized practices which make use of a symbol system and a technology for producing and disseminating it" (p. 236). Like them, we are in search of a "framework which situates cognitive skills in culturally organized practices [in order to provide] one way of moving beyond the antonymic terms that dominate much thinking about thinking: general versus specific, higher order versus lower order" (p. 259). At the same time, our experience as teachers pressures us to account for the commonalities, for the familiar patterns of success and failure we see in these data.

Academic discourse, even the freshman version of the species, is not the result of a unified cognitive or social process, but is made up of a variety of context-specific practices, some of which, such as the systematic consideration of rival hypotheses, are associated with disciplines and genres. Other practices, such as analyzing one's own assumptions, are common across disciplines but are more or less relevant depending on the task at hand. Given this diversity, we want to be explicit about the particular expectations we brought to this freshman course and this study and to acknowledge the different priorities other academic microcommunities might set. However, we also want to argue for commonality. In this course and our analysis we concentrated on two sets of practices and expectations we believed many teachers would share, which cut across disciplines and, we hypothesize, may be at the root of other apparent problems students face in negotiating various academic practices. These two practices are (1) integrating information from sources with one's own knowledge and (2) interpreting one's reading/adapting one's writing for a purpose. From our perspective these two practices stand as critical features of academic discourse that often limit entry and full participation in the academic community. Insofar as other teachers and other rhetorical situations share these goals, our study can be said to be about "academic discourse" more generally and to speak to common problems that cross our multiple communities.

In this case I can be even more specific about some of the shared assumptions operating within our local community which helped shape the course under study and our expectations for students. One such premise was that reading and writing are constructive acts (see Flower, 1987; Spivey, 1987). Readers do not simply absorb and store information, they create meaningful interpretations through selective attention, connections to prior knowledge, and evaluation of what they read. On one level, this individual construction of meaning is neither good nor bad; it is merely the nature of this cognitive and social process. However, the ideal reader of academic discourse manages this event in order to build a rich and integrated personal representation of a text (see McCormick & Waller, 1987). We expect writers to carry this integrative process even further. People join the academic community by contributing to both a conversation and a shared body of knowledge (see Bazerman, 1985; Kaufer, Geisler, & Neuwirth, 1989; Nelson & Hayes, 1988). They enter the discourse by offering us research, scholarship, and theory. In addition to these finished thoughts, academic discourse also encourages and values writing that presents new ideas, hypotheses and mysteries, issues for negotiation, and thoughtful reflections.

This is not to say that reader/teachers invoke these ideals at every turn, on every paper, but they are part of the unwritten curriculum and unstated criteria that set expectations. Moreover, these ideals embrace conflicting values the writer must balance. Although academic communities prize openness and exploration, their expectations for thoughtful, supported claims are typically high, even for freshman writing. As readers we expect (student) writers not only to recognize and understand other points of view, but to investigate such claims with their own prior knowledge and experience, to think critically. When writers present those ideas, we expect them not only to recount their knowledge, but to adapt, even transform it to address a shared purpose. Student writers must manage the conflicting roles of being at once learners and contributors. As partners in an academic discourse, writers are expected to explore questions that matter, to teach us, to surprise us at any opportunity—in essence, to contribute to a serious and energetic conversation. This, we felt, was not an image of school discourse that entering students often possess.

THE TRANSFORMATION OF KNOWLEDGE

This image of academic discourse as a rhetorical act also assumes that writers often need to transform their knowledge in response to a problem, issue, or purpose. Yet in the school writing studied by Bereiter and Scardamalia (1987) and Applebee (1984a), the shift from knowledge telling to knowledge transforming did not happen easily, if at all. Transformation appears to be a complex cognitive process that is heavily influenced by the plans and goals writers give themselves, which in turn are highly dependent on the support and incentives for such effort provided by the context. Bazerman's (1985) study of the reading process of seven physicists highlights the intensely goal-directed process that leads these academic writers to transform not only the information they read but their own prior knowledge. The researchers he studied work within a socially constructed body of scientific knowledge and current problems. However, in the act of selecting and interpreting what they read, they construct a personal schema of the field built around their own research goals. "The way [they] read is a strategic consequence of what [they are] trying to accomplish" (p. 11). In a similar way, when the biologists studied by Myers (1985a) revised their proposals, they responded to critics but preserved the original intent of their work by revamping the conceptual framework of their proposals to reflect consensus and common goals. In essence, they had to rethink and re-present their work from the theoretical perspective of their readers.

Studies of college students suggest some of the specific ways transformation is carried out in reading-to-writing, in which "knowledge" can include information both from sources and from memory. Looking at the synthesis texts produced by more and less able comprehenders, Spivey (1984) found that the better readers not only achieved higher overall quality, but their texts contained fewer, more tightly connected, and fully developed thematic chunks. In constructing meaning from sources, these students had actively *selected, connected,* and *organized* information. This same trio of constructive processes accounts for much of the picture that is emerging in modern cognitive research on reading (Spivey, 1987). Tracking the reading and writing process through think-aloud protocols, Kennedy (1985) found that fluent readers were more active in planning and manipulating their sources (by taking, rereading, and using their own notes) than less fluent readers. They also engaged more frequently in "higher level processing and study-type" actions during reading (e.g., elaboration, evaluation, marking the text).

However, when Kantz (1987) presented students with a more rhetorically complex reading-to-write task, she found that traditionally valued "active" reading strategies did not predict the quality of the paper or tell the full story of the transformation process. Students in this study were asked to help certain freshman writers be more "creative," drawing on diverse sources that included Kurt Vonnegut, Ken Macrorie, and William Perry. In this open-ended, audience-driven synthesis task, students who engaged in elaborating on and critically evaluating their source texts—but *without* a consistent rhetorical purpose beyond that of response— did not necessarily write good papers or even use their responses made during reading. Good writing was predicted, instead, by the extent of planning and by the students' purposeful use of reading strategies which let them select rhetorically relevant information and begin their constructive process as writers even as they read through the sources.

The particular patterns of reading, writing, and knowledge transformation Kantz observed were shaped by the rhetorical stance writers took to their material and audience. Students who, based on their own comments, approached this task as *summarizers* did relatively little manipulation compared to students who saw themselves as *explicators* of their sources for a student audience. In this study transformation not only led to radical decisions about what to select, what to jettison, and how to organize it, but also led writers to draw inferences and see implications in order to adapt their personal experiences and the source information for a hard-to-impress reader. Once again, the goals writers set and the task they give themselves emerged as powerful influences on both the process and the text.

Sometimes, however, the decision *not* to transform information may also reflect what the student feels able to do. Although the sophomore literature student observed by Herrington (1988) had been asked to write an "argument" about an "issue," she apparently "perceived an 'interesting issue' to be something that interested her and that she didn't understand"—a mismatch with the instructor's goals (p. 158). By the second paper, the student perceived "proving a point" to be her purpose; however, her paper remained a descriptive summary reflecting a writer "trying to figure out a story for herself, exploring her ideas, and admitting to her . . . professor, what she doesn't understand" (p. 160). As Herrington concludes, this student probably needed more "guidance as to *how* to go about formulating an issue and working out an interpretation to resolve it" (p. 160). In support, Graff (1985) has argued that our teaching of literature may even tend to suppress this awareness of contradictions and issues. His image of the "guidance" that might lead to transformed knowledge is a social one: students would be plunged into the cultural context of literary theory and its debates—a context in which issues of interpretation become meaningful.

When Nelson and Hayes (1988) tracked students from different courses over the extended process of writing a research paper, they found some behavioral indicators of how knowledge is transformed and what conditions support it. Some students approached the paper with a low-investment strategy guided by a content-driven search for information. Starting two to three days before the paper was due, they did their research in one visit to the library, based on a random search of books on the topic. Copying down quotes and paraphrases from books in the order found in the sources, they subsequently incorporated that information directly, in much the same order, in their own papers. Other students took a high-investment, and issue-driven writing and search strategy. Starting three to four weeks in advance, they began with questions, hypotheses, or at least an intent to find an issue, which guided their multiple trips to the library. They read for background and took notes not intended for the final text. Their revisions reflected conceptual as well as textual changes. They also felt good about the work. These work patterns suggest some of the conditions that support or work against the transformation of knowledge. This study also suggests ways the context of academic writing, whether in a class or a community of physicists, supports these work habits by encouraging planning, drafts, reflection, and public presentation.

GROWTH AS A PROCESS OF ADAPTATION AND NEGOTIATION

If the goal of the freshman transition is to begin performing with confidence within a shared discourse that may call for the transformation of knowledge, what does it take to get there? David Bartholomae's (1985) study of underprepared students used the metaphor of "initiation" to capture the outsider status students may feel. It described this transition as a social process of "imitation"—picking up the commonplaces of thought and the conventions of text that go with the territory. Our view is a complementary one that emphasizes the *insider* status students also possess—the important legacy of schooling and academic know-how they bring to college. Entering this partly new discourse appears to be an act of negotiation that involves a good deal of experimentation and discovery, uncertainty and failure, success and growth. It also involves adapting old strategies and retuning and reinterpreting old understandings to meet this new situation.

Some recent case studies of academic writers help us sketch some of the specific literate practices called for in different academic settings, practices that range from developing a formal proposal for biological research to writing an interpretive paper in a poetry course. These studies emphasize the distinctiveness of each practice, but together they help us picture the larger strategic repertoire students are developing in these courses. This repertoire includes not only text conventions, rhetorical patterns, and domain-specific organizing ideas, but also strategies for reading and writing and (in some cases) meta-level strategies for interpreting what these different discourses expect. "Learning to write" in these studies often involves negotiating a transition from one discourse (e.g., from writing personal essays in freshman comp) to another discourse (e.g., to writing literary analyses in sophomore poetry). The student's task is to interpret this change.

For instance, when Herrington's (1985) chemical engineering students moved from a lab course to a design course, they had to move from what she described as a school-based forum and argumentative rhetoric (in which claims and warrants were based on technical theory and accuracy) to a professional forum that called for deliberative rhetoric (in which reasons were based on expediency and advantages to the client audience). The change in textual conventions reflected a change in the way writers were expected to use their technical knowledge. Students often had difficulty making this shift. As McCarthy (1987) showed, even when a student understood the broad goals for an assignment (e.g., to accurately use scientific concepts from a biology article or to marshal appropriate evidence to interpret a poem), the student could have trouble turning those goals into actions. Although her case study student, Dave, had successfully learned to use a thesis–subpoint analytical structure in his first semester composition course, he depended (with little success) on summary in his poetry papers and asserted that the writing tasks for his composition, biology, and poetry classes were "totally different from each other and totally different from anything he had ever done before" (p. 243). In his unsuccessful negotiation with the poetry course, Dave appeared to be preoccupied with the new conventions of interpreting and quoting poetry and unable to see how his old strategies, such as thesis and support, were still required, though in a new guise, within this altered context.

Berkenkotter, Huckin, and Ackerman (1988) were able to track an extended process of negotiation and knowledge transformation that took place at the level of graduate work. The student they describe came to a research-oriented graduate program with a strong background in expressive writing. In trying to make the shift to a new body of knowledge couched in the discourse of rhetoric and social science, he went through a process of "reframing" the new information in light of his prior knowledge, that is, trying to transform the issues raised in the new and unfamiliar discourse into personally relevant terms as a way to understand them. However, the informal and playful style of expressive writing he brought with him did not help him write an explicit, cohesive analysis of the key issues in his sources. Over the semester, he negotiated this transition first by simply switching discourses—writing a personal memo to the instructor of the course talking through the issues his formal paper had failed to address. In subsequent papers he continued to negotiate this transition by relaxing some of the constraints of genre and register to produce a hybrid text—a mixture of personal talk and research-based analysis of issues. The process Berkenkotter et al. describe is interesting for our purposes. Rather than leading to the loss of an earlier "voice" or "style," which some students say they fear, this process of negotiation can lead to a multiregister fluency in which the writer is able to command alternative modes of discourse and create, in this case, a distinctive blend of both old and new. However, this multiregister ability did not emerge overnight, and the hybrid and ad hoc variations on "research talk" the writer made along the way seemed necessary to support his attempt to comprehend and transform new knowledge into his own intellectual framework and goals.

When we look at the discourse conventions and strategies freshmen exhibited in the present study, we see a repertoire that is at once robust, limited, and ripe for change. Some parts of this repertoire, such as drawing comparisons, seem well learned, widely shared, and adaptable. Other rhetorical moves, such as the superficial essay "frame" which suggests a synthesis but delivers a summary, appear to be dead-end strategies, unlikely to help students meet the higher expectations of the discourse. Other parts of the repertoire observed were strategies, such as elaboration, that had high potential for testing and transforming knowledge which students, however, used in tentative or limited ways. Strategies such as recognizing contradictions but still making a statement were conspicuous by their absence. Although these students often demonstrated the underlying cognitive abilities to analyze, synthesize, or reconceptualize that would support these high potential strategies, some students rarely made such intellectual moves. In celebrating the strengths of these freshmen, we must note that such strategies do not appear to be live options in their repertoire. Why?

In a study like this—and in the classroom—we often cannot tell why a student's strategic process fails or runs among the shallows. Are certain strategies missing from the repertoire of a student who, like Darlene, seems to see no options ("But then they [the sources] don't agree—There's nothing you can say about this.")? Or is the student simply failing to use abilities he or she has because of task representation, narrow assumptions, rigid rules, or a cost/benefit choice? Or is the writer, like some of the Intenders, actively trying but still struggling to control a new, developing, or difficult strategy? Although researchers and teachers may catch glimpses of unused potential and skill in the making, readers are concerned with the bottom line. What finally matters is not what writers *might be able to do,* but the strategic repertoire they *actually invoke* on normal tasks. Learning when and how to use strategies one already has may be as difficult as learning new conventions and new rules.

This image of growth as negotiation and adaptation predicts that metacognition could play a large role in helping students to learn and engage in new types of discourse. The growth of *strategic awareness means an increased sense of rhetorical options and an expanded power to direct one's own cognition.* We can see the tracks of strategic choice (with or without awareness) in the alternative task representations students created, in the cost/benefit decisions they made about their own goals, and in the theories they held about what was possible and appropriate in academic writing, including their assumptions that older students would handle this task differently (see Chapters 1, 3, and 8). We see the need for awareness perhaps most poignantly in the students who plan and intend purposeful revisions that the reader never sees and in those who engage in critical thinking and constructive elaborations, but never transfer that self-generated knowledge to their texts (see Chapters 5 and 6). And at the same time, we see signs of growth in students' options as they reflect on their own process:

> So I decided I was just gonna like sit down and read it and try not to think (laughter across the class). So I did that and read straight through and then came to the part where I had to write. And then I realized that I really did not understand what I was reading. . . . So I had to go back and reread like each point. And I kinda got an idea of where I should start and what kind of direction I was going in. . . . I looked [each point] over really carefully in my mind, and I tried to figure out what it was saying— and then I wrote about it.
>
> And I think that worked really good for me—because I never wrote like that before—I usually just like sat down and wrote. . . . And somehow things never used to come out the way I wanted them. And this paper came out better than I had expected.

UNIQUENESS AND COMMONALITY: BUILDING A COMPOSITE PICTURE

The conceptual frame proposed here sees students trying to negotiate an entry into the seemingly familiar, yet surprisingly new, and always ill-defined community of academic discourse in which the goals of integrating and transforming knowledge for a rhetorical purpose present a major hurdle. It describes students' performance in terms of strategic knowledge (i.e., goals, strategies, and awareness), seen as a form of knowledge that bridges cognition and context. This attempt to link individual cognition and a school context is at best a tentative and partial one, focused on a limited number of areas—task representation, elaboration, the legacy of school, the role of certain cultural assumptions—and affected by our particular emphasis on cognitive data. Even so, this examination of cognition in context has led us to some seemingly alternative interpretations of "what happened" that might be useful to confront since they are inherent in the individual/social nature of strategic knowledge.

On one level of analysis, strategic knowledge can be seen as a response to the immediate environment—a rhetorical action that mirrors the local, even idiosyncratic, context of this class and this open-ended assignment. The students' performance reveals the strategic decisions prompted by this particular situation; our analysis documents a situated action.

However, strategic knowledge, seen as a form of procedural knowledge or "knowing how," depends on an interpretive process in which writers "read" a situation by their own lights. The context that matters most is the one constructed by the writer. A freshman, writing for a history course, describes an act of "rereading" the situation to his planning collaborator:

So anyway, . . . So I wrote five or six pages on nothing, but I included the words "African nationalism" in there once in awhile. I thought, why this is just like high school, I can get away with doing this. I got the paper back, and it was a C minus or a C or something like that. It said "no content." And I was introduced to the world of college writing.

A fine-grained analysis of the reading/writing process itself paints a picture of individual differences in task representation, in strategies, and in awareness— differences that have a visible effect on texts and, one can predict, on students' success and failure in school writing. This level of analysis highlights writers' cognitive, interpretive engagement with their context and the way in which they translate that context into action—a constructive process that teachers may not always see.

And, yet, an analysis of strategic knowledge appears to describe more than the immediate situation and individual writers' processes. The context writers "see" and the patterns of interpretation they bring develop over time; they reflect experience, prior contexts, and cultural and social influences. At this level of analysis we begin to see patterns across the diversity that we can recognize as a typical "freshman paper" and a familiar freshman writing dilemma. From that perspective, these data on how sixty-nine students interpreted a given assignment may offer us an indepth look at a process and a reading of the situation that other students share.

We believe that a full understanding of what these students did has to honor all of these levels of analysis. When attention is focused on not only the immediate context, but on individual differences within it, and on the larger social and cultural context that informs both, we not only see the process differently, we are in a position to contextualize, qualify, or conditionalize each level of analysis with the other. Using each of these perspectives to describe students' strategic response helps us chart their engagement with academic writing in more precise ways.

For example, in describing this transition, we must not assume that *this performance* is a measure of general competence, but must ask: Did the immediate context elicit the best performance these students could muster, or are we seeing a different (perhaps even more relevant) picture of how they approach such tasks? This picture of performance has an interesting status: The assignment was given as part of the freshman writing course in a competitive school where freshman grades can put you in or out of programs. Papers matter. However, in its immediate context, this particular assignment was not graded and was presented with some fanfare as an occasion for examining one's own writing process. Moreover, it is easy to imagine that a highly motivated assignment on a topic chosen by the student could elicit a higher level of commitment, energy, and imagination, and to predict that on such an assignment we would see more sophisticated critical thinking and planning, and a sharper sense of purposiveness than we saw. We have no doubt that under ideal, supportive circumstances these students, like most writers, *could* write better papers and think more rigorously than they did. This study, then, should not be read as an evaluation study or an attempt to mark the upper or lower limits of this group's ability.

On the other hand, the interviews showed us a group of freshmen trying very hard to succeed at their first term in college, drawing on their best guesses from high school about how to do it. Moreover, the students who did the thinking-aloud protocols at home were receiving special attention. It was clear that we thought their writing strategies were important and that they wanted to look good to themselves and the class. The protocols make it apparent that nearly all of these students were engaged with the task, that they set standards they could not always reach, and that, as they ran into dilemmas, they were willing to worry and struggle with this problem even when they could not figure out what to do. As one student says in her protocol, trying to account for why she is in such a jam:

> How can I possibly make this into anything? Now I sound like one of the kids in the survey [a student survey in the source materials which discussed procrastination]. Yes, I put it off till the last minute.—But I did not. It's 12:58 p.m. It's noon time. I'm sitting here thinking about rehearsal tonight. I'm sitting here thinking about anything but— That's not true. I'm thinking about time management. And I'm thinking that I'm not doing well, but I don't know why.

What then should we make of this picture of "freshman performance" with its complex mix of motives? As an analysis of the immediate context tells us, this picture does not intend or pretend to measure students' highest potential or developmental limits. Yet the analysis of individual writers shows genuine engagement and persistence (to a point) with difficulties beyond the writer's immediate power to resolve. Despite this effort, however, the papers and the goals students set failed to meet the expectations of both instructors and many students. Here we find that a broader social perspective on writing in school may help us see coherence in this mixed performance. From our experience with freshman writers, this mixture of limited goals, reasonable effort, and perplexity at the result is not surprising—the papers failed to meet our expectations in some expected ways. Perhaps the most useful way to read these data is as a picture of the *standard repertoire* of writing strategies these particular students control with comfort and call up without question for tasks they expect school to present. In their second month of college, they come with a prior context of writing in school, especially of writing based on reading. *Their performance shows us the skills they have mastered, the criteria they believe are appropriate, and the strategies they can draw on at will and manage with confidence.*

The notion of a partially shared standard repertoire for school writing stresses commonality. A more fine-grained analysis of the individual writer at work does not just reveal uniqueness but lets us glimpse the cutting edge of personal growth. In the process data we could see places where this standard repertoire was hitting its limits, failing to deal with inherent problems in the task (such as embedded contradictions), and failing to meet other expectations for academic sophistication. All these images are necessary parts of the picture. While a broader, social reading of this performance foregrounds a familiar pattern we are calling the standard repertoire, a closer process analysis of individuals trying to use that repertoire on a new task shows it coming into conflict with the demands of the rhetorical situation. Moreover, in the crucible of their own writing process, these limits were becoming apparent to students.

This composite picture of the individual experience and the larger pattern suggests a starting place for teaching. Under special circumstances, all of us can do extraordinary things. But one goal of education is to make certain abilities and strategies, such as forming an astute anticipation of a reader's response, subject to the conscious choice to use such strategies even when circumstances do not elicit our best. Being able to engage in what Bereiter and Scardamalia (1987) call "intentional cognition" means that we can think well and write effectively even if the topic is new, the goals are set by circumstance rather than choice, and our heart is not on the line. The "standard repertoire" of goals and writing strategies a given group of students shows us is not all they can do, but it represents the working knowledge on which these students rely, even in the face of problems. It shows us the foundation on which our instruction needs to build if we hope to extend that standard set and it reveals some student assumptions about academic writing we might want to challenge. This analysis also raises a question about other populations of students. Do they bring a similar shared repertoire of goals and strategies and assumptions to academic writing? Does such strategic knowledge vary in significant ways across groups?

The first section of this chapter has laid out a conceptual framework for understanding how freshmen deal with academic writing as a cognitive and social process. In the next section we take a close look at one set of strategies students used to construct an organizing idea. It shows us how a growing strategic awareness might let students adapt and extend the processes they already use, to enter the more sophisticated discourse of our expectations. However, in the final section I want to end with the disquieting possibility that cognitive and social forces may be working together against this awareness.

Our study has repeatedly observed that students' very success with school writing and recitation may be part of the problem. Their assumptions, like their assured opening moves, create a legacy writers must resist and revise. When students begin to struggle with this problem, the transition seems well underway. But some students, I will suggest at the end of this chapter, may never fully register the difference between the school tasks they do so well and the more complexly constructive act we have in mind. Given our own teacherly task representations, which set such store in critical thinking and purposeful reading and writing, we have no trouble seeing an important transition in front of our students, and we know that it can entail some significant changes in recognition. But for some students, this intellectual initiation, so evident to us, may be a *tacit transition:* that is, the range of goals and the intellectual strategies one needs to employ has expanded, but the task (writing an essay in response to reading) and the rhetorical context (student writing to teacher) look remarkably the same. Moreover, the familiar cognitive processes of comprehension and knowledge telling are so robust, able to do so much of the writer's intellectual work, that some students never realize that significant strategic changes are called for. They may simply fail to see what all the fuss is about.

Developing an Organizing Idea

The work of a constructive process is most evident when knowledge resists easy translation into text. When students in this study looked at the protocol record of their own process and talked about it in class, the difficulty they referred to most was "getting good ideas." For an essay like this the key problem seemed even more specific: where do you find that central good idea that will then organize the paper for you? To pursue this part of the freshman repertoire that seems to loom large for both students and teachers, we decided to track down the process by which each of these seventeen freshmen arrived at their final organizing idea. We framed the analysis to answer questions a teacher would ask, such as What process do these students actually use to get an organizing idea? Are half of my students doing something the other half doesn't even consider doing? How is it that three (but only three) students created surprising and original ideas when I encouraged everyone to do so? And what about the two students in the back who turned in three semi-coherent paragraphs with no organizing ideas? What happened when these seventeen students wrote?

Without even looking at the protocol data or listening to the students, we can predict some reasonable answers to the question How do students get their organizing ideas? One solution to the problem draws heavily on available topic knowledge. That is, the student could simply *select* an important or relatively inclusive idea from the source text. Another solution depends on knowing the conventions of academic discourse. For example, one authority in the source text, William James, admonishes us to push through fatigue to new energy. But another authority, Jean Guitton, says to rest at the first sign of mental fatigue. Now in such a situation the conventions of academic discourse might come to one's rescue and provide a commonplace or conventional posture which a writer who was savvy to such discourse could take.

And, indeed, that happened. One popular commonplace—six students used this—was a variation on the theme, "Time management is a very important topic (and here are some things I have to say on it. . . .)." A somewhat more sophisticated commonplace was the academic waffle which begins with the statement, "There are many theories about time management." However, knowing a commonplace was not always enough to solve the problem. Here is the difficulty, in Bob's words, as he is describing "this most interesting feature" of his process in class:

> I started with "There are several theories as to the most efficient strategies concerning time management." Which is really bad—And I wrote like a page of this. I just stopped and I went: This is just so bad—And I just said, like—I have to take this totally from my own point of view. [pause] But first I have to get a point of view.

His rueful final comment brought the whole room into sympathetic laughter.

The thinking-aloud protocols revealed five reading-to-write strategies freshmen used in the face of this dilemma to get a point of view and an organizing idea, each of which had some distinctive costs and benefits. Three were primarily reading strategies, which we labeled the gist and list, the TIA, and the dialogue strategy. The other two strategies, knowledge-driven planning and constructive planning, are ones that support writing. In describing them I want to raise two questions which we can only partly answer. First, what does each strategy offer a writer? And second, do the students who use only some of these strategies possess the awareness of and option to use the others?

STRATEGIES FOR READING

Although strategies are revealing, we must first recognize that the foundation of the reading-to-write process is the basic process of *comprehension* itself (see Chapter 4). The comprehension process described in recent reading research and theory is much like composing, a highly constructive process. In simply reading for understanding, students are doing much of the cognitive work we associate with writing. For instance, they read James and recognize his main idea. They read Guitton and notice the contradiction. They get the gist of a passage. And they put these gists into some sort of meaningful structure—*simply in the act of comprehending the text.*

Some students merely extended this constructive comprehension process into a more systematic strategy which we called *gist and list*. For these students, gist and list is a well-learned strategy. The writer goes through the text looking for the main points, finds an idea or term that links them, and uses that to organize the text. This familiar strategy, the product of years of paraphrasing, summarizing, and recitation in school, is dominated by the text and fueled by the reading process (see Chapter 7). It is fast, efficient, and faithful to the source.

By contrast, a second strategy we observed was driven less by the text and more by the reader's own knowledge. Eleven of the seventeen students used a strategy which took on the rhythm of a private, mental call and response. Students would read a line of text and say to themselves in the protocol:

[Text] Yeah, I agree.
[Text] That's probably true.
[Text] Yeah, I do this.
[Text] What does that mean? [further thought] Oh if that's what it means, then I agree.
[Text] That's ridiculous.
[Text] That says absolutely nothing to me.
[Text] That's nice; I've done that.

We ended up calling this the *True, Important, I Agree strategy*—or the *TIA* for short. The student using the TIA strategy goes through the text with a special, evaluative filter. Certain ideas appear to be tagged, or stamped like USDA Prime with this is True, this is Important, or I Agree with this. TIA is an effective method for selecting the ideas you like, already know about, and could write on—and for deleting the rest. For one student, Suzie, the "most interesting thing" about her protocol was learning that she had this strategy. As she reports in class:

> So this time, since I was talking out loud, I was very conscious of the fact that I was making connections to what everyone was saying. Using my own—using things that have happened to me to connect to the people that were talking about time management. . . . And I realized that I actually do have strategies to read—I thought I didn't—I thought I was some kind of odd person who didn't have any strategies ever. [She ends her statement with an uncertain laugh.]

TIA is a very powerful strategy for reading to write. Like gist and list it builds on the foundation of the comprehension process, but then uses the writer's own response to create a pool of ideas the writer likes, understands, and can elaborate on. If one true, important, or agreeable idea stands out at the end of this reading, it can automatically take on the role of an organizing idea. Here, in Suzie's protocol, we can see the TIA at work as an invention strategy as she monitors her current thinking and develops a plan:

> I'm writing down things I agree with—that I can comment on because I agree with. He's not saying things I disagree with. There are some people in this article that are saying things I disagree with. I guess I'll put it in two different parts of my paper. The things that I agree with and the things that I don't agree with. All right.

However, TIA has an important limitation. It is a one-way communication in which the student selects or rejects the claims of others but does not appear to listen to what the voice in the text is saying about them. The writer who depends exclusively on the TIA strategy either selects her own congenial company, ignoring the rest of the "unselected" information, or simply organizes the paper into sheep and goats based on her prior attitudes on the subject. Evidence is not an issue. The writer is not open to argument or learning.

Given this limitation it was exciting to see that some students brought an additional strategy to this process. More precisely, what they did was to *embed* the useful TIA and gist and list strategies in a more complex process we will call a *dialogue* strategy (Figure 16).

In a dialogue, the text is not simply selected or dismissed; it is in a sense listened to and allowed to talk back. By questioning what the text means, the writer using the dialogue strategy begins to move toward a *qualified, negotiated understanding of the ideas in question*. In these dialogues the sources are also allowed to talk to each other: James says to push on despite mental fatigue, Guitton says to rest at the first sign, and the writer says, "What should I make of this?"

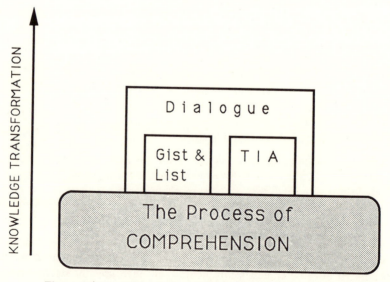

Figure 16. Reading strategies and knowledge transformation.

The dialogue strategy in these protocols was identified by four key features (interrater reliability .83), all of which create relations among ideas. One form of dialogue was simply a comparison between the two authorities in the source text: "This one says X and/but that one says Y." A second form of dialogue generates examples. Building on a TIA response, the student goes on to extend or elaborate the source's meaning with an inference, an example, or a reason (a supportive dialogue). For instance, in response to James's advice to push on, the writer responds, "It's like having a second wind." Or the reader may present a counterexample (a critical dialogue). In the excerpt below, Bob has just read a sentence in which one authority points out that students who schedule lots of study time seem to get higher grades. He responds: "He's saying work all day. That's stupid.—You have to eat. You have to take showers. You have to sleep. You might schedule time to sleep also." Bob's sarcastic tone suggests that long work days may be a new idea to him. Nevertheless, the dialogue is started. (Note that our coding excluded inferences which were deemed to be so obvious as to be nearly a paraphrase of the source. A response had to contribute new information to be termed a dialogue.)

A third form of the dialogue leads to qualified and contextualized ideas. The reader responds by imagining a scenario or an instance in which the idea in question might operate or by imagining a hypothetical situation in which a claim from the source text might be tested. In this process of contextualizing an idea (e.g., the idea that it helps to schedule study time), dialogues often spell out cause and effect relations or they tie a claim to certain conditions in which it is valid (as in, "Oh that [scheduling] works sometimes, until everything piles up on you."). As a result of these contextualizing dialogues, readers end up adding qualifications to their own ideas or to those of the supposed authorities. They start seeing claims as conditional.

In the following brief dialogue Jordan entertains three voices—his own, the text's, and "most people's"—as he thinks through a statement in the text advocating music as white noise.

> That's what I always thought. Most people say to me, don't listen to music. But if you get a quiet music going on all the time, which flows, as he says, steady, then it definitely helps.

Even though Jordan already agreed with the claim, his dialogue, unlike a TIA response, led him to establish its range of validity. This move to qualify ideas is typically signaled in the dialogues by certain conditionalizing linguistic patterns observable in Jordan and the previous example. Following are three skeleton dialogues in which the content words have been removed to highlight this qualifying play of mind.

1. True, if . . . and if. . . , but, . . . because. . . . If . . , then. . . .
2. At times, . . . because. . . . But not necessarily, . . . If. . . .
3. Yeah, but. . . . It's stupid to say "never," and so. . . . [The writer concludes] It's gonna help in the long run.

Finally, the combination of comparisons, examples, and qualifications in these dialogues sometimes led to a fourth form—a statement that synthesized two claims by qualifying both or at least putting them into relation with one another. Such syntheses may offer genuinely new insights, or perhaps just an accommodation, as in one dialogue which moved from a claim to a "but sometimes" counterexample, and then concluded with, "But to each his own, I guess."

As these examples show, the dialogue strategy is not characterized by moments of rigorous, formal, or logical examination of the sort presented in books on inductive logic or critical thinking. On the other hand this informal elaborative strategy seems to yield a qualitatively different representation of meaning than that created by TIA or gist and list. In it, authorities, prior knowledge, and the student's current inferences are brought face to face with one another. Claims are tested against other evidence or other experiences, and often emerge as qualified, more fully contextualized ideas.

The contrast I have drawn between the gist and list and the TIA strategies, on one hand, and the dialogue strategy on the other is particularly important if we are interested in asking students to use writing to *transform* their knowledge not just to express it. If we imagined a continuum defined in Figure 16 as the Knowledge Transformation Continuum, we could conclude that the gist and list and TIA strategies *can* lead to changes in knowledge. At the least, they help students learn new information and reorganize their prior knowledge, but those two categories of information rarely interact with one another. Gist and list is highly dependent on the text. The TIA strategy is driven by the student's prior experience and beliefs. If one thinks William James's advice is bunk, that is the end of the matter. Students using the TIA did not ask themselves: What is the evidence? How could I decide which claim is true? Or even *why* do these people disagree? When the TIA or gist and list is embedded in a dialogue, however, the opportunity for *examining, questioning, qualifying, and extending knowledge* goes up. This option for transformation applies both to one's own knowledge and to the claims of the "authorities."

MAKING A PLAN TO WRITE

The gist and list, TIA, and dialogue strategies are three ways in which students used their reading to write. But this raises the question, how does one go from response as a reader to forming an organizing idea and a text of one's own? The answer is not simple, but I would like to contrast two particular strategies students used because this contrast may help explain why the transition to academic discourse, the real focus of this chapter, is often difficult. The contrast shows us a powerful, efficient—and limited—strategy operating in a situation that calls for more.

As Figure 17 shows, some students simply embedded the processes we have already looked at within a knowledge-telling and/or a schema-driven plan. That is, their reading had created a mental representation organized around the topic and their response to it or around the plan supplied by a familiar text schema. Writing was essentially a process of communicating that knowledge.

Dotty, for example, was the "TIA Speed Queen" in this study. She started the assignment at 12:30 A.M., using the TIA strategy. Within five seconds of completing the reading, an organizing idea rolled off her pen as final text. She used the commonplace "Time Management is important" for her introductory sentence and then wrote about a short list of "important things to remember" based on ideas she had selected by TIA. Dotty shows us a low-effort, knowledge-driven plan at work.

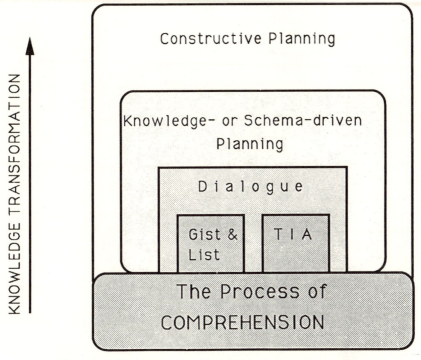

Figure 17. Knowledge- or schema-driven constructive planning.

A high-effort version of a knowledge-driven plan can look quite different. One of the most careful planners of the seventeen picked her way through the source text, carefully classifying, defining, and synthesizing. She and Dotty produced very different papers, but both relied on a planning strategy that focused exclusively on organizing and presenting knowledge.

This knowledge-driven (and to some extent format- or schema-driven) approach accounts for the planning process of ten of these seventeen students, and for good reason. A knowledge-telling plan for writing, especially when it is based on a TIA response, has both academic virtues and practical advantages. It is not only highly efficient, but allows writers to show they have read the source *and* to translate their own ideas directly into text as a response. A student can write a highly rated, well-organized summary, synthesis, or personal response with the strategy, as well as quick and superficial paper. However, if one wants the writing process to also lead to a transformation of knowledge, it is likely that knowledge-driven planning will short-circuit much of that process. A plan to *tell* one's knowledge is different from a plan to *transform* that knowledge for a clear intellectual or rhetorical purpose or to *adapt* it to the needs of a reader. This is not to say that all writing needs to create such transformations, but this ability is often critical in carrying out academic discourse.

From this perspective, then, an alternative strategy seemed particularly important. Seven students in this group placed their work in the still larger context of their own *constructive planning*. That is, these seven students who engaged in constructive planning *spent time thinking about not only content, as did everyone, but about goals for this paper, about criteria for judging it, about problems in designing it, and/ or about alternative ways to handle the task.* They became reflective, strategic thinkers, looking at their writing as a rhetorical problem and a constructive act. (We should note that in reading research, the term "constructive" is used as a broad statement about epistemology—an assertion that all reading involves inference drawing and meaning making [Spivey, 1987]. In the present distinction between knowledge-driven, schema-driven, and constructive planning, "constructive" refers to a more narrowly defined act—a more fully conscious, attention-absorbing, problem-solving process that some planners may engage in at some times [Flower, Schriver, Carey, Haas, & Hayes, in press].)

Constructive planning, when it happened, often came as a response to a problem. Collene has just written a predictable sentence defining time management. It is followed by a paragraph on the theme of "there are different theories." She looks at her work and says in the protocol:

> Garbage. Well, this is not enough. I have to write some more. [This evaluation appears to push her into an episode of constructive planning that goes on in a sort of musing, sing-song tone.] Ok so what? What do I think about this. Time management. What do I know about time management. . . .
>
> [A little later] "The key" nah—I wish I could get an angle on this. How am I going to do this? *Why* [vocal emphasis] do I want to do this? What good will it do me? Time management? "Time management. What good will it do me?"—"How can I time manage." No. How am I going to do this? "What good will it do for me?" [And then, flipping back to the assignment, she discovers another possible angle on the subject and says to herself:] My opinion—[paraphrasing the text] write down my statement, based on my interpretation of this data.

This episode of constructive planning may not be brilliant, but it shows a student's explicit, reflective attempt to set goals for herself and to consider alternative rhetorical approaches to her subject. The problem of making a plan and writing a paper has itself become the subject of thought. This planning strategy, as I have suggested in Figure 17, often builds on the other strategies we have discussed. A knowledge-driven plan, for instance, is often embedded within and guided by a constructive, rhetorical plan for how to use that information.

In using the term "constructive planning" I have distinguished between this reflective effort to solve a rhetorical problem and the bulk of planning which goes on in these protocols—that is, content planning, which is focused exclusively on selecting, structuring, and expressing content information—without apparent reference to rhetorical goals. An ideal description of students' planning would integrate both, including not only the organizing plans discussed in Chapters 1 and 2, but other aspects of content planning, such as topical structure and development (Witte, 1983). One limitation of this analysis, then, is that it does not describe the way in which the rhetorical plans these writers made produced specific manipulations of content. Another limitation to bear in mind is that some constructive planning is certain to be carried out tacitly, so that students are making decisions the protocols do not capture. However, this absence is also informative: it tells us that the attention students are giving to these decisions is so fleeting there is nothing to articulate, or so automatic that it fails to rise to conscious attention. The protocols show us to what extent students are engaging in conscious, articulated planning over which they can exercise some reflective control. There are reasons to think this is valuable. In an extended study of the planning process and how effective writers use it (Flower et al., in press), we found that students often relied on knowledge-driven or schema-driven plans to guide their composing. Experts used such plans, too, but they embedded them within the larger designs of constructive planning.

The constructive planning observed here served at least three interestingly different functions: intention setting, creating a plan, and monitoring progress. Collene's episode begins with intention setting in the form of a very open-ended call for a plan when she says, "Ok, so what? What do I think about this?" Her later, more specific decision to "get an angle" refines that intention. Intention setting, as Collene uses it, initiates and directs a search of both her own memory and of the text. And in its small way it sets certain criteria (e.g., I need an "angle") that help her manage her search and her attempt to construct a rhetorical plan for the paper.

A more obvious function of constructive planning is to create a plan itself (e.g., Collene's final plan to use her opinion as the angle for the paper). However, we should note that these plans were often tentative: the act of planning let writers hold an idea up for consideration. Finally, many of these moments of constructive planning were devoted to evaluating a plan, evaluating a piece of text in light of a plan, or managing the writer's own process on the basis of goals or a plan. In general, these episodes let people monitor their progress and keep contact between their goals for this text and the result so far.

In the following example we can see Fred not only doing constructive planning, but considering and rejecting a knowledge-driven plan based on "just restat[ing] a lot of this stuff." In these excerpts he uses his plan to direct his reading, which leads to a different interpretation of Guitton than he held before planning. The plan itself also develops as he works, and he ends with a very satisfied evaluation of his progress:

> Unless I just restate a lot of this stuff, talk about the fact that, you know, it is important, . . . but that's not what they want. They want me to assimilate this, come up with some conclusions, they [should] be related to something. . . .
>
> [He rereads the assignment and appears to conceive a new goal.] I guess I'm gonna have to deal with how, how to attack the problem of time management. It sounds good, write this down, and attack problem. Yeah! Great! Things I can think of off hand, you got to put in there about. . . . [At this point he begins to review his notes, to search the text and to rethink his response to Guitton. A few minutes later he returns to his plan.]
>
> I guess I can do a little bit more than restate what they have in the text. I can relate to my situation as a college student. It would be easier to relate to a college student! Well, wonderful.

STRATEGIES AND ACADEMIC DISCOURSE

Examining the strategies these students used to develop their organizing ideas has given us a close look at one small but probably critical part of the freshman repertoire. Our analysis here is both exploratory and descriptive: it cannot assert a cause and effect relation or show us what to teach. But it can prompt us to question some assumptions about learning to write in this context, and it can help us build a more articulate, data-based hypothesis about what these students were doing. Let us return to the question that began this chapter: What is going on when students negotiate their transition into the discourse community of academic writing, when the goal of such writing is full and critical literacy? That is, what happens when we expect students not only to read others and *summarize* accurately, and to *respond* insightfully, but also to *interpret* and apply their reading and their own thinking to a new *problem* or for a *purpose* of their own? How might strategies such as these contribute to this vision of academic discourse?

As a group these students demonstrated an impressively complex and flexible body of strategies for writing. Although there is much we could gladly teach them, many of their thinking strategies have the potential for sophisticated, critical thinking, for learning, and for building a crafted piece of work. Moreover, when students turned their attention to figuring out what the assignment and situation required, we could see them actively compensating for the practiced moves and easy reliance on conventions a more experience writer would have. We can catch a glimpse of how constructive planning lets writers compensate for some of the topic knowledge and the discourse knowledge they, by definition, lack when they are learning to write in some new way or when they are writing to learn new information. We saw little to suggest that these students need to learn radical new ways of thinking or make a developmental leap to use strategies such as dialoguing or constructive planning. But it is also clear that not all of the students used all of these strategies. The study showed us, on the one hand, a repertoire of powerful and seemingly accessible strategies and, on the other, a number of students who relied on the more familiar but limited process of comprehension, summary, and response.

And yet, even if we grant the potential of these writers and the power of an expanded repertoire, we must still explain how this or any set of strategies actually operates in the context of writing in school. How does such a process work and what might teachers teach? Let me contrast two ways of imagining the role of strategies, which I will describe as the "good process" conceptualization and a "strategic process" view.

THE MYTH OF THE "GOOD PROCESS"

As teachers we are sometimes overeager to formalize knowledge worth having into a set of activities we can teach, especially ones we can also observe in class or in a text. The process movement in writing, for all its virtues, has become at times absorbed in the search for a mythical and canonical "good process." Is it possible to identify certain processes or activities (e.g., the holy trinity of prewrite, write, and rewrite) as inherently valuable and to build a composite, obligatory good process for students to walk through? Or are we dealing with a far more radically goal-directed, strategic process in which a mental activity is only as good as the uses to which the writer chooses to put it?

For instance, one could imagine that the strategies sketched in Figure 17 reflect a meaningful progression; that is, that gist and list, TIA, dialogue, knowledge-driven, and constructive planning form a "natural" or desirable *sequence* that good writers go through as they compose—or which students *should* go through as a set of steps. However, there was no indication in this study that students used these strategies in any standard order or that one *needs* to perform one strategy (e.g., knowledge telling) in order to do another (e.g., constructive planning).

We might ask if these strategies fit into a developmental sequence, with constructive planning as a more abstract, more complex process. However, a developmental explanation of why these college-age adults chose to do knowledge telling would be a weak hypothesis—there are too many better alternative explanations. Moreover, there is no evidence that it is inherently "easier" to summarize (gist and list) than it is to question and elaborate (dialogue). When students discover dialoguing as a new strategy they can now consciously use, the leap they make, I would argue, is not a developmental change in ability but a change in the way they represent the task and their options. As the student quoted at the beginning of the introductory chapter said: "What I wasn't used to was interjecting my own feelings about the assignment as I went along. And when I think back on that, the fact that I stopped and responded to what the author had just said . . . that was a new experience for me."

Another possible, but I think inaccurate, way to conceptualize strategies is to imagine a context-free "good process" in which strategies form a hierarchy based on their value—each one better (more sophisticated, more literate, more useful, etc.) than the last. And yet, as we discussed in Chapter 1, what criteria would we use to define "valuable"? A dialogue strategy is good for stimulating critical thinking, and we want students to be able to do such thinking when they need to. On the other hand, if Walter Pauk, one of the authorities quoted in the source text, were asked to do this assignment, his deep knowledge of the topic and well-developed schemas for such a piece might make a mental dialogue or constructive planning quite unnecessary for writing a good essay. It would be a mistake to force these processes into a simple, ascending taxonomy of intellectual skills. A more accurate description would have to plot their *strategic value* for the task at hand—did the writer need the strategy to accomplish what he or she wanted to do or what the situation demanded? The apparent value of the dialogue strategy in this study was a function of the task we gave students. Even though this task is an important one in school, we should not be lured into a simpler theoretical view of value.

The limitations of a good process conceptualization become even more problematic if we consider what we actually want students to learn. When, for instance, I look at the constructive planning of Fred and Collene, I am inclined to echo the sentiments of Fred, who concluded his planning with "Well, wonderful." It is, I believe, reasonable to infer that these particular students may have an ace up their sleeve; they appear to have valuable strategies in their repertoire that help them solve problems, transform their knowledge, and write good papers. And it appears that other students do not have or use such strategies. The next reasonable inference is that if teachers could get students to engage in mental dialogues and to do constructive planning—if they could make that a part of students' process on every assignment—students' writing would improve.

There is, however, a problem with that inference. In this study, only three of the seven students used constructive planning to create what I, as a teacher, would value most—a purposeful, rhetorically aware text. And a fourth planned her way to a thoughtful synthesis of the source texts. The remaining students who did constructive planning, however, used it to turn their TIA notes into a paper in which they essentially commented on ideas they agreed with. Constructive planning was, in fact, useful to them; but it did little more than help them think a lot about how to write a limited paper. Or consider the students Stein (Chapter 5) describes who made impressive use of elaboration and dialogue during reading, but used almost none of that material in their final texts. Strategies and writing activities alone, even "good ones," are only as good as the uses to which writers put those processes.

THE EMBEDDED STRUCTURE OF A STRATEGIC PROCESS

In place of attempting to prescribe a canonical "good process," I think we need to conceptualize academic writing and the attempt to learn it as a strategic process in which the writer's goals and metacognitive awareness play a critical part. We would then see, for instance, how the writing process operates in intimate response to context as the writer sees it and how writing strategies are ordered in a *structural* hierarchy. That is, the hierarchy these data do point to is not based on value; rather it is a structural metaphor for how these strategies *function* with one another. Actions that are higher in the hierarchy operate by incorporating other strategies as supporting parts of a larger process. As the simplified schematic diagrams in Figures 16 and 17 attempt to show, these strategies are recursive in the sense used in linguistics: they can embed other strategies within themselves. The dialogue strategy, for instance, is not an esoteric or independent new cognitive process that bursts on the scene in these protocols. Instead, it builds on the students' well-developed abilities to locate important points and to create gists, but adds to those processes the additional goals of questioning, conditionalizing, and testing. It embeds the gist and list and TIA within an expanded effort. And the constructive planning we observed is not a different species from knowledge-driven planning; rather it adds an additional set of goals (beyond knowledge telling) to the planning process. These goals, generated by the writer, dictate how knowledge will used. Constructive planning embraces the TIA, the gisting and the dialoguing that has gone on before in order to use them and to transform the knowledge they yield for a special purpose.

One of the advantages recursion offers is the ability to embed complex processes such as comprehending, summarizing, and knowledge telling within another strategy, such as constructive planning, and thus to extend their use. The relation we observed, then, is a structural hierarchy (rather than a procedural, developmental, or value hierarchy) in which certain strategies incorporate other processes within themselves, as the writer attempts to meet a new set of goals or personal criteria. Whether a writer is fully conscious of it or not, these cognitive processes are in fact moves in a strategic process which takes its meaning and its shape from the unfolding goals and needs of the writer.

Recently, both Applebee (1986) and Hillocks (1986) have argued that the process movement in teaching writing has sometimes lost sight of the fact that writing is a *goal-directed process*. Teachers lose sight of this fact when they teach the writing process as a sequence of exercises that are presumed to be good, in and for themselves. As Applebee has shown, teachers may treat journal keeping, peer review, or revising as obligatory behaviors in a "good" process, even when the success of a paper depends on quite different strategies, such as the careful reading of a science textbook. Students begin to see the "required good process" as irrelevant to the real goals of their papers because we have failed to make it clear that these activities (e.g., journal keeping) are really *optional strategies in the writer's repertoire,* which are especially useful in certain tasks, for certain purposes.

The same problem occurs when researchers, trying to describe the process of good writers, simply count behaviors: for example, how many times writers plan or how many global corrections they make. In both cases the teachers and researchers are working with a psychologically impoverished version of the writer's process. They have failed to account for the logic that drives successful problem solving. Because writing is a constructive, rhetorical process, it can not be equated with simple behaviors or classroom techniques: we are dealing with a strategic, contextualized action, a thinking process that is guided by the writers' goals and by their interpretation of the writing situation. Although constructive planning and dialoguing, for instance, are strategies with high potential and ones I tend to value as a teacher, they can be put to widely differing uses. They neither predict nor ensure success.

To understand the repertoire of freshman writers, then, we have to look at the *goals* as well as the *strategies* students employ and at the task as they are representing it to themselves. The *awareness* and *metacognitive control* students bring to their own goals and process are difficult to assess and to teach. Yet this third element of strategic knowledge may be more critical than we have realized as we try to chart the transition into academic discourse and to explain why this necessarily challenging journey may become unnecessarily difficult for some students.

The Tacit Transition to Academic Discourse

This study presents us with a perplexing picture. We see students who are relatively efficient readers and writers, who are skillful and fluent with some forms of academic discourse; nevertheless, the texts they produce fall short of our larger expectations, and students themselves often feel confused about why. What might this situation look like from the students' point of view? Are our new expectations less self-evident, is this transition more tacit than we have assumed? We suggest that the context of school writing and the cognition that supports reading-to-write may conspire to make this transition seem both invisible and unnecessary to some students. Let us begin with cognition.

THE COMPREHENSION AND RESPONSE STRATEGY

A look at the cognitive basis of the reading-to-write process suggests one reason students' paper-writing habits might be so resistant to change. Although the theoretical description of a comprehension/response strategy proposed here will go beyond what our study can confirm or deny, it offers us a research-based way to understand students' experiences. The reading-to-write process can be said to be built on the foundation of two strategies, or rather two large, interlinked families of strategies that are central to school—comprehension and response. The cognitive processes that underlie this comprehension/response strategy, as we will call it, are so robust and so well-learned, that this strategy can handle most school writing and important parts of more complex academic discourse, as long as the writers are not asked to purposefully invent and transform their knowledge.

Consider for a moment the cognitive processes that are a normal part of reading for comprehension. At one time reading was described as a receptive process of "decoding" and storing information for later recall. However, the cognitive perspective in recent reading research has built an impressive picture of a "constructive" process in which readers organize, select, and connect information to build their own mental representation of a text (see Spivey, 1987, for a review of this work). Readers not only bring their prior knowledge in the form of schemata and assumptions, but use a combination of their prior knowledge and the text to make a meaningful interpretation. Furthermore, this constructive, meaning-making process is itself guided by the goals of the reader, who may be reading to follow an argument, pick a fight, or enjoy a cup of tea and a good book.

If people who are ostensibly reading for comprehension are, in fact, building a unique representation of meaning, what sort of representation do they produce? Would that mental representation—created simply by reading for comprehension— look at all like an essay a student might be asked to write? A brief review of what the subjects described in this reading research are typically doing suggests that many features of a standard "freshman" essay might be supplied by this reading process alone.

1. *Readers select and recall the main points or important information from the text.*

   Ideas that are high in the text structure or idea hierarchy of a text are better remembered (Meyer, 1982), although good and poor readers differ on what they think is important (Winograd, 1984).

2. *Readers also create "gists," which condense or collapse related ideas in a text into more abstract or inclusive concepts.*

   These gists and inferences play an important role in comprehension, serving as anchor points that readers refer to as they try to build a coherent meaning or a "connected text base" out of the unrolling text (Afflerbach, 1985; Kintsch & Vipond, 1979).

3. *Readers not only select and invent main points, they link this information in various structured ways.*

   The macrostructures people build during comprehension and at the point of recall can take the form of a loose collection or a highly structured hierarchy (Meyer, 1982). These structures may reflect personal or cultural schemata readers bring to the text more than the structure cued by the author (Bartlett, 1932; Meyer, Brandt, & Bluth, 1980). Good readers are more likely to be able, on request, to build a macrostructure that resembles the author's than are poor readers (Meyer, 1982; Winograd, 1984), and readers differ in their ability to restructure information (Mandler & DeForest, 1979).

4. *Readers do not stop with these handy blueprints of the text. They create extended elaborations and inventive inferences that become woven into the meaning of the text.*

   These elaborations and inferences often help resolve problems in comprehension (Bransford, 1979; Haas & Flower, 1988), but they may also be highly personal associations triggered by the text (Reder, 1980). Many of these inferences become a part of the meaning to the extent that readers cannot distinguish between what they actually read and what they inferred (Bransford, 1979; Kintsch, 1974).

5. *Finally, this comprehension process—and the representation it builds—is highly subject to the individual reader's goals.*

   If the goal is to find connections, readers might well ignore contradictions that do not fit the picture (see Spivey, 1984). If the goal is to find the "author's" structure, a more inclusive representation will be created (Meyer, 1982). And if the goal is practical action, such as planning a burglary, the reader of a household description is more likely to remember the TV set than the leak in the roof—a fact which the prospective buyer would recall (Pichert & Anderson, 1977).

To sum up, in "simply" reading for comprehension, readers are building a mental macrostructure based on main points and larger gists cued by the text, extended by elaborations and inferences, and sensitive to the readers' own goals. They have created a complex and highly structured private representation of meaning.

What does this tell us about reading-to-write? Many people, such as Tierney and Pearson (1984), are urging us to see the parallels between reading and writing as constructive processes. Readers too, they argue, can "revise" their understanding as they read, and they can set goals for themselves, such as the goal to reread and see the text from a different perspective. However, we do not want to overstate the probability of large transformations. This expanded view of reading, Tierney and Pearson point out, is "almost contrary to some well-established goals readers proclaim for themselves (e.g., that efficient reading is equivalent to maximizing recall based on a single fast reading)" (p. 42).

My point is based on a more limited claim about reading. Although it *may* at times work radical transformations on knowledge, even the smaller transformations are significant. The relatively straightforward process of reading for comprehension is a vigorously constructive, inventive act. It generates a selective, organized, and elaborated structure of ideas in memory—all in a normal day's work. If we look at that mental construction as a product, it is a rather impressive product. This product of comprehension would not make a bad "essay" in some school settings if the student were asked to write it out. My point is that the process of comprehension is not only a robust, well-learned process, but in the hands of a student who has just negotiated twelve years of schooling, it can do much of the work reading-to-write calls for. It is capable of producing a structured, elaborated mental representation of meaning.

But comprehension alone is not an adequate explanation for this performance. To account for more of the success and fluency of these students we need to posit a somewhat more complex combination of goals and strategies, which I will call a comprehension/response strategy. In the class presentations and in the search for an organizing idea seen in the protocols, students make it clear that "getting a good idea" is at the heart of writing a short paper. Without one you are in danger of sounding unintelligent or boring, and you have nothing onto which to hook all the material you have just comprehended. School asks for intelligent, if brief responses. Bereiter and Scardamalia (1982) have shown how children build their early writing on the foundation of conversation, using the patterns of turn-taking and conversational response to manage their writing process. Generating an "acceptable" response, whether it is in conversation or in reply to questions, is a basic discourse skill these college freshmen brought to writing. We see this pattern of comprehension and response formalized in the standard high school assignment that asks the student to read a short passage, summarize it, and then write his or her own "opinion" as the final paragraph. Of course, short papers and essay exams demand more than a conversational response. They ask the writer to stay on topic and to use some of the standard conventions of written text that maintain topical focus and that link adjacent sentences and paragraphs. And we saw in Chapter 2, the college students in this study often had firm control over many conventions of surface coherence, including introductory paragraphs, topic sentences, repeated referents and key words, even when that coherence was only skin deep.

What I am suggesting is that the comprehension/response strategy—really, this large happy family of strategies—is at the heart of the standard repertoire these students brought to college. Moreover, it can, by itself, account for *much* of the underlying cognitive process of reading-to-write. Now look at the situation from the learner's point of view: if comprehension and response, even in their relative straightforward forms, are central to so much of reading and writing in school, if they are robust, constructive processes that can give you a focused, developed set of things to say, and if they are processes you have learned to manage with some success, then why assume you need to do anything else? The answer, I believe, is that many students indeed see no reason to initiate changes in cognition. They approach these new academic writing tasks with a set of familiar goals and strategies that do appear to fit. And they are right—to a point. From a cognitive perspective, the comprehension/response process continues to stand at the center of reading-to-write. It is not replaced—it is only embedded in new goals. And that, perhaps, is what makes this transition tacit—what allows teachers to assume the difference is self-evident while students are not fully aware it exists.

EMBEDDING THE COMPREHENSION/RESPONSE STRATEGY IN A RHETORICAL PLAN

For all its virtues, a comprehension/response strategy is not geared to examining, testing, and transforming one's own knowledge. It does not push the reader/writer to take advantage of the "writerly" reading process Tierney and Pearson (1984) and Greene (in preparation) describe. The goals it sets and the strategies it draws on, like the TIA, are designed to tell one's current knowledge rather than transform it. This does not preclude insight, discovery, or reintegration, but the strategy is not designed to seek and nurture these actions.

Comprehension/response can handle some writing occasions with efficiency and flair. Unfortunately, the academic discourse community (as defined in this study) often expects student writers to transform their knowledge, not tell it, and to adapt it to new or special readers by filling in gaps of implicit meaning, anticipating a reader's response, or imagining the reader's needs. In many classes, the writer must adapt, restructure, or synthesize knowledge in order to answer complex questions or write a paper that applies the student's reading and thinking to some larger issue in the field. If knowledge transformation is the cognitive trademark of academic discourse, speaking with authority and purpose is one of its social manifestations. Full-fledged members of this community are also expected to speak as contributors with the authority of their own thinking, guided by an intellectual or rhetorical purposes of their own making. When we perceive that an essayist's dominant purpose is to recite his or her reading or relate a response to it, we often ask, "But what is the point? Why are you telling me this?" We expect a rhetorical purpose, beyond the purpose of comprehension and response. And, as all writers know, discovering, shaping, and using that unique purpose to construct a text is one of the most demanding and creative acts of writing.

If a comprehension/response strategy cannot meet all of these expectations, despite its constructive power and familiarity, what must the student do: abandon it, replace it, move on to different or "higher" processes? The answer, we will argue, is not to abandon but to embed. Strategic knowledge is the ability to put old strengths to new purposes. Imagine the writer as a ballet dancer who has spent the last twelve years perfecting the basic movements of ballet—the first, second, third positions, the grand plie, the arabesque, and so on. Eventually these movements are combined into exercises at the barre and across the room (like the "school exercises" in figure skating)—basic movements requiring skill and dedication, which are never abandoned. However, when the dancer walks onto the stage as a performer in his or her own right, we expect a new thing. Those basic movements are *transformed* into dance and they are used, not for themselves, but to carry out the expressive, interpretive *purpose* of the dancer and the dance.

The dancer is a metaphor for the growth of a strategic, recursive process. The basic movements of ballet, like the intellectual moves of comprehension and response, are never left behind—they are the center and the heartbeat of any performance. But as student becomes performer, these moves become embedded in a process with expanded horizons and new goals. Just as sentences are embedded within sentences in linguistic recursion, complex intellectual acts are often embedded within the more complex hierarchy of a recursive cognitive process.

This picture of strategic development suggests natural and evolutionary change. And yet, sometimes a recursive, adaptive process—in which old strategies and abilities need to be put to new uses—may be the hardest change for a learner to see. Students may be caught in a tacit transitions in which the cues to change are subtle, but their significance is far-reaching. We want to explore the possibility that the context of college writing may offer such indirect cues that some students fail to perceive that a change in goals has occurred.

BUILDING A THEORY OF THE TASK

Just as writers have to build an individual task representation of each new assignment, students entering college also appear to build what we call a theory of the task
for college writing. Although informal and often implicit, this more general "theory" emerges when freshmen talk about the questions many share (or the conclusions
they have already reached): Is college writing really different from high school
writing? Are each teacher's expectations idiosyncratic? Is writing in each discipline
largely unrelated to the others? (See Chapter 8.) Imagine this theory-building process (which may itself be tacit, casual, shrewd, or conscious and desperate) from the
students' point of view.

The Process of Theory Building

Like the stranger Burke (1941) describes who drifts into a knot of people in an
ongoing conversation at a party and must infer the direction and the shape of the
discourse she would enter, a student enters the ongoing conversation of academic
writing. In doing so, the rules of the game she must infer are not only those of
academic papers in general, but of the discipline and the individual class. Standing
on the edge of the assigned conversation, the student must construct a theory of the
task from available evidence. Like that of Burke's stranger, the student's "theory"
making may well be intuitive and unexamined.

If we focus on the cognition of theory making (rather than on the patterns and
conventions it invents), we might predict a scenario of the following sort. The
student will, first of all, notice and even look for familiar clues in this situation that
let her call on prior knowledge. Much of that knowledge will be organized as well-
structured schemas (e.g., the "English theme" schema, which has slots for obligatory key features such as format and style, and carries assumptions about the level of
effort and the place of one's own ideas). The great cognitive convenience of such
schemata, of course, is that when some part of the schema is triggered in the writer's
memory, the whole organized structure becomes active. Using our prior schemas is
at the heart of cognitive efficiency: hearing a few words of the conversation lets us
quickly, almost automatically infer an entire web of meaning. However, depending
on these prefabricated knowledge structures does not direct the perceiver's attention
to the new or to modified features of a situation. In fact, like stereotypes and
prejudice, which are other forms of schemata, they may suppress awareness of the
facts that do not fit.

Familiar Features, Changing Goals

Imagine, then, the student, faced with constructing a theory of the task and bringing
her previous experience with school writing to the job. How easy will it be for her to
see new features or to recognize that familiar features have undergone a sea change?

On the surface, various sorts of academic and school writing have much in
common. Standard features of clear exposition and organization, the conventions of
introductions and conclusions, topic sentences and transitions, and the informational focus and transactional voice of such writing are so visible and reassuringly
concrete that they may become defining features in the student's schema. Moreover,

the standard organizing plans one learns in school—the personal response, the summary, the synthesis of outside sources—are still standard plans in all sorts of later college-level and professional academic writing. But there is an important difference between doing a summary or synthesis for its own sake, as a genre so to speak, and embedding those forms in a piece of writing that has its own purpose within a community of readers. Experienced academic writers may *use* a summary to present two points of view or use a source-based synthesis to establish context to their own credibility; but those plans and their attending conventions of format and style are typically in the service of grander goals, larger motives—in short, they serve the writer's rhetorical purpose.

For the student, whom we left in the throes of constructing a theory of the task, this means that the main visible features of the task look remarkably unchanged. The classroom context, the teacher's concern with content, and the role of the paper as a tool in the grading process, all these are likely to fit a familiar schema for theme writing. *What has changed most is not the apparent genre or conventions, but the goals. The goals of self-directed critical inquiry, of using writing to think through genuine problems and issues, and of writing to an imagined community of peers with a personal rhetorical purpose—these distinguish academic writing from a more limited comprehension and response.* This is not to say that all college assignments pose this task, but many do (including the set of assignments designed by the Reading-to-Write teachers to highlight these goals [presented in McCormick, 1989]). These new goals are part of what makes the transition problematic. Moreover, college teachers may simply expect and reward such thinking (from the "good students") without ever articulating their criteria for such college work. Without awareness of these goals it is also hard to make sense of many of the discourse conventions of academic papers, such as examining counterpositions to achieve a balanced appraisal or using a literature review to define issues and establish credibility rather than to survey information (see Bazerman, 1985; Myers, 1985a).

This fuller form of academic discourse is not limited to college. When students are asked to make such a transition by high school teachers, the change in goals may be even more difficult to communicate without the social reinforcement for change and the new authority college can confer. In either case this shift in goals may be faintly signaled by our assignments, which offer only weak indicators that old schemas do not fit. In this scenario of transition, the signals may begin to accumulate in the form of paper grades and comments that seem to ask for something different (or only idiosyncratic?), while the evidence from which to construct a theory of the task and its new goals may still be indirect.

The Contextual Evidence for a Change in Goals

We should also consider the *nature* of the evidence the context supplies to our theory builders. Learning to "discourse" as a member of the academic community is, of course, related to some other unmistakable changes going on in a freshman's emotional and intellectual life. It typically coincides with a change in adult status. It has many parallels to the intellectual struggle with authority and the problem of relative values that William Perry (1968) describes. The generative, purposeful process we hope to see in students as *writers* is not a gift teachers have the power to give; it is part of a larger hard-won authority students are achieving for themselves.

On the other hand, this potential for speaking with new authority *as a writer* may be a dimly perceived change compared to the change in status that goes with graduating from being a high school "student" to being a college "man" or "woman." Even though that more public transition to intellectual and social independence can be rocky, it is clearly marked and modeled by society; the goals are quite visible to all. By comparison, the strategic transition we expect within a student's writing calls for a private and internal change—within a largely unaltered social context of students writing to and being graded by a professor. The need to assume authority calls for alterations in well-learned and heretofore successful habits of mind, rather than the acquisition of an obvious new skill, such as doing statistics. It calls for new goals that embed old means.

To make the matter more mysterious, transforming one's current knowledge and adapting it to a purpose are dynamic intellectual events: actions, not products. Because they refer to a process of mind, they are sometimes hard to demonstrate with written products, even with "before and after" versions of a text. And even then the learner must infer the process from the product; one cannot observe knowledge transformation happening by reading "model" texts or see the shifting shape of a purpose in the making. Instructors try to overcome this problem when in conferences, they elicit, reify, and celebrate the student's own meaning making. But because this process is normally tacit, students are often not aware of their own constructive process. And even when a paper does succeed, thanks to a transforming and purposeful act of mind, it is easy for students to assume that the paper succeeded because this time they possessed the "right" topic knowledge or were lucky to have a bright idea—not because of any repeatable strategic process they could use again. Finally, our attempts to teach thinking processes in writing and other disciplines are still in their infancy. For all the sense of potential in this area, in strategic teaching, in cognitive apprenticeship, in critical thinking (see Collins, Brown, & Newman, in press; Jones, Palincsar, Ogle, & Carr, 1987), we have to remember that a tacit transition is the norm for strategic knowledge. Students are often expected to leap into a complex problem-solving process with little instruction or even acknowledgment that such a task is there.

This may seem to paint an overly bleak picture of this transition, since in fact many students confront the change in expectations, feel the confusion of entry, but do eventually construct a workable theory of the task of academic writing. On the other hand, many students may succeed in college courses with comprehension and response and never cross this particular threshold as writers, while others find college writing an enigmatic, even pointless, business. The task representation our students need to construct is not the theory of an easy task. A richer representation will not make the hurdles go away. But, this study suggests, we might give students more authority over this transition by dealing more directly with *the strategic knowledge—the goals, strategies, and awareness*—that support the construction of academic discourse.

References

Afflerbach, P. (1985). *The influence of prior knowledge on expert readers' main idea construction processes (Importance, Prose, Verbal Reports, Hypothesis Testing, Comprehension).* (Monograph for Outstanding Dissertation Award). Newark, DE: International Reading Association.

Althusser, L. (1971). *Lenin and philosophy and other essays* (Ben Brewster, Trans.). New York: Monthly Review Press.

Anderson, J. R. (1980). *Cognitive psychology and its implications.* San Francisco: Freedman.

Anderson, J. R. (1983). *The architecture of cognition.* Cambridge, MA: Harvard University Press.

Applebee, A. N. (1981). *Writing in the secondary school.* (Research Monograph No. 21). Urbana, IL: National Council of Teachers of English.

Applebee, A. N. (1984a). *Contexts for learning to write.* Norwood, NJ: Ablex.

Applebee, A. N. (1984b). Writing and reasoning. *Review of Educational Research, 54,* 577–596.

Applebee, A. N. (1986). Problems in process approaches: Toward a reconceptualization of process instruction. In A. R. Petrosky & D. Bartholomae (Eds.), *The teaching of writing* (pp. 95–113). Eighty-fifth Yearbook of the National Society for the Study of Education. Chicago: National Society for the Study of Education.

Applebee, A. N., Durst, R., & Newell, G. (1984). The demands of school writing. In A. N. Applebee (Ed.), *Contexts for learning to write: Studies of secondary school instruction* (pp. 55–77). Norwood, NJ: Ablex.

Arnheim, R. (1954). *Visual thinking.* Berkeley: University of California Press.

Ausubel, D. P. (1963). *The psychology of meaningful verbal learning.* New York: Grune & Stratton.

Baker, L. (1979). Comprehension monitoring: Identifying and coping with text confusions. *Journal of Reading Behavior, 11* (4), 365–374.

Baker, L., & Brown, A. L. (1983). Cognitive monitoring in reading. In J. Flood (Ed.), *Understanding reading comprehension.* Newark, DE: International Reading Association.

Baker, L., & Brown, A. L. (1984). Metacognitive skills in reading. In P. D. Pearson, R. Barr, M. L. Kamil, & P. Mosenthal (Eds.), *Handbook of reading research* (pp. 353–394). New York: Longman.

Balibar, E., & Machery, P. (1981). On literature as ideological formation. In R. Young (Ed.), *Untying the text: A post-structuralist reader* (pp. 79–99). Boston: Routledge & Kegan Paul.

Barthes, R. (1981). Textual analysis of Poe's "Valdemar." In R. Young (Ed.), *Untying the text: A post-structuralist reader* (pp. 32–47). Boston: Routledge & Kegan Paul.

Bartholomae, D. (1983). Writing assignments: Where writing begins. In P. L. Stock (Ed.), *Fforum*. Upper Montclair, NJ: Boynton/Cook.

Bartholomae, D. (1985). Inventing the university. In M. Rose (Ed.), *When a writer can't write: Studies in writer's block and other composing problems* (pp. 134–165). New York: Guilford Press.

Bartholomae, D. (1986). Words from afar. In A. R. Petrosky & D. Bartholomae (Eds.), *The teaching of writing* (pp. 1–7). Eighty-fifth Yearbook of the National Society for the Study of Education. Chicago: National Society for the Study of Education.

Bartlett, F. C. (1932). *Remembering: A study in experimental and social psychology*. Cambridge: Cambridge University Press.

Bazerman, C. (1981a). *The informed writer*. Boston: Houghton Mifflin.

Bazerman, C. (1981b). What written knowledge does: Three examples of academic discourse. *Philosophy of the Social Sciences, 11*, 361–382.

Bazerman, C. (1985). Physicists reading physics: Schema-laden purposes and purpose-laden schema. *Written Communication, 2*, 3–23.

Benton, S., Glover, L., & Plake, M. (1984). Employing adjunct aids to facilitate elaboration in writing. *Research and the Teaching of English, 18*, 2.

Bereiter, C., & Bird, M. (1985). Uses of thinking aloud in identification and teaching of reading comprehension strategies. *Cognition and Instruction, 2*, 131–156.

Bereiter, C., & Scardamalia, M. (1982). From conversation to composition: The role of instruction in a developmental process. In R. Glaser (Ed.), *Advances in instructional psychology* (Vol. 2, pp. 1–64). Hillsdale, NJ: Erlbaum.

Bereiter, C., & Scardamalia, M. (1983). Schooling and the growth of intentional cognition: Helping children take charge of their own minds. In Z. Lamm (Ed.), *New Trends in education* (pp. 73–100). Tel-Aviv: Yachdev United Publishing Company.

Bereiter, C., & Scardamalia, M. (1985). Cognitive coping strategies and the problem of inert knowledge. In S. F. Chipman, J. W. Segal, & R. Glaser (Eds.), *Thinking and learning skills: Research and open questions* (Vol. 2, pp. 65–80). Hillsdale, NJ: Erlbaum.

Bereiter, C., & Scardamalia, M. (1987). *The psychology of written communication*. Hillsdale, NJ: Erlbaum.

Berkenkotter, C., Huckin, T., & Ackerman, J. (1988). Conversation, conventions, and the writer: Case study of a student in a rhetoric Ph.D. program. *Research in the Teaching of English, 22*, 9–41.

Bitzer, Lloyd F. (1968). The rhetorical situation. *Philosophy and Rhetoric, 1* (1), 1–14.

Bizzell, P. (1982a). Cognition, convention, and certainty: What we need to know about writing. *Pre/Text, 3*, 213–244.

Bizzell, P. (1982b). College composition: Initiation into the academic discourse community. *Curriculum Inquiry, 12* (2), 191–207.

Bizzell, P., & Herzberg, B. (1986). Review of "What makes writing good." *College Composition and Communication, 37*, 244–247.

Bloom, B. S. (Ed.). (1956). *Taxonomy of educational objectives: Cognitive domain* (Vols. 1–2). New York: McKay.

Booth, W. C., & Gregory, M. W. (1987). *The Harper & Row Rhetoric: Writing as thinking, thinking as writing* (pp. 138–139). New York: Harper & Row.

Bracewell, R., Frederiksen, C., & Frederiksen, J. (1982). Cognitive processes in composing and comprehending discourse. *Educational Psychologist, 17*, 146–164.

Bransford, J. D. (1979). *Human cognition: Learning, understanding, and remembering*. Belmont, CA: Wadsworth.

Bransford, J. D., & McCarrell, N. S. (1974). A sketch of a cognitive approach to comprehension: Some thoughts about understanding what it means to comprehend. In W. B. Weimer & D. S. Palermo (Eds.), *Cognition and the symbolic processes* (pp. 189–229). Hillsdale, NJ: Erlbaum.

Braxton, J. M., & Nordvall, R. C. (1985). Selective liberal arts colleges: Higher quality as well as higher prestige? *Journal of Higher Education, 5*, 538–554.

Bridgeman, B., & Carlson, S. B. (1984). Survey of academic writing tasks. *Written Communication, 1*, 247–280.

Bridwell, L. (1980). Revising strategies in twelfth grade students: Transactional writing. *Research in the Teaching of English, 14*, 107–122.

Britton, J., Burgess, T., Martin, N., McLeod, A., & Rosen, H. (1975). *The development of writing abilities* (pp. 11–18). London: Macmillan.

Brodkey, L. (1987a). Modernism and the scene(s) of writing. *College English, 49*, 396–418.

Brodkey, L. (1987b). Writing critical ethnographic narratives. *Anthropology & Education Quarterly, 18*, 67–76.

Brown, A. L. (1980). Metacognitive development and reading. In R. J. Spiro, B. C. Bruce, & W. F. Brewer (Eds.), *Theoretical issues in reading comprehension: Perspectives from cognitive psychology, linguistics, artificial intelligence, and education* (pp. 453–481). Hillsdale, NJ: Erlbaum.

Brown, A. L. (1985). Metacognition: The development of selective attention strategies for learning from texts. In H. Singer & R. B. Ruddell (Eds.), *Theoretical models and processes of reading* (pp. 501–526). Newark, DE: International Reading Association.

Brown, A. L., & Day, J. D. (1983). Macrorules for summarizing texts: The development of expertise. *Journal of Verbal Learning and Verbal Behavior, 22*(1), 1–14.

Brown, A. L., & Palincsar, A. M. (1989). Guided cooperative learning and individual knowledge acquisition. In L. B. Resnick (Ed.), *Knowing, learning, and instruction: Essays in honor of Robert Glaser* (pp. 393–451). Hillsdale, NJ: Erlbaum.

Brown, R. (1986). Evaluation and learning. In A. R. Petrosky & D. Bartholomae (Eds.), *The teaching of writing*. Eighty-fifth Yearbook of the National Society for the Study of Education. Chicago, IL: National Society for the Study of Education.

Bruffee, K. A. (1986). Social construction, language and the authority of knowledge: A bibliographical essay. *College English, 48*, 773–790.

Burke, K. (1941). *The philosophy of literary form: Studies in symbolic action*. Berkeley: University of California Press.

Burtis, P. J., Bereiter, C., Scardamalia, M., & Tetroe, J. (1983). The development of planning in writing. In B. M. Kroll & G. Wells (Eds.), *Explorations in the development of writing* (pp. 153–174). Chichester, England: Wiley.

Chase, G. (1988). Accommodation, resistance and the politics of student writing. *College Composition and Communication., 39*, 13–22.

Chase, W. G. (1982). *Spatial representations of taxi drivers* (Tech. Rep. No. 6). Pittsburgh, PA: Learning Research & Development Center, The University of Pittsburgh.

Cohen, J. (1960). A coefficient of agreement for nominal scales. *Educational and Psychological Measurement, 20*, 37–46.

Coles, W. E., Jr. (1969). Freshman composition: The circle of unbelief. *College English, 31*, 134–142.

Coles, W. E., Jr. (1978). *The Plural I*. New York: Holt, Rinehart & Winston.

Collins, A., Brown, J. S., & Newman, S. E. (1989). Cognitive apprenticeship: Teaching the craft of reading, writing, and mathematics. In L. B. Resnick (Ed.), *Knowing, learning, and instruction: Essays in honor of Robert Glaser* (pp. 453–494). Hillsdale, NJ: Erlbaum.

Consigney, S. (1974). Rhetoric and its situations. *Philosophy and Rhetoric, 7*, 175–185.

deBeaugrande, R. (1984). *Text production* (Vol. 11). Norwood, NJ: Ablex.

Doyle, W. (1983). Academic work. *Review of Educational Research, 53*, 159–199.

Dyson, A. H. (1986). Transitions and tensions: Interrelations between the drawing, talking, and dictating of young children. *Research in the Teaching of English, 20*, 379–409.

Eagleton, T. (1985). *Literary theory: An introduction*. Minneapolis: University of Minnesota Press.

Elbow, P. (1981). *Writing without teachers*. New York: Oxford University Press.

Elbow, P. (1985). The shifting relationship between reading and writing. *College Composition and Communication, 36*, 283–303.

Faigley, L. (1986). Competing theories of process: A critique and a proposal. *College English, 48*, 527–542.

Faigley, L., & Witte, S. (1981). Analyzing revision. *College Composition and Communication, 32*, 400–414.

Fiske, S. T., & Linville, P. W. (1980). What does the schema concept buy us? *Personality and Social Psychology Bulletin, 6,* 543–557.

Flower, L. (1981). Revising writer-based prose. *Journal of Basic Writing, 3,* 62–74.

Flower, L. (1987). Interpretive Acts: Cognition and the construction of discourse. *Poetics, 16,* 109–130.

Flower, L. (1988). The construction of purpose in writing and reading. *College English, 50,* 528–550.

Flower, L. (1989a). Taking thought: The role of conscious processing in the making of meaning. In E. Maimon, B. Nodine, & F. O'Connor (Eds.), *Thinking, reasoning, and writing.* New York: Longman.

Flower, L. (1989b). Cognition, context, and theory building. *College Composition and Communication, 40,* 282–311.

Flower, L., Carey, L., & Hayes, J. (1986). *Diagnosis in revision: The expert's option* (Communications Design Center Tech. Rep.). Pittsburgh: Carnegie Mellon University.

Flower, L., & Hayes, J. R. (1980). The cognition of discovery: Defining a rhetorical problem. *College Composition and Communication, 31,* 21–32.

Flower, L., & Hayes, J. R. (1981a). Plans that guide the composing process. In C. H. Frederiksen & J. F. Dominic (Eds.), *Writing: The nature, development and teaching of written communication* (pp. 39–58). Hillsdale, NJ: Erlbaum.

Flower, L., & Hayes, J. R. (1981b). The pregnant pause: An inquiry into the nature of planning. *Research in the Teaching of English, 15,* 229–243.

Flower, L., & Hayes, J. R. (1981c). A cognitive process theory of writing. *College Composition and Communication, 32,* 365–387.

Flower, L., & Hayes, J. R. (1984). Images, plans and prose: The representation of meaning in writing. *Written Communication, 1,* 120–160.

Flower, L., Hayes, J. R., Carey, L., Schriver, K., & Stratman, J. (1986). Detection, diagnosis, and the strategies of revision. *College Composition and Communication, 37,* 16–55.

Flower, L., Schriver, K. A., Carey, L., Haas, C., & Hayes, J. R. (in press). *Planning in writing: The cognition of a constructive process.* In S. Witte, N. Nakadote, & R. Cherry (Eds.), *A Rhetoric of doing.* Carbondale: Southern Illinois University Press.

Foucault, M. (1980). *Power/Knowledge: Selected interviews and other writings, 1972–1977.* (C. Gordon, Ed.) (C. Gordon, L. Marshall, J. Mepham, & K. Soper, Trans.). New York: Pantheon.

Foucault, M. (1981). The order of discourse. In R. Young (Ed.), *Untying the text: A post-structuralist reader* (pp. 48–78). Boston: Routledge & Kegan Paul.

Frase, L. (1976). Reading performances and document design. *Proceedings of Society for Applied Learning Technology.* Washington, D.C.

Frederiksen, C. H. (1972). Effects of task-induced cognitive operations on comprehension and memory processes. In R. O. Freedle & J. B. Carroll (Eds.), *Language comprehension and the acquisition of knowledge* (pp. 211–245). New York: Wiley.

Freedman, A., & Pringle, I. (1980). Writing in the college years: Some indices of growth. *College Composition and Communication, 31,* 311–324.

Freedman, S. W. (1979a). How characteristics of student essays influence teachers' evaluations. *Journal of Educational Psychology, 71,* 328–338.

Freedman, S. W. (1979b). Why do teachers give the grades they do? *College Composition and Communication, 30,* 162.

Freedman, S. W. (1982). Some reasons for the grades we give compositions. *English Journal, 71,* 86–89.

Freedman, S. W., Dyson, A. H., Flower, L., & Chafe, W. (1987). *Research in writing: Past, present and future* (Tech. Rep. No. 1). Berkeley: University of California and Carnegie Mellon University, Center for the Study of Writing at University of California, Berkeley, and Carnegie Mellon.

Freire, P. (1970). *Pedagogy of the oppressed* (M. B. Ramos, Trans.). New York: Continuum.

Geertz, Clifford. (1983). *Local knowledge.* New York: Basic Books.

Gilbert, N. G., & Mulkay, M. (1984). *Opening Pandora's box: A sociological analysis of scientists' discourse.* Cambridge: Cambridge University Press.

Giroux, H. (1983). *Theory and resistance in education.* South Hadley, MA: Bergin.

Glaser, R. (1986). On the nature of expertise. In F. Klix & H. Hagendorf (Eds.), *Human memory and cognitive capabilities: Mechanisms and performances* (pp. 915–928). Amsterdam: Elsevier North Holland.

Glick, J. (1975). Cognitive development in cross-cultural perspective. In F. D. Horowitz (Ed.), *Review of child development research* (Vol. 4). Chicago: University of Chicago Press.

Goodlad, J. (1984). *A place called school*. New York: McGraw-Hill.

Goodnow, J. J. (1976). The nature of intelligent behavior: Questions raised by cross-cultural studies. In L. B. Resnick (Ed), *New approaches to intelligence* (pp. 168–188). Potomac, MD: Erlbaum.

Graff, G. (1985). The university and the prevention of culture. In G. Graff & R. Gibbons (Eds.), *Criticism in the university* (pp. 62–82). Evanston, IL: Northwestern University.

Greene, S. (in preparation). *Mining texts in reading to write.* (Occasional paper). Berkeley: University of California and Carnegie Mellon University, Center for the Study of Writing at University of California, Berkeley, and Carnegie Mellon.

Gumperz, J. (1982). *Discourse strategies*. New York: Cambridge University Press.

Haas, C., & Flower, L. (1988). Rhetorical reading strategies and the construction of meaning. *College Composition and Communication, 39,* 167–183.

Hamilton, S. (1987, April). *Effects of elaboration on concept learning from prose*. Paper presented at the American Educational Research Association Conference, Washington, DC.

Hare, V. C. (1981). Reader's problem identification and problem-solving strategies for high- and low-knowledge comprehenders. *Journal of Reading Behavior, 13,* 359–365.

Hayes, J. R. (1981). *The complete problem solver*. Philadelphia: Franklin Institute Press.

Hayes, J. R. (1985). Three problems in teaching general skills. In J. W. Segal, S. F. Chipman, & R. Glaser (Eds.), *Thinking and learning skills: Research and open questions* (Vol. 2, pp. 391–406). Hillsdale, NJ: Erlbaum.

Hayes, J. R., & Flower, L. (1981). Writing as problem solving. *Visible Language, 14,* 388–389.

Hayes, J. R., Flower, L., Schriver, K., Stratman, J., & Carey, L. (1987). Cognitive processes in revision. In S. Rosenberg (Ed.), *Advances in applied psycholinguistics: Reading, writing, and language processing.* Cambridge: Cambridge University Press.

Heath, S. B. (1983). *Ways with words: Language, life and work in communities*. Cambridge: Cambridge University Press.

Herrington, A. (1985). Writing in academic settings: A study of the contexts for writing in two college chemical engineering courses. *Research in the Teaching of English, 19,* 331–361.

Herrington, A. (1988). Teaching, writing and learning: A naturalistic study of writing in an undergraduate literature course. In D. Jolliffe (Ed.), *Advances in writing research: Vol. 2. Writing in academic disciplines* (pp. 133–166). Norwood, NJ: Ablex.

Hillocks, G. (1986). *Research on written composition*. Urbana, IL: National Council of Teachers of English.

Huckin, T. N. (1987, March). *Surprise value in scientific discourse*. Paper presented at the Conference on College Composition and Communication, Atlanta, GA.

Hudson, R. A. (1980). *Sociolinguistics*. Cambridge: Cambridge University Press.

Hymes, D. (1972). Introduction. In C. B. Cazden, V. P. John, & D. Hymes (Eds.), *Functions of language in the classroom* (pp. xi–lvii). New York: Teachers College Press.

Jameson, F. (1980). *The political unconsciousness*. Princeton, NJ: Princeton University Press.

Jones, B. F., Palincsar, A. M., Ogle, D. S., & Carr, E. G. (1987). *Strategic teaching and learning: Cognitive instruction in the content areas.* Alexandria, VA: Association for Supervision and Curriculum Development.

Just, M., & Carpenter, P. A. (1986). *The psychology of reading and language comprehension.* New York: Allyn and Bacon.

Kantz, M. (in preparation). *Reading strategies and success in synthesizing: It's what you do with them that counts.* Berkeley: University of California and Carnegie Mellon University, Center for the Study of Writing at University of California, Berkeley, and Carnegie Mellon.

Kantz, M. (1987). *Composing from textual sources: Rhetorical stances for writing syntheses.* Unpublished doctoral dissertation, Carnegie Mellon University, Pittsburgh.

Kaufer, D., Geisler, C., & Neuwirth, C. (1989). *The architecture of argument: Cross-disciplinary rhetoric.* San Diego, CA: Harcourt Brace Jovanovich.

Kennedy, M. L. (1985). The composing process of college students writing from sources. *Written Communication, 4,* 434–456.

Kintsch, W. (1974). *The representation of meaning in memory.* Hillsdale, NJ: Erlbaum.

Kintsch, W., & van Dijk, T. (1978). Towards a model of text comprehension and production. *Psychological Review, 85,* 363–394.

Kintsch, W., & Vipond, D. (1979). Reading comprehension and readability in educational practice and psychological theory. In L. G. Nilsson (Ed.), *Perspectives in memory research* (pp. 329–365). Hillsdale, NJ: Erlbaum.

Kroll, B. M. (1978). Cognitive egocentrism and the problem of audience awareness in written discourse. *Research in the Teaching of English, 12,* 269–281.

Kucer, S. L. (1985). The making of meaning: Reading and writing as parallel processes. *Written Communication, 2,* 317–336.

Kuhn, T. S. (1970). *The structure of scientific revolution* (2nd ed.). Chicago: University of Chicago Press.

Labov, W. (1972). *Language in the inner city* (pp. 201–254). Philadelphia: University of Pennsylvania Press.

Langer, J. A. (1984a). Effects of topic knowledge on the quality and coherence of informational writing. In A. N. Applebee (Ed.), *Contexts for learning to write.* Norwood, NJ: Ablex.

Langer, J. A. (1984b). Relation between levels of prior knowledge and the organization of recall. In M. Kamil & A. J. Moe (Eds.), *Perspectives in reading research and comprehension* (pp. 28–33). Washington, DC: National Reading Conference.

Langer, J. A. (1986). Reading, writing, and understanding: An analysis of the construction of meaning. *Written Communication, 3,* 219–267.

Langston, M. D. (1989). *Engagement in writing.* Unpublished doctoral dissertation, Carnegie Mellon University, Pittsburgh.

Larkin, J. (1983). Understanding, problem representation and skill in physics. In *Learning, cognition and college teaching.* San Francisco: Jossey-Bass.

LeFevre, Karen B. (1987). *Invention as a social act.* Carbondale: Southern Illinois University Press.

Levin, J. R. (1987). *Memorable learning strategies: Powerful theory-powerful application.* Paper presented at the Annual Meeting of the American Education Research Association, Washington, DC.

Lunsford, A. (1980). The content of basic writer's essays. *College Composition and Communication, 31,* 278–290.

Lunsford, A., & Ede, L. (1986). Why write . . . together: A research update. *Rhetoric Review, 51,* 71–81.

Macherey, P. (1978). *A theory of literary production* (G. Wall, Trans.). Boston: Routledge & Kegan Paul.

Macrorie, K. (1968). To be read. *English Journal, 57,* 686–692.

Mandler, J. M., & DeForest, M. (1979). Is there more than one way to recall a story? *Child Development, 50,* 886–889.

McCarthy, L. P. (1987). A stranger in strange lands: A college student writing across the curriculum. *Research in the Teaching of English, 21,* 233–265.

McCormick, K. (1985). Theory in the reader: Bleich, Holland and beyond. *College English, 47,* 836–850.

McCormick, K. (Ed.). (1989). *Expanding the repertoire: An anthology of practical approaches for the teaching of writing.* (Tech. Rep. No. 30). Berkeley: Center for the Study of Writing at University of California, Berkeley, and Carnegie Mellon.

McCormick, K., & Waller, G., with L. Flower (1987). *Reading texts: Reading, responding, writing.* Lexington, MA: Heath.

Meyer, B. J. F. (1982). Reading research and the composition teacher: The importance of plans. *College Composition and Communication, 33,* 34–49.

Meyer, B. J. F., Brandt, D. M., & Bluth, G. J. (1980). Use of top-level structure in text: Key for comprehension of ninth-graders. *Reading Research Quarterly, 16,* 72–103.

Myers, G. (1985a). The social construction of two biologists' proposals. *Written Communication, 2,* 219–245.

Myers, G. (1985b). Texts as knowledge claims: The social construction of two biologists' articles. *Social Studies of Science, 15,* 593–630.

National Assessment of Educational Progress. (1981). *Reading, thinking and writing: Results from the 1979–81 National Assessment of Reading and Literature.* Denver: Education Commission of the States.

Nelson, J. (1988). *Examining the practices that shape student writing: Two studies of college freshmen writing across the disciplines.* Unpublished doctoral dissertation, Carnegie Mellon University, Pittsburgh.

Nelson, J., & Hayes, J. R. (1988). *How the writing context shapes college students' strategies for writing from sources.* (Tech. Rep. No. 16). Berkeley: University of California and Carnegie Mellon University, Center for the Study of Writing at University of California, Berkeley, and Carnegie Mellon.

Newell, A., & Simon, H. A. (1972). *Human problem solving.* Englewood Cliffs, NJ: Prentice-Hall.

Nickerson, R. S., Perkins, D. N., & Smith, E. E. (1985). *The teaching of thinking.* Hillsdale, NJ: Erlbaum.

Nystrand, M. (1986). *The structure of written communication: Studies in reciprocity between writers and readers.* New York: Academic Press.

Odell, L., & Goswami, D. (1985). *Writing in nonacademic settings.* New York: Methuen.

Ong, W. (1982). *Orality and literacy.* New York: Methuen.

Palincsar, A., & Brown, A. L. (1983). *Reciprocal teaching of comprehension-monitoring activities.* (Tech. Rep. No. 269). Urbana: Center for the Study of Reading at the University of Illinois.

Penrose, A. M., & Sitko, B. (in preparation). *Studying cognitive processes in the classroom: A sourcebook for teachers of writing.* Pittsburgh: Center for the Study of Writing, Carnegie Mellon University.

Perry, W. G. (1968). *Forms of intellectual and ethical development in the college years.* New York: Holt, Rinehart and Winston.

Piaget, J. (1932). *The language and thought of the child* (M. Gabin, Trans.). New York: Harcourt, Brace.

Pichert, J. W., & Anderson, R. C. (1977). Taking different perspectives on a story. *Journal of Educational Psychology, 69,* 309–315.

Porter, J. E. (1986). Intertextuality and the discourse community. *Rhetoric Review, 5,* 34–47.

Reder, L. M. (1979). The role of elaborations in memory for prose. *Cognitive Psychology, 11,* 221–234.

Reder, L. M. (1980). The role of elaboration in the comprehension and retention of prose: A critical review. *Review of Educational Research, 50,* 5–53.

Reder, L. M., Charney, D. H., & Morgan, K. I. (1986). The role of elaborations in learning a skill from an instructional text. *Memory and Cognition, 14,* 64–78.

Richardson, R. C., Jr., Fisk, E. C., & Okun, M. A. (1983). *Literacy in the open-access college.* San Francisco: Jossey-Bass.

Rohman, D. G. (1965). Pre-writing: The stage of discovery in the writing process. *College Composition and Communication, 16,* 106–112.

Rohman, D. G. (1985). Pre-writing: The stage of discovery in the writing process. *College English, 47,* 620–628.

Rose, M. (1980). Rigid rules, inflexible plans, and the stifling of language: A cognitivist analysis of writer's block. *College Composition and Communication, 31,* 389–401.

Rose, M. (1984a). Complexity, rigor, evolving method and the puzzle of writer's block: Thoughts on composing-process research. In M. Rose (Ed.), *When a writer can't write: Studies in writer's block and other composing-process problems* (pp. 227–260). New York: Guilford Press.

Rose, M. (1984b). *Writer's block: The cognitive dimension.* Carbondale: Southern Illinois University Press.

Rose, M. (1985). The language of exclusion: Writing instruction in the university. *College English, 47,* 341–359.

Rose, M. (1988). Narrowing the mind and page: Remedial writers and cognitive reductionism. *College Composition and Communication, 39,* 267–302.

Rothkopf, E. Z. (1976). Writing to teach and reading to learn: A perspective on the psychology of written instruction. In N. L. Gage (Ed.), *The psychology of teaching methods* (pp. 91–129). Seventy-fifth Yearbook of the National Society for the Study of Education, Part I). Chicago: National Society for the Study of Education.

Ruth, L., & Murphy, S. (1984). Designing topics for writing assessment: Problems of Meaning. *College Composition and Communication, 35,* 410–422.

Scardamalia, M., & Bereiter, C. (1987). Knowledge telling and knowledge transforming in written composition. In S. Rosenberg (Ed.), *Advances in applied psycholinguistics: Vol. 2. Reading, writing, and language learning* (pp. 142–175). Cambridge: Cambridge University Press.

Schoenfeld, A. H. (1979). Can heuristics be taught? In R. Lesch (Ed.), *Applied problem solving.* (ERIC 315–338).

Schwegler, R., & Shamoon, L. (1982). The aims and process of the research paper. *College English, 44,* 817–824.

Scribner, S. (1984). Studying working intelligence. In B. Rogoff & J. Lave (Eds.), *Everyday cognition: Its development in social context.* Cambridge, MA: Harvard University Press.

Scribner, S., & Cole, M. (1981). *The psychology of literacy.* Cambridge, MA: Harvard University Press.

Schank, R. C., & Abelson, R. P. (1977). *Scripts, plans, goals and understanding: An inquiry into human knowledge structures.* Hillsdale, NJ: Erlbaum.

Shaughnessy, M. (1977). Some needed research in writing. *College Composition and Communication, 28,* 317–321.

Simon, H. A. (1973). The structure of ill-structured problems. *Artificial Intelligence, 4,* 181–201.

Smith, W. L., Hull, G. A., Land, R. E., Jr., Moore, M. T., Ball, C., Dunham, D. E., Hickey, L. S., & Ruzich, C. W. (1985). Some effects of varying the structure of a topic on college students' writing. *Written Communication, 2,* 73–89.

Sommers, N. I. (1980). Revision strategies of student writers and experienced adult writers. *College Composition and Communication, 31,* 378–388.

Spivey, N. N. (1984). *Discourse synthesis: Constructing texts in reading and writing* (Outstanding Dissertation Monograph Series). Newark, DE: International Reading Association.

Spivey, N. N. (1987). Construing constructivism: Reading research in the United States. *Poetics, 16,* 169–192.

Stein, V. E. (in preparation). Lives of a skill: Cognitive and academic perspectives on critical literacy.

Stewart, D. (1983). Prose with integrity: A primary objective. *College Composition and Communication, 34,* 278–283.

Sticht, T. G. (1977). Comprehending reading at work. In M. A. Just & P. A. Carpenter (Eds.), *Cognitive Processes in Comprehension* (pp. 221–246). Hillsdale, NJ: Erlbaum.

Swales, J. (1984). Research into the structure of introductions to journal articles and its application to the teaching of academic writing. In R. Williams, J. Swales, & J. Kirkman (Eds.), *Common ground: Shared interests in ESP and communications studies* (pp. 77–86). Oxford: Pergamon.

Swales, J. (1987, March). *Approaching the concept of discourse community.* Paper presented at the Convention on College Composition and Communication, Atlanta.

Thoreau, H. D. (1964). In C. Bode (Ed.), *The portable Thoreau.* New York: Viking Press.

Tierney, R. J., & Pearson, P. D. (1984). Toward a composing model of reading. In J. M. Jensen (Ed.), *Composing and comprehending* (pp. 33–45). Urbana, IL: ERIC Clearinghouse on Reading and Communication Skills and National Conference on Research in English.

Tierney, R. J., & Pearson, P. D. (1985). Learning to learn from text: A framework for improving classroom practice. In H. Singer & R. B. Ruddell (Eds.), *Theoretical models and processes of reading* (pp. 860–878). Newark, DE: International Reading Association.

Tulving, E. (1972). Episodic and semantic memory. In E. Tulving & W. Donaldson (Eds.), *The organization of memory.* New York: Academic Press.

Vatz, R. E. (1973). The myth of the rhetorical situation. *Philosophy and Rhetoric, 6,* 154–161.

Voss, J. F., & Post, T. A. (1988). On the solving of ill-structured problems. In M. T. H. Chi, R. Glaser, & M. J. Farr (Eds.), *The nature of expertise* (pp. 261–286). Hillsdale, NJ: Erlbaum.

Voss, J. F., Greene, T. R., Post, T. A., & Penner, B. C. (1983). Problem solving skills in the social sciences. In G. Bower (Ed.), *The psychology of learning and motivation: Advances in research and theory* (Vol. 17). New York: Academic Press.

Wagoner, S. A. (1983). Comprehension monitoring: What it is and what we know about it. *Reading Research Quarterly, 18* (3), 328–346.

Waller, G., McCormick, K., & Fowler, L. (1986). *The Lexington introduction to literature.* Lexington, MA: Heath.

Weinstein, C. E., Underwood, V. L., Wicker, F. W., & Cubberly, W. E. (1979). Cognitive learning strategies: Verbal and imaginal elaboration. In H. F. O'Neil & C. D. Spielberger (Eds.), *Cognition and affective learning strategies*. New York: Academic Press.

Whitney, P. (1987). Psychological theories of elaborative inferences: Implications for schema-theoretic views of comprehension. *Reading Research Quarterly, 22,* 299–309.

Winograd, P. (1984). Strategic difficulties in summarizing texts. *Reading Research Quarterly, 19,* 404–425.

Witte, S. (1983). Topical structure and revision: An exploratory study. *College Composition and Communication, 34,* 313–341.

Witte, S. (1987). Pre-text and composing. *College Composition and Communication, 38,* 397–425.

Witte, S., Cherry, R., & Meyer, P. (1982). *The goals of freshman writing programs as perceived by a national sample of college and university writing program directors and teachers*. (Tech. Rep. No. 5). Austin: Writing Assessment Project, University of Texas. (ERIC Doc. No. ED 216 395).

Witte, S., Meyer, P., with Miller, T. (1982). *A national survey of college and university writing teachers*. (Tech. Rep. No. 4). Austin: Writing Program Assessment Project.

Index